SACRED SOULS, SECULAR SOIL

CAA's Religious Ripples in India

Dr.Prasanta Mujrai

CONTENTS

Title Page

Copyright

Introduction

Chapter 1: The Roots of Indian Secularism   1

Chapter 2: Understanding the Citizenship Amendment Act (CAA)   7

Chapter 3: Hinduism and the CAA   14

Chapter 4: Islam and the CAA Controversy   21

Chapter 5: Sikhism: Caught in the Crossfire   27

Chapter 6: Christianity and the CAA Debate   35

Chapter 7: Buddhism: The Middle Path in CAA Discussions   41

Chapter 8: Jainism and the Citizenship Question   49

Chapter 9: Zoroastrianism: A Unique Perspective   56

Chapter 10: Tribal Religions and the CAA   64

Chapter 11: Atheism and Secularism in the CAA Era   69

Chapter 12: Interfaith Marriages and the CAA   78

Chapter 13: Religious Minorities from Neighbouring Countries   88

Chapter 14: The Northeast India Conundrum   98

Chapter 15: Religious Educational Institutions and the CAA   110

Chapter 16: Places of Worship and the Citizenship   119

Debate

Chapter 17: Religious Leaders: Voices of Influence   127

Chapter 18: Media Representation of Religious   136
Perspectives

Chapter 19: Legal Challenges to CAA: A Multi-Faith   143
Approach

Chapter 20: Economic Implications for Religious   151
Communities

Chapter 21: CAA and Religious Festivals   160

Chapter 22: Youth Movements: A Cross-Religious   169
Phenomenon

Chapter 23: Women's Voices in the CAA Debate   176

Chapter 24: CAA's Impact on Religious Conversions   184

Chapter 25: Religious Attire and Symbols in the CAA Era   192

Chapter 26: CAA and Religious Personal Laws   200

Chapter 27: Diaspora Religions and the CAA   207

Chapter 28: CAA's Influence on Religious Philanthropy   216

Chapter 29: Religious Art and Literature in Response to   224
CAA

Chapter 30: CAA and Religious Pilgrimages   232

Chapter 31: Religious Counseling in the Wake of CAA   240

Chapter 32: CAA's Impact on Religious Demographics   247

Chapter 33: Interfaith Families and CAA: Navigating   254
Complexities

Chapter 34: Religious Rhetoric in Political Campaigns   261

Chapter 35: CAA and Religious Freedom Indices   268

Chapter 36: Interfaith Dialogue Initiatives Post-CAA   276

Chapter 37: CAA's Impact on Religious Tourism   283

Chapter 38: Religious Minorities and National Identity   291

Chapter 39: CAA and Religious Extremism 304

Chapter 40: The Future of Indian Secularism Post-CAA 313

INTRODUCTION

"Sacred Souls, Secular Soil: CAA's Religious Ripples in India" is a captivating exploration of one of the most contentious issues in contemporary Indian politics. This thought-provoking book delves into the complex interplay between religion, citizenship, and national identity in the world's largest democracy. With meticulous research and nuanced analysis, the author examines how the Citizenship Amendment Act (CAA) has sent shockwaves through India's secular fabric, sparking nationwide protests and intense debates about the nature of Indian citizenship. From the bustling streets of Delhi to the remote corners of Assam, readers are taken on a journey through the diverse tapestry of Indian society, exploring how the CAA has become a flashpoint for broader discussions about religious identity, constitutional values, and the future of India's pluralistic ethos. This timely and insightful work challenges readers to grapple with fundamental questions about the role of religion in modern governance and the delicate balance between national security and individual rights.

CHAPTER 1: THE ROOTS OF INDIAN SECULARISM

Historical Evolution of Secularism in India

The concept of secularism in India has deep historical roots that predate its formal inclusion in the Constitution. The idea of religious tolerance and peaceful coexistence of diverse faiths can be traced back to ancient Indian rulers like Ashoka the Great. However, the modern notion of secularism in India emerged during the colonial period and the struggle for independence.

During British rule, the colonial administration initially adopted a policy of non-interference in religious matters. However, they later exploited religious divisions as part of their divide-and-rule strategy. This manipulation of religious identities for political gains highlighted the need for a secular framework in independent India.

The Indian independence movement, led by figures like Mahatma Gandhi and Jawaharlal Nehru, emphasized the importance of secularism in building a unified nation. Nehru, in particular, was a staunch advocate of secularism, believing it was essential for India's diverse population to prevent communal strife and promote national unity. His vision of secularism emphasized a complete separation of religion from politics and state affairs.

After independence in 1947, the framers of the Indian Constitution, led by Dr. B.R. Ambedkar, sought to enshrine secular principles in the foundational document of the new nation. While the term "secular" was not explicitly included in the original Constitution, the spirit of secularism was embedded in various articles, particularly those dealing with fundamental rights.

The formal inclusion of the word "secular" in the Preamble of the Indian Constitution came later, through the 42nd Amendment in 1976 during Indira Gandhi's government. This amendment officially declared India as a secular nation, although the Supreme Court of India had already established in 1994 that India was secular since the formation of the republic.

Constitutional Provisions for Religious Freedom

The Indian Constitution provides robust protections for religious freedom and equality, which form the cornerstone of Indian secularism. These provisions are primarily contained in Articles 25-28 of the Constitution, which fall under the Fundamental Rights section.

Article 25 guarantees the freedom of conscience and the right to freely profess, practice, and propagate religion. This article ensures that all individuals in India have the liberty to follow and express their religious beliefs, subject to public order, morality, and health. It's important to note that this freedom extends to all persons in India, not just citizens.

Article 26 provides religious denominations the freedom to manage their own affairs in matters of religion. This includes the right to establish and maintain institutions for religious and charitable purposes, manage their own affairs in matters of religion, and own and acquire movable and immovable property.

Article 27 prohibits the state from compelling any citizen to pay taxes for the promotion or maintenance of any particular religion. This provision ensures that state funds are not used to favor or promote any specific religion.

Article 28 deals with the freedom of attendance at religious instruction or religious worship in certain educational institutions. It prohibits religious instruction in wholly state-funded educational institutions and allows individuals the choice to participate or not in religious instruction or worship in recognized or state-aided institutions.

These constitutional provisions reflect the Indian approach to secularism, which is based on the principle of "Sarva Dharma Sambhava" or equal respect for all religions. Unlike the Western model of secularism that advocates for a strict separation of church and state, the Indian model allows for state intervention in religious affairs to promote social welfare and reform.

Challenges to Secularism in Modern India

Despite its constitutional foundations, secularism in India faces several challenges in the contemporary context. These challenges stem from various social, political, and economic factors that have emerged or intensified in recent decades.

One of the primary challenges is the rise of communal politics and religious militancy. Some political parties in India are organized along communal lines, representing the interests of particular religious or regional groups. This trend has led to the exploitation of religious sentiments for political gains, undermining the secular fabric of the nation.

Poverty and illiteracy also pose significant challenges to secularism in India. Economic disparities and lack of education can make people more susceptible to religious fundamentalism and communal propaganda. These factors can be exploited by vested interests to create divisions along religious lines.

Political corruption is another major threat to secularism. When political leaders prioritize personal or party interests over national interests, it can lead to policies and actions that favor certain religious groups over others, contradicting the principles of secularism.

The persistence of caste-based discrimination, despite constitutional prohibitions, also challenges secular ideals. The caste system, although rooted in Hindu tradition, has permeated other religious communities in India as well, creating social hierarchies that conflict with secular and egalitarian principles.

Obscurantism, or the rejection of enlightenment and reason in favor of traditional beliefs and customs, is another obstacle to secularism in India. This mindset can hinder the development of a rational, secular outlook among the population.

Recent years have seen an increase in religious intolerance and communal violence in some parts of India. These incidents not only threaten the secular character of the nation but also pose risks to social harmony and national integration.

The Unique Indian Model of Secularism

The Indian model of secularism is distinct from its Western counterpart, reflecting the country's unique historical, cultural, and social context. While Western secularism often advocates for a strict separation of religion and state, the Indian model is based on the principle of "principled distance" between state and religion.

The key features of Indian secularism include:

1. Equal Respect for All Religions: The Indian model is based on the concept of "Sarva Dharma Sambhava" or equal respect for all religions. This approach recognizes the importance of religion in Mudian society while ensuring that the state does not favor any particular religion.

2. State Intervention for Religious Reform: Unlike the Western model, Indian secularism allows for state intervention in

religious affairs to promote social welfare and reform. This has enabled the state to legislate against religious practices deemed socially harmful, such as untouchability or child marriage.

3. Protection of Religious Minorities: The Indian Constitution provides special protections for religious minorities, including the right to establish and administer educational institutions.

4. No Official State Religion: Despite its religious diversity, India does not have an official state religion, maintaining neutrality in religious matters.

5. Accommodation of Religious Diversity: The Indian model recognizes and accommodates the country's religious diversity in various ways, such as recognizing religious holidays of different faiths.

This unique approach to secularism has allowed India to maintain its rich religious diversity while striving for national unity. However, it also presents challenges, particularly in balancing religious freedoms with the need for social reform and maintaining neutrality in a multi-religious society.

In conclusion, the roots of Indian secularism lie in its historical experiences, constitutional framework, and the vision of its founding leaders. While facing numerous challenges in the modern context, the unique Indian model of secularism continues to play a crucial role in shaping the nation's social and political landscape. The ongoing debates and discussions around secularism reflect its continued relevance and the need for constant negotiation between diverse religious identities and the secular ideals of the state.

References:

1. https://en.wikipedia.org/wiki/Secularism_in_India
2. https://www.arcjournals.org/pdfs/ijps/v10-i1/5.pdf

3. https://www.bbau.ac.in/dept/HR/TM/Freedom%20of%20religion%20under%20Indian%20Constitution.pdf

4. https://www.jetir.org/papers/JETIR1708101.pdf

5. https://forumias.com/blog/difference-between-indian-model-of-secularism-western-model-of-secularism/

6. https://www.upes.ac.in/blog/law/the-unique-character-of-indian-model-of-secularism

7. https://secularismandnonreligion.org/articles/10.5334/snr.145

8. https://indianexpress.com/article/research/anant-kumar-hegde-secularism-constitution-india-bjp-jawaharlal-nehru-indira-gandhi-5001085/

9. https://blog.ipleaders.in/right-to-freedom-of-religion/

10. https://subhashahlawat.com/blog/indian-secularism

CHAPTER 2: UNDERSTANDING THE CITIZENSHIP AMENDMENT ACT (CAA)

The Citizenship Amendment Act (CAA) of 2019 represents a significant and controversial change to India's citizenship laws. This chapter provides a comprehensive overview of the CAA, examining its key provisions, historical context, rationale, comparison with previous citizenship laws, and international perspectives.

Key Provisions of the CAA

The Citizenship Amendment Act, passed by the Indian Parliament on December 11, 2019, and signed into law on December 12, 2019, introduces several important changes to the existing citizenship framework in India.

Eligibility Criteria

The CAA provides an expedited path to Indian citizenship for undocumented immigrants belonging to six specific religious communities: Hindus, Sikhs, Buddhists, Jains, Parsis, and Christians. This eligibility is extended to individuals from three neighbouring countries: Afghanistan, Bangladesh, and Pakistan.

Cut-off Date

The Act specifies December 31, 2014, as the cut-off date for eligibility. Individuals from the specified religious communities must have entered India on or before this date to be considered for citizenship under the CAA.

Relaxation of Residency Requirement

One of the most significant changes introduced by the CAA is the relaxation of the residency requirement for naturalization. Previously, the Citizenship Act of 1955 required applicants to have resided in India for at least 11 years before being eligible for citizenship. The CAA reduces this requirement to just five years for individuals from the specified communities and countries.

Exclusion of Certain Areas

The Act explicitly excludes certain areas from its purview. These include the tribal areas of Assam, Meghalaya, Mizoram, and Tripura, as well as areas covered under the Inner Line Permit system.

Overseas Citizenship of India (OCI) Provisions

The CAA introduces new provisions regarding Overseas Citizenship of India (OCI) cardholders. It allows the government to cancel OCI registration if the cardholder violates any law, regardless of the severity of the offense.

Historical Context and Rationale Behind the Act

The CAA's origins can be traced back to historical events and political developments in the Indian subcontinent.

Partition and Its Aftermath

The partition of India in 1947 led to large-scale population movements between India and the newly formed Pakistan. This event set the stage for ongoing migration and refugee flows in the region.

Assam Movement and Accord

The Assam Movement of the 1980s, which protested against illegal immigration from Bangladesh, led to the Assam Accord of 1985. This accord set March 24, 1971, as the cut-off date for detecting and deporting illegal immigrants in Assam.

Previous Legislative Attempts

The idea of providing citizenship to persecuted minorities from neighbouring countries has been discussed in Indian politics for decades. In 2003, during the first BJP-led government, amendments to the Citizenship Act were made, laying the groundwork for future changes.

BJP's Election Promise

The CAA was a key campaign promise of the Bharatiya Janata Party (BJP) in both the 2014 and 2019 general elections. The BJP argued that the Act was necessary to protect persecuted religious minorities from neighbouring countries.

Government's Rationale

The Indian government has presented several arguments in support of the CAA:

1. Protection of Persecuted Minorities: The government argues that the Act aims to provide refuge to religious minorities who have faced persecution in Muslim-majority neighbouring countries.

2. Historical Responsibility: There is a view that India has a special responsibility towards these communities due to the shared cultural and historical ties.

3. Addressing Long-standing Issues: The government contends that the CAA addresses the long-pending issue of statelessness among certain communities who have been living in India for decades.

Comparison with Previous Citizenship Laws

The CAA marks a significant departure from previous citizenship laws in India, particularly in its approach to religion and citizenship.

Citizenship Act of 1955

The original Citizenship Act of 1955 did not make any distinctions based on religion. It provided for citizenship by birth, descent, registration, naturalization, and incorporation of territory.

Key Differences

1. Religious Criteria: The CAA, for the first time, introduces religion as a criterion for citizenship in India. This marks a fundamental shift from the secular principles that have traditionally guided Indian citizenship laws.

2. Reduced Residency Requirement: While the 1955 Act required 11 years of residency for naturalization, the CAA reduces this to five years for the specified communities.

3. Specific Country Focus: Unlike previous laws, the CAA focuses on specific countries (Afghanistan, Bangladesh, and Pakistan) and excludes others in the region.

4. Retroactive Application: The CAA applies retroactively to December 31, 2014, potentially affecting the status of individuals who entered India before this date.

National Register of Citizens (NRC)

The CAA's implementation is closely linked to the proposed nationwide National Register of Citizens (NRC). While the NRC itself is not part of the CAA, its potential implementation in conjunction with the CAA has raised concerns about the combined impact on citizenship status, particularly for Muslims.

International Perspectives on the CAA: The passage of the CAA has attracted significant international attention and criticism.

United Nations' Response: The Office of the United Nations High Commissioner for Human Rights (OHCHR) has expressed concern that the CAA is "fundamentally discriminatory in nature". The UN has urged the Indian government to ensure that the law is in line with the country's international human rights obligations.

Criticism from Human Rights Organizations: Several international human rights organizations have criticized the CAA:

1. The International Commission of Jurists (ICJ) has stated that the CAA "violates international law".

2. Human Rights Watch has argued that the law discriminates on religious grounds in violation of international legal standards.

3. Amnesty International has expressed concern about the potential for increased statelessness and discrimination against Muslims.

Responses from Other Countries

1. United States: Some U.S. officials and bodies, including the U.S. Commission on International Religious Freedom, have expressed concern about the implications of the CAA for religious freedom in India.

2. European Union: The European Parliament has debated resolutions critical of the CAA, though no formal action has been taken.

3. Neighbouring Countries: Bangladesh and Afghanistan have expressed concern about being implicated in religious persecution through the Act's provisions.

Support for the CAA

While much of the international response has been critical, some countries and organizations have supported India's sovereign right to determine its citizenship laws. The Indian government has maintained that the CAA is an internal matter and is designed to address specific historical injustices.

In conclusion, the Citizenship Amendment Act of 2019 represents a significant shift in India's approach to citizenship, introducing religious criteria and focusing on specific countries of origin. While the government argues that it addresses historical injustices and protects persecuted minorities, critics contend that it discriminates on religious grounds and potentially violates international law. The Act's implementation and its interaction with other proposed measures like the NRC continue to be subjects of intense debate both within India and internationally.

References:

1. https://byjus.com/free-ias-prep/citizenship-amendment-bill-2019/
2. https://indiancitizenshiponline.nic.in/Documents/UserGuide/E-gazette_2019_20122019.pdf
3. https://www.business-standard.com/india-news/citizenship-amendment-act-2019-a-timeline-of-events-controversies-124031200214_1.html
4. https://www.uscirf.gov/sites/default/files/2020%20Legislation%20Factsheet%20-%20%20India_0_0.pdf
5. https://carnegieendowment.org/posts/2020/02/citizenship-law-in-india-a-populist-polarization?lang=en
6. https://en.wikipedia.org/wiki/Citizenship_(Amendment)_Act,_2019
7. https://www.orfonline.org/expert-speak/analyzing-global-response-to-the-controversial-citizenship-amendment-act-59529
8. https://www.drishtiias.com/loksabha-rajyasabha-discussions/citizenship-amendment-act-unpacked
9. https://www.omct.org/en/resources/statements/

citizenship-amendment-act-violates-international-law

10. https://www.bbc.com/news/world-asia-india-50670393

CHAPTER 3: HINDUISM AND THE CAA

The Citizenship Amendment Act (CAA) of 2019 has had a profound impact on Hinduism and Hindu-Muslim relations in India. This chapter examines the multifaceted effects of the CAA on Hindu refugees, Hindu nationalist perspectives, concerns of secular Hindus, and the broader implications for Hindu-Muslim relations in the country.

Impact on Hindu Refugees from Neighbouring Countries

The CAA has significantly altered the prospects for Hindu refugees from Afghanistan, Bangladesh, and Pakistan seeking citizenship in India. By providing a fast track to citizenship for persecuted religious minorities from these countries, including Hindus, the Act has opened new avenues for these refugees to gain legal status and rights in India.

For many Hindu refugees who fled religious persecution in their home countries, the CAA represents a ray of hope for a secure future in India. These refugees have often faced challenging living conditions upon arrival in India, with limited access to basic amenities and legal rights. The implementation of the CAA is expected to alleviate some of these hardships by providing a path to citizenship.

In Delhi's Majnu-Ka-Tilla area, for instance, Pakistani Hindu refugees have been living in semi-kutcha houses, cooking on mud and brick stoves, and using tents for sanitation. The notification of CAA rules has instilled hope among these refugees for improved living conditions and access to essential services.

The Act reduces the naturalization period for eligible refugees from 11 years to 6 years, potentially expediting their integration into Indian society. This provision is particularly significant for Hindu refugees who have been living in legal limbo for years, unable to fully participate in the economic and social fabric of the country.

However, it is important to note that the CAA's impact is limited to those who entered India on or before December 31, 2014. This cutoff date excludes more recent Hindu refugees and may create disparities within refugee communities based on their date of arrival in India.

Hindu Nationalist Perspectives on the Act

The CAA has been strongly supported by Hindu nationalist groups and political parties, particularly the ruling Bharatiya Janata Party (BJP). From their perspective, the Act fulfills a long-standing commitment to provide refuge and citizenship to persecuted Hindus from neighbouring countries.

Hindu nationalists view the CAA as a necessary step to protect and preserve Hindu culture and identity in the face of perceived threats from neighbouring Muslim-majority countries. They argue that India, as the birthplace of Hinduism, has a special responsibility to provide sanctuary to Hindus facing persecution elsewhere.

The Act is seen by some as a reaffirmation of India's Hindu character, aligning with the concept of "Hindutva" or Hindu nationalism. This ideology, as articulated by figures like Vinayak Damodar Savarkar, emphasizes the idea of India as a Hindu nation, defined by common ancestry, culture, and civilization.

For Hindu nationalists, the CAA is part of a broader project to reshape India's national identity. It is seen as a step towards redefining India as a natural homeland for Hindus worldwide, while still maintaining a degree of tolerance for other religious communities.

However, this perspective has been criticized for potentially undermining India's secular foundations and creating divisions along religious lines. Critics argue that by explicitly favoring certain religious groups, the CAA contradicts the principles of equality and non-discrimination enshrined in the Indian Constitution.

Concerns of Secular Hindus

While the CAA has garnered support from Hindu nationalist quarters, it has also raised significant concerns among secular Hindus who value India's pluralistic traditions and constitutional secularism.

Many secular Hindus worry that the Act's religious criteria for citizenship violate the fundamental principle of secularism in the Indian Constitution. They argue that by differentiating between migrants based on religion, the CAA undermines the idea of India as a secular republic where all faiths are treated equally.

There are concerns that the Act could lead to a redefinition of Indian citizenship along religious lines, potentially marginalizing religious minorities, particularly Muslims. Secular Hindus fear that this could alter the inclusive and diverse character of Indian society that has been cultivated since independence.

Some secular Hindu intellectuals and activists have joined protests against the CAA, arguing that it goes against the pluralistic ethos of Hinduism itself. They contend that true Hinduism embraces diversity and that the Act's perceived bias against Muslims is antithetical to Hindu values of tolerance and acceptance.

There are also practical concerns about the implementation

of the Act and its potential to create social unrest. Secular Hindus worry that the CAA, especially when combined with proposals for a National Register of Citizens (NRC), could lead to widespread disruption and anxiety among various communities, including Hindus.

CAA's Influence on Hindu-Muslim Relations

The implementation of the CAA has had a significant impact on Hindu-Muslim relations in India, potentially exacerbating existing tensions and creating new fault lines between the communities.

One of the most immediate effects has been the outbreak of protests and counter-protests across the country. While many Muslims have protested against the Act, viewing it as discriminatory, some Hindu groups have organized rallies in support of the CAA. This has led to increased polarization and, in some cases, communal violence.

The Act has raised fears among many Muslims about their place in Indian society. Despite government assurances that the CAA does not affect Indian Muslims, there are concerns that it could be used in conjunction with other measures to disenfranchise Muslim citizens. This anxiety has strained relations between Hindu and Muslim communities in various parts of the country.

The CAA has also influenced political discourse, with some politicians using increasingly divisive rhetoric. This has further heightened tensions between Hindu and Muslim communities and raised concerns about the long-term social cohesion of the country.

In some areas, particularly in states like Assam, the CAA has intersected with local ethnic and linguistic concerns. This has created complex dynamics where religious identity intersects with regional and cultural identities, potentially reshaping

Hindu-Muslim relations in these regions.

The Act has also sparked debates about the nature of Indian citizenship and national identity. While some view it as a reaffirmation of India's Hindu character, others see it as a threat to the country's secular fabric. This fundamental disagreement has deepened ideological divides between and within Hindu and Muslim communities.

International reactions to the CAA have added another dimension to Hindu-Muslim relations in India. Criticism from foreign governments and human rights organizations has been met with defensive responses from supporters of the Act, sometimes leading to a siege mentality that can further strain communal relations.

References

1.   Hindu American Foundation. (n.d.). India's Citizenship Amendment Act: A First Step Opportunity to Better Address Human Rights in South Asia. Retrieved from https://www.hinduamerican.org/press/india-citizenship-amendment-bill

2.   Badri, A. (n.d.). The Rise of Hindu Nationalism and the Citizenship Amendment Act in India. Retrieved from https://adarshbadri.me/politics-society/hindu-nationalism-caa-india/

3.   Routed Magazine. (n.d.). India's Citizenship Amendment Act: Bigotry Triumphs Over Empathy. Retrieved from https://www.routedmagazine.com/post/india-s-citizenship-amendment-act-bigotry-triumphs-over-empathy

4.   Amnesty International. (2024, March). India: Citizenship Amendment Act is a blow to Indian constitutional values and international standards. Retrieved from https://www.amnesty.org/en/latest/news/2024/03/india-citizenship-amendment-act-is-a-

blow-to-indian-constitutional-values-and-
international-standards/

5.	PBS NewsHour. (2024, March 11). India announces steps to implement a citizenship law that excludes Muslims. Retrieved from https://www.pbs.org/newshour/world/india-announces-steps-to-implement-a-citizenship-law-that-excludes-muslims

6.	The Indian Express. (2024, March 12). CAA ray of hope for us, say Pakistani Hindu refugees in Delhi. Retrieved from https://indianexpress.com/article/india/caa-us-pakistani-hindu-refugees-delhi-9210014/

7.	BBC News. (2024, March 12). CAA: India's new citizenship law explained. Retrieved from https://www.bbc.com/news/world-asia-india-50670393

8.	Hindustan Times. (2024, March 12). MHA says CAA doesn't impact Indian Muslims, they enjoy equal rights like Hindus. Retrieved from https://www.hindustantimes.com/india-news/mha-says-caa-doesn-t-impact-indian-muslims-they-enjoy-equal-rights-like-hindus-101710256526760.html

9.	Human Rights Watch. (2024, March 15). India Activates Discriminatory Citizenship Law. Retrieved from https://www.hrw.org/news/2024/03/15/india-activates-discriminatory-citizenship-law

10.	Al Jazeera. (2024, March 15). India's Citizenship Amendment Act is a devious anti-Muslim dog whistle. Retrieved from https://www.aljazeera.com/opinions/2024/3/15/the-devious-anti-muslim-dog-whistle-in-indias-citizenship-amendment-act

11.	NDTV. (2024, March 19). "Deeply Concerned About Impact Of CAA On Muslims In India": US Senator. Retrieved from https://www.ndtv.com/india-news/deeply-concerned-about-impact-of-caa-on-muslims-in-india-us-senator-5267318

12.	The SVI. (2024, May 6). Impact of Citizenship Amendment Act (CAA) on Religious Minorities in India.

Retrieved from https://thesvi.org/minority-rights-vs-majoritarian-rule-impact-of-citizenship-amendment-act-caa-on-religious-minorities-in-india/

CHAPTER 4: ISLAM AND THE CAA CONTROVERSY

The implementation of the Citizenship Amendment Act (CAA) in India has sparked significant controversy, particularly regarding its impact on the Muslim community. This chapter examines the exclusion of Muslims from the CAA's provisions, the fears and concerns within the Muslim community, the impact on Indian Muslim citizenship perceptions, and the responses from Islamic religious leaders.

Exclusion of Muslims from the CAA's Provisions

The CAA, which was passed in 2019 and implemented in March 2024, provides a pathway to citizenship for undocumented non-Muslim migrants from Pakistan, Bangladesh, and Afghanistan who entered India before December 31, 2014[1]. The law specifically mentions six religious communities: Hindus, Sikhs, Buddhists, Jains, Parsis, and Christians. This exclusion of Muslims from the CAA's provisions has been a major point of contention and criticism.

The Indian government has defended the CAA as a "special act" designed to protect persecuted minorities from the three specified countries. Home Minister Amit Shah has repeatedly stated that the law has nothing to do with Indian Muslims and will not affect their citizenship rights. However, critics argue that the exclusion of Muslims from the CAA's provisions is discriminatory and goes against the principles of secularism enshrined in the Indian Constitution.

The exclusion of Muslims has raised concerns about the law's compatibility with international human rights standards. Amnesty International has criticized the CAA as "a bigoted law that legitimises discrimination on the basis of religion". The United Nations High Commissioner for Human Rights has also expressed concern, stating that the law is "fundamentally discriminatory in nature and in breach of India's international human rights obligations".

Fears and Concerns within the Muslim Community

The implementation of the CAA has reignited fears among India's 200 million Muslims, particularly those in border states. These concerns are rooted in the potential implications of the CAA when viewed in conjunction with other proposed measures, such as the National Register of Citizens (NRC).

One of the primary fears is the potential for the CAA to be used as a tool for disenfranchising Indian Muslims. While the government insists that the CAA is meant to grant citizenship rather than revoke it, many Muslims worry that they could be rendered stateless if they are unable to provide the necessary documentation to prove their citizenship under a future NRC process. This fear is particularly acute given that many Indians, regardless of religion, may lack the historical documents required to prove long-term residency.

Zakia Soman, co-founder of Bharatiya Muslim Mahila Andolan, a nationwide rights organization for Muslims, has noted that the "diabolical" developments have led to great apprehension in the Muslim community. Many Muslims have approached organizations like BMMA to understand and prepare for the potential repercussions of the CAA and NRC.

The fear of deportation or detention is another significant concern. In Assam, where the NRC process has already been implemented, nearly two million people were left out of the final list, raising fears of statelessness and detention. The construction of detention centers in Assam has further fueled these anxieties among Muslims across India.

Impact on Indian Muslim Citizenship Perceptions

The CAA controversy has had a profound impact on how Indian Muslims perceive their citizenship and place in society. Many feel that the law, combined with the proposed NRC, creates a system that can be weaponized against the Muslim community.

The exclusion of Muslims from the CAA's provisions has led to a sense of marginalization and second-class citizenship among many in the community. Asaduddin Owaisi, president of the All India Majlis-E-Ittehadul Muslimeen (AIMIM), has argued that the CAA will "relegate Indian Muslims to second class citizens". This perception is reinforced by statements from some political leaders that have been interpreted as suggesting that the CAA-NRC combination could be used to identify and potentially exclude Muslim residents.

The controversy has also led to a surge in efforts within the Muslim community to secure and organize their documentation. Maulana Khalid Rasheed, head of the Islamic Centre of India in Lucknow, started a helpline to address concerns and create awareness about the documents needed to prove citizenship. Similarly, the Karnataka State Board of Auqaf issued a circular to mosques, calling on them to maintain registers with important documents of all Muslims in their jurisdiction.

These efforts reflect a growing anxiety within the community about the need to constantly prove their citizenship and belonging. This anxiety is particularly acute among poorer and less educated Muslims, who may have limited access to official documentation or face challenges in navigating bureaucratic processes.

Responses from Islamic Religious Leaders

The responses from Islamic religious leaders to the CAA have been varied, reflecting the diversity of opinions within the Muslim community.

Some prominent Muslim organizations have come out in support of the CAA. The All India Muslim Jamaat (AIMJ) has backed the law; with its president Maulana Shahabuddin Razvi Bareilvi stating that the CAA will not negatively impact the status of Indian Muslims. Bareilvi attributed previous protests against the CAA to miscommunication and urged Indian Muslims to embrace the law.

Other religious bodies have taken a more cautious approach. The All India Muslim Personal Law Board (AIMPLB) decided to reserve its reaction, with its legal committee studying the CAA notification before issuing any statement. Maulana Khalid Rasheed Farangi Mahali of AIMPLB appealed to community members to maintain peace while the notification is being studied.

The All India Shia Muslim Personal Law Board (AISMPLB) has also called for calm, with its speaker Maulana Mohammad Mirza Yasoob Abbas stating that there is no need to panic over the notification. However, Abbas also appealed to the government to take everyone into confidence before bringing in any law.

Some religious leaders have taken a more critical stance. Zafarul-Islam Khan, former chairman of the Delhi Minorities Commission, has alleged that the sudden implementation of the CAA, after years of delay and weeks before general elections, suggests that the government is using it to polarize society for electoral benefits.

The diversity of responses from Islamic religious leaders reflects the complex and nuanced reactions within the Muslim community to the CAA. While some see the law as benign or even potentially beneficial, others view it as a threat to the secular fabric of India and the citizenship rights of Muslims.

The CAA controversy has highlighted the complex interplay between religion, citizenship, and national identity in India. The exclusion of Muslims from the CAA's provisions has raised significant concerns about discrimination and the potential for the law to be used in ways that marginalize the Muslim community.

While the government insists that the CAA is not anti-Muslim and will not affect the citizenship rights of Indian Muslims, the fears and anxieties within the community persist. The potential combination of the CAA with the proposed NRC has particularly heightened these concerns, leading to efforts within the Muslim community to secure documentation and prepare for potential challenges to their citizenship status.

The responses from Islamic religious leaders have been varied, reflecting the diversity of opinions within the community. As India moves forward with the implementation of the CAA, it will be crucial to address the concerns of the Muslim community and ensure that the law does not lead to further marginalization or discrimination.

The CAA controversy underscores the need for ongoing dialogue and engagement between the government, religious communities, and civil society to address concerns about citizenship, religious discrimination, and national identity. As India continues to navigate these complex issues, it will be essential to uphold the principles of secularism, equality, and non-discrimination enshrined in its Constitution.

References:

1. Amnesty International. (2024). India: Citizenship Amendment Act is a blow to Indian constitutional values and international standards. Retrieved from https://www.amnesty.org/en/latest/news/2024/03/india-citizenship-amendment-act-is-a-blow-to-indian-constitutional-values-and-

international-standards/
2. Foreign Policy. (2020). India's Muslims Fear Deportation Under Citizenship Law. Retrieved from https://foreignpolicy.com/2020/02/21/india-muslims-deported-terrified-citizenship-amendment-act-caa/
3. NDTV. (2024). Does CAA Put Any Restrictions On Muslim Migrants? What Government Said. Retrieved from https://www.ndtv.com/india-news/citizenship-amendment-act-does-caa-put-any-restrictions-on-muslim-migrants-what-government-said-5226063
4. SCObserver. (n.d.). CAA: Writ Petition Summary (Indian Union Muslim League). Retrieved from https://www.scobserver.in/reports/indian-union-muslim-league-citizenship-amendment-act-caa-writ-petition-summary-indian-union-muslim-league/
5. Swarajya. (2024). What Prominent Muslim Leaders And Islamic Organisations Said About CAA. Retrieved from https://swarajyamag.com/politics/what-prominent-muslims-leaders-and-islamic-organisations-said-about-caa
6. Voice of America. (2024). India's Muslims See Discrimination in New Religion-Based Citizenship Law. Retrieved from https://www.voanews.com/a/india-muslims-see-discrimination-in-new-religion-based-citizenship-law/7531377.html

CHAPTER 5: SIKHISM: CAUGHT IN THE CROSSFIRE

The Citizenship Amendment Act (CAA) of 2019 has brought the complex history of Sikh migration and the community's relationship with India's religious landscape into sharp focus. This chapter explores the multifaceted impact of the CAA on Sikhs, tracing their historical migration patterns, examining the divided opinions within the community, and analyzing the potential consequences for Sikh-Muslim relations in border states.

Sikh Refugees and the CAA

The CAA, passed by the Indian Parliament in December 2019, aims to provide a path to Indian citizenship for persecuted religious minorities from Afghanistan, Bangladesh, and Pakistan who entered India before December 31, 2014[5]. The Act specifically includes Hindus, Sikhs, Buddhists, Jains, Parsis, and Christians, but notably excludes Muslims. For many Sikhs who fled religious persecution in neighbouring countries, the CAA represents a potential lifeline to legal status and citizenship in India.

The Akal Takht Jathedar, Giani Harpreet Singh, welcomed the inclusion of Sikhs in the CAA, acknowledging its potential benefits for the community:

"It is a good development and a welcome step. The CAA will be of big relief for the Sikhs who were facing religious persecution. There are Afghan Sikhs who have been attacked and forced to leave their birth place. They will benefit from this Act".

This sentiment reflects the experiences of many Sikh refugees who have sought safety in India after facing discrimination and violence in countries like Afghanistan and Pakistan. The CAA offers these individuals a formal pathway to citizenship, potentially alleviating years of uncertainty and legal limbo.

However, the exclusion of Muslims from the CAA has sparked controversy and debate, even within the Sikh community. The same Akal Takht Jathedar who praised the Act's benefits for Sikhs also expressed concern about its exclusionary nature:

"According to principles of Sikhism, we Sikhs cannot differentiate against anyone on the basis of religion and caste. In the same way, the Constitution also does not differentiate on the basis of religion and caste. So, there was no need to keep the Muslims out".

This statement highlights the tension between the potential benefits for Sikh refugees and the Act's perceived departure from principles of religious equality, which are central to both Sikh teachings and India's secular constitution.

Historical Context of Sikh Migration to India

To understand the significance of the CAA for Sikhs, it is crucial to examine the historical context of Sikh migration to India, particularly in the aftermath of the 1947 Partition.

The Partition and Its Aftermath

The Partition of India in 1947 had a profound and traumatic impact on the Sikh community. As the British colonial rule came to an end, the division of the subcontinent into India and Pakistan led to one of the largest mass migrations in human history. The Punjab region, home to a significant Sikh population, was split between the two new nations.The consequences for Sikhs were particularly severe:

1. Displacement: Approximately 40% of Sikhs were forced to

leave their homes in what became Pakistan, abandoning lands, properties, and sacred shrines.

2. Violence: Sikhs faced widespread violence during the partition, with some estimates suggesting they suffered the highest proportion of casualties relative to their population size.

3. Demographic shifts: The Sikh community, which had been concentrated in Punjab, found itself divided across new national borders.

4. Loss of heritage: Many important Sikh religious sites and historical landmarks were left on the Pakistani side of the border.

The trauma of Partition has left an indelible mark on the Sikh psyche, influencing community attitudes towards issues of citizenship, religious identity, and national belonging for generations.

Post-Partition Migrations

In the decades following Partition, Sikhs continued to migrate to India from neighbouring countries, often in response to political instability, economic factors, or religious persecution. Notable waves of migration included:

1. Afghan Sikhs: Following the Soviet invasion of Afghanistan in 1979 and the subsequent rise of the Taliban, many Sikhs fled to India seeking refuge.

2. Economic migrants: Some Sikhs from Pakistan and Bangladesh moved to India in search of better economic opportunities.

3. Conflict-driven displacement: Political unrest and targeted violence against religious minorities in Pakistan and Afghanistan periodically drove Sikhs to seek safety in India.

These ongoing migrations have contributed to the formation of a diverse Sikh diaspora within India, with varying legal statuses and levels of integration into Indian society.

Divided Opinions Within the Sikh Community

The CAA has elicited a range of responses from within the Sikh community, reflecting the complex interplay of religious identity, political affiliations, and historical experiences.

Support for the CAA

Some Sikh leaders and organizations have expressed support for the CAA, viewing it as a necessary measure to protect persecuted religious minorities. The Act's potential to provide citizenship to Sikh refugees who have long resided in India without legal status is seen as a positive development.

Proponents argue that the CAA addresses a historical injustice, providing a legal framework to accommodate Sikhs who were forced to flee their homes due to religious persecution. This perspective often emphasizes the shared experiences of Hindus and Sikhs as minority communities in Muslim-majority countries like Pakistan and Afghanistan.

Opposition and Concerns: However, significant voices within the Sikh community have raised concerns about the CAA's implications:

1. Religious discrimination: Many Sikhs object to the Act's exclusion of Muslims, viewing it as a violation of the principle of religious equality that is central to Sikh teachings.

2. Secular values: Some Sikh leaders argue that the CAA undermines India's secular constitution by introducing religion as a criterion for citizenship.

3. Potential for division: There are concerns that the Act could exacerbate religious tensions and lead to further marginalization of minority communities.

4. Incomplete protection: Critics point out that the CAA does not address the needs of all persecuted groups, such as Ahmadiyya Muslims or Rohingya refugees.

These diverse perspectives reflect the heterogeneity of the Sikh community and the complex historical relationships between Sikhs, other religious groups, and the Indian state.

Impact on Sikh-Muslim Relations in Border States

The implementation of the CAA has the potential to significantly impact Sikh-Muslim relations, particularly in Border States with sizeable populations of both communities. This dynamic is especially relevant in Punjab, which shares a border with Pakistan and has a history of both interfaith harmony and periodic tensions.

Historical Context of Sikh-Muslim Relations: Sikh-Muslim relations in India have been shaped by a long and complex history:

1. Mughal era: While some Mughal emperors persecuted Sikh Gurus, there were also periods of cooperation and cultural exchange between Sikhs and Muslims.

2. Partition violence: The communal violence during Partition strained relations between Sikhs and Muslims, leaving lasting scars on both communities.

3. Post-independence cooperation: In many areas, Sikhs and Muslims have coexisted peacefully, often finding common cause as religious minorities in a Hindu-majority nation.

4. Shared cultural heritage: Punjab's cultural traditions often transcend religious boundaries, with Sikhs and Muslims sharing linguistic and cultural ties.

Potential Consequences of the CAA: The implementation of the CAA could affect Sikh-Muslim relations in several ways:

1. Increased polarization: The Act's differential treatment of religious groups could exacerbate existing divisions and lead to further polarization between communities.

2. Solidarity among minorities: Conversely, the shared experience of being religious minorities might strengthen bonds between Sikhs and Muslims in opposition to perceived majoritarianism.

3. Refugee integration: The influx of Sikh refugees granted citizenship under the CAA could alter local demographics and potentially impact established community dynamics.

4. Political realignments: The CAA debate might lead to new political alliances or divisions based on attitudes towards the Act, potentially cutting across traditional religious lines.

5. Border security concerns: In Punjab and other border states, changes in citizenship policies could raise complex questions about national security and cross-border movements.

The ultimate impact of the CAA on Sikh-Muslim relations will likely depend on how the Act is implemented, how local communities respond, and the broader political and social context in which these changes occur.

The Citizenship Amendment Act has placed the Sikh community at a complex intersection of historical trauma, religious identity, and contemporary politics. While the Act offers potential benefits to Sikh refugees, it has also sparked debates about religious equality, secularism, and the nature of Indian citizenship.

The divided opinions within the Sikh community reflect broader questions about the balance between addressing historical injustices and maintaining India's secular character. As the CAA move from legislation to implementation, its impact on Sikh-Muslim relations and the broader social fabric of Border States remains to be seen.

Ultimately, the Sikh experience with the CAA underscores the challenges of navigating religious identity and citizenship in a diverse and rapidly changing India. It highlights the need for policies that address the legitimate concerns of persecuted minorities while upholding the principles of equality and inclusivity that are fundamental to both Sikh teachings and India's constitutional values.

References:

1.	Axel, B. K. (2001). The nation's tortured body: Violence, representation, and the formation of a Sikh "diaspora". Duke University Press.

2.	BBC. (2024, March 12). CAA: India's new citizenship law explained. https://www.bbc.com/news/world-asia-india-50670393

3.	Britannica. (2024, November 27). Partition of India. https://www.britannica.com/event/Partition-of-India

4.	Economic Times. (2024, December 28). CAA notification: Religious leaders from Jain, Sikh and other communities support Citizenship Amendment Act, say opposition lacks the vision. https://economictimes.indiatimes.com/news/politics-and-nation/caa-notification-religious-leaders-from-jain-sikh-and-other-communities-support-citizenship-amendment-act-say-opposition-lacks-the-vision/videoshow/108480921.cms

5.	Indian Express. (2019, December 18). Sikhs stand for equality, include Muslims in CAA: Akal Takht Jathedar. https://indianexpress.com/article/india/sikhs-stand-for-equality-include-muslims-in-caa-akal-takht-jathedar-6172454/

6.	Minority Rights Group. (2024). Sikhs in India. https://minorityrights.org/communities/sikhs/

7.	Supreme Court Observer. (n.d.). Citizenship Amendment Act. https://www.scobserver.in/

cases/constitutionality-of-the-citizenship-amendment-act-2019-caa/

8.   Tatla, D. S. (1999). The Sikh diaspora: The search for statehood. UCL Press.

9.   Wikipedia. (n.d.). Islam and Sikhism. https://en.wikipedia.org/wiki/Islam_and_Sikhism

10.   Wikipedia. (n.d.). Sikh diaspora. https://en.wikipedia.org/wiki/Sikh_diaspora

CHAPTER 6: CHRISTIANITY AND THE CAA DEBATE

The Citizenship Amendment Act (CAA) of 2019 has sparked significant controversy and debate in India, with implications extending to various religious communities, including Christians. This chapter explores the multifaceted relationship between Christianity and the CAA, examining its impact on Christian refugees, reactions from Indian Christian communities, potential influences on missionary activities, and the role of interfaith dialogue in addressing the challenges posed by this legislation.

Christian Refugees from Neighbouring Countries

The CAA aims to provide expedited citizenship to non-Muslim refugees, including Christians, from Afghanistan, Bangladesh, and Pakistan who entered India before December 31, 2014 (Singh, 2024). This provision has direct implications for Christian refugees from these countries who have sought asylum in India due to religious persecution.

Christians, particularly those from Pakistan and Afghanistan, have faced significant challenges in their home countries. In Pakistan, Christians have been subjected to blasphemy laws, forced conversions, and targeted violence (Guha, 2024). Similarly, in Afghanistan, especially under Taliban rule, Christians have faced severe persecution and threats to their lives and freedom of religion.

The CAA's inclusion of Christians among the eligible groups for expedited citizenship has been viewed positively by some Christian refugees. It offers them a potential path to legal status and citizenship in India, which could provide greater security and opportunities for integration into Indian society. However, the implementation of the CAA has raised concerns about the process and criteria for proving religious persecution, which may pose challenges for some Christian refugees seeking to benefit from this provision.

It is important to note that while the CAA provides a pathway for Christian refugees from the specified countries, it does not extend the same benefits to Christian refugees from other neighbouring countries such as Myanmar or Sri Lanka, where Christians have also faced persecution. This limitation has been criticized by some human rights organizations and Christian advocacy groups as being inconsistent and potentially discriminatory.

Reactions from Indian Christian Communities

The response to the CAA from Indian Christian communities has been mixed, reflecting the diverse perspectives within this religious minority. Some Christian leaders and organizations have expressed support for the Act, viewing it as a measure to protect persecuted religious minorities. They argue that the CAA aligns with India's historical tradition of providing refuge to those fleeing religious persecution.

However, many Indian Christian leaders and institutions have voiced strong opposition to the CAA, citing concerns about its implications for India's secular fabric and constitutional values. The National Council of Churches in India (NCCI), representing 30 churches and 14 million Christians, has taken a firm stance against the CAA. In their official statement, the NCCI emphasized:

"We strongly believe that any amendment to say legislation should keep in mind the secular ethos of the Constitution. We believe that an India without its many multiplicities is not the India that we know and any attempt to homogenize religion, culture, language, and practices will only polarise communities".

The NCCI's position reflects a broader concern among many Indian Christians that the CAA, by introducing religion as a criterion for citizenship, undermines the principles of secularism and equality enshrined in the Indian Constitution. They argue that while the Act may benefit some Christian refugees, its overall impact on India's pluralistic society could be detrimental.

Some Christian leaders have also expressed solidarity with Muslim communities, who are excluded from the CAA's provisions. This interfaith solidarity was particularly evident during the anti-CAA protests in 2019-2020, where Christians joined hands with Muslims and other religious groups in opposing the legislation.

The Catholic Bishops' Conference of India (CBCI) has also weighed in on the debate, emphasizing the need for a comprehensive and non-discriminatory approach to addressing the refugee issue. While acknowledging the plight of persecuted religious minorities, the CBCI has called for a more inclusive policy that considers the humanitarian needs of all refugees, regardless of their religious background.

Influence on Christian Missionary Activities

The implementation of the CAA has raised questions about its potential impact on Christian missionary activities in India. While the Act itself does not directly address missionary work, its broader implications for religious minorities and the socio-political climate it has created may indirectly affect such activities.

One potential consequence is increased scrutiny of foreign Christian organizations and missionaries operating in India. The CAA, coupled with other measures such as stricter regulation of foreign funding for NGOs, has led to concerns about heightened government oversight of religious activities, particularly those involving foreign nationals or funding.

Some Christian leaders worry that the polarized atmosphere surrounding the CAA debate may lead to increased suspicion or hostility towards missionary activities, particularly in regions where such work is already viewed with skepticism. This could potentially result in greater challenges for Christian organizations engaged in educational, healthcare, and social welfare activities.

Conversely, the CAA's provisions for expedited citizenship for persecuted Christians from neighbouring countries could potentially facilitate the entry and integration of Christian workers from these nations into India. This could lead to new opportunities for cross-border religious and cultural exchange within Christian communities.

It is important to note that the long-term impact of the CAA on Christian missionary activities remains to be seen and will likely depend on various factors, including its implementation, judicial review, and broader societal responses.

Interfaith Dialogue in the Wake of CAA

The controversy surrounding the CAA has underscored the importance of interfaith dialogue and cooperation in addressing social and political challenges. The Act has prompted renewed efforts among religious communities to engage in constructive dialogue and build solidarity across faith lines.

Initiatives like "In Sync," India's first forum for Interfaith Arts and Dialogue, have emerged as platforms for fostering understanding and cooperation between different religious communities. These efforts draw inspiration from the interfaith solidarity witnessed during the anti-CAA protests, where people of various faiths came together to oppose what they perceived as discriminatory legislation.

Christian leaders and organizations have played a significant role in these interfaith initiatives. Many have emphasized the need for a united front among religious minorities to address shared concerns about religious freedom, equality, and social harmony. The NCCI, for instance, has called for efforts to "ensure peace in our country" and has pledged support for maintaining communal harmony.

Interfaith dialogue in the context of the CAA debate has focused on several key themes:

1. Shared values of secularism and religious pluralism

2. The importance of constitutional rights and equal citizenship

3. Addressing misconceptions and stereotypes about different religious communities

4. Collaborative approaches to social justice and human rights issues

These dialogues have not been without challenges. The polarized nature of the CAA debate has sometimes made it difficult to find common ground. However, many religious leaders see these challenges as opportunities to build stronger interfaith relationships and to work towards a more inclusive and harmonious society.

Christian participation in these interfaith efforts has been particularly significant given Christianity's status as both a minority religion in India and one of the beneficiary groups under the CAA. This unique position has allowed Christian leaders to bridge divides and advocate for a more comprehensive approach to addressing religious persecution and refugee rights.

References:

1.   Bhat, M. A. (2019). The constitutional case against the Citizenship Amendment Bill. Economic and Political Weekly, 54(3), 12-14.

2.   Guha, R. (2024). Understanding the Citizenship Amendment Act: A comprehensive analysis. Indian Journal of Political Science, 85(2), 245-260.

3.   National Council of Churches in India. (n.d.). National Council of Churches in India on Citizenship Amendment Act. Retrieved from https://www.globalministries.org/nccindia_responds_to_caa/

4.   Singh, A. (2024). The Citizenship Amendment Act: Implications for religious minorities in India. South Asian Survey, 31(1), 78-95.

5.   United States Institute of Peace. (2020). Combating Religious Discrimination in India and Beyond. Retrieved from https://www.usip.org/publications/2020/05/combating-religious-discrimination-india-and-beyond

CHAPTER 7: BUDDHISM: THE MIDDLE PATH IN CAA DISCUSSIONS

The Citizenship Amendment Act (CAA) of 2019 has sparked intense debates across India and internationally, touching on fundamental questions of religious identity, citizenship, and human rights. Within this complex discourse, the Buddhist perspective offers a unique lens through which to examine the implications and ethical considerations of the CAA. This chapter explores the multifaceted relationship between Buddhism and the CAA, delving into the experiences of Buddhist refugees, the diverse viewpoints within Buddhist communities, the impact on Indo-Tibetan relations, and the application of Buddhist principles of compassion in the context of citizenship legislation.

Buddhist Refugees and the CAA

The CAA explicitly includes Buddhists among the religious minorities eligible for expedited citizenship if they fled from Afghanistan, Bangladesh, or Pakistan due to religious persecution. This inclusion recognizes the historical and ongoing challenges faced by Buddhist communities in these predominantly Muslim nations.

Historical Context

Buddhism has a long and complex history in South Asia, with its influence waxing and waning over centuries. In the countries specified by the CAA, Buddhist populations have often found themselves in vulnerable positions:

- Afghanistan: Once a center of Buddhist culture,

Afghanistan saw the destruction of its Buddhist heritage, most notably the Bamiyan Buddhas, by the Taliban in 2001. The Buddhist population in Afghanistan has been virtually non-existent for centuries.

- Bangladesh: Despite a rich Buddhist heritage, the Buddhist minority in Bangladesh has faced discrimination and occasional violence. The 2012 Ramu violence, where Buddhist temples and homes were attacked, highlights the precarious situation of Buddhists in the country.
- Pakistan: The Buddhist population in Pakistan is extremely small, primarily concentrated in Sindh and Khyber Pakhtunkhwa provinces. They often face marginalization and lack of recognition.

Impact of the CAA on Buddhist Refugees: The inclusion of Buddhists in the CAA potentially offers a lifeline to those facing persecution in these countries. However, the actual impact on Buddhist refugees may be limited due to several factors:

1. Small Population: The number of Buddhist refugees from these countries is relatively small compared to other religious groups mentioned in the Act.

2. Tibetan Exclusion: The CAA does not address the situation of Tibetan refugees in India, who form a significant Buddhist refugee population but are not from the specified countries.

3. Documentation Challenges: Like other refugee groups, Buddhist refugees may face difficulties in providing the necessary documentation to prove their religious affiliation and date of entry into India.

Perspectives from Different Buddhist Sects: The Buddhist community is not monolithic, and different sects and schools of Buddhism have varying perspectives on the CAA and its implications.

Theravada Perspective

Theravada Buddhism, prevalent in South and Southeast Asia, emphasizes individual enlightenment and strict adherence to the monastic code. Some Theravada leaders have expressed support for the CAA, viewing it as a means to protect persecuted Buddhists. However, others have raised concerns about the potential for the Act to create divisions and conflict, which goes against Buddhist principles of harmony and non-violence.

Mahayana Perspective

Mahayana Buddhism, with its emphasis on compassion for all sentient beings, presents a more complex view of the CAA. Some Mahayana leaders have argued that the Act's selective approach to citizenship contradicts the Buddhist ideal of universal compassion. They contend that protection should be extended to all persecuted groups, regardless of religious affiliation.

Vajrayana Perspective

The Vajrayana tradition, particularly influential in Tibetan Buddhism, brings unique considerations to the CAA debate. While Tibetan refugees are not directly addressed by the Act, the Vajrayana perspective often emphasizes the interconnectedness of all beings and the importance of compassionate action.

Ambedkarite Buddhist Perspective

Followers of B.R. Ambedkar's interpretation of Buddhism, particularly prevalent among Dalit communities in India, have expressed mixed views on the CAA. Some see it as a potential tool for upliftment of marginalized Buddhist communities, while others critique its exclusion of Muslim refugees and its potential to exacerbate social divisions.

Impact on Indo-Tibetan Relations

The CAA has significant implications for Indo-Tibetan relations, despite not directly addressing Tibetan refugees. The Act's focus on religious persecution in neighbouring countries raises questions about India's stance towards Tibetan Buddhists who have sought refuge in India since the 1950s.

Historical Context of Tibetan Refugees in India

India has been home to a large Tibetan refugee population since the Dalai Lama's exile in 1959. The Indian government has generally maintained a supportive stance towards Tibetan refugees, allowing them to establish settlements and institutions across India.

CAA's Indirect Impact on Tibetan Refugees: While the CAA does not directly affect the status of Tibetan refugees, it has sparked discussions about India's refugee policies more broadly. Some key considerations include:

1. Citizenship Aspirations: The CAA has reignited debates about potential pathways to citizenship for long-term Tibetan residents in India.

2. Geopolitical Implications: India's approach to Tibetan refugees is intertwined with its complex relationship with China. The CAA's focus on religious persecution in specific countries may indirectly influence India's stance on Tibet-related issues.

3. Buddhist Solidarity: The Act's inclusion of Buddhists from other countries may strengthen feelings of Buddhist solidarity, potentially benefiting Tibetan communities in India.

Tibetan Government-in-Exile's Response

The Central Tibetan Administration (CTA), often referred to as the Tibetan government-in-exile, has maintained a cautious stance on the CAA. While not directly commenting on the Act, the CTA continues to advocate for the rights and welfare of Tibetan refugees in India.

Buddhist Principles of Compassion in the CAA Context

Buddhist teachings on compassion, non-violence, and interdependence offer a valuable framework for examining the ethical implications of the CAA.

Karuna (Compassion) and the CAA

The Buddhist concept of karuna, or compassion, emphasizes the alleviation of suffering for all beings. In the context of the CAA, this principle raises questions about the Act's selective approach to citizenship:

- Universal Compassion: Does the CAA align with the Buddhist ideal of extending compassion to all, regardless of religious affiliation?
- Alleviating Suffering: To what extent does the Act address the suffering of persecuted minorities, and does it potentially create new forms of suffering for excluded groups?

Ahimsa (Non-violence) and Social Harmony: The Buddhist principle of ahimsa, or non-violence, extends beyond physical harm to include the avoidance of actions that create discord or suffering. The CAA's impact on social harmony in India can be examined through this lens:

- Potential for Conflict: Critics argue that the Act's religious-based criteria for citizenship may exacerbate existing social tensions.
- Peaceful Coexistence: Buddhist teachings emphasize the importance of creating conditions for peaceful coexistence among diverse communities.

Pratityasamutpada (Interdependence) and Citizenship: The Buddhist concept of pratityasamutpada, or interdependent origination, highlights the interconnectedness of all phenomena. Applied to the CAA, this principle invites reflection on the broader implications of citizenship policies:

- Global Interconnectedness: How does the Act reflect or challenge the reality of global interdependence and human migration?
- Long-term Consequences: What are the potential ripple effects of the CAA on India's social fabric and international relations?

Middle Path Approach: Buddhism's emphasis on the Middle Path, avoiding extremes, offers a potential framework for addressing the complex issues surrounding the CAA:

- Balancing Compassion and Security: How can India address genuine concerns about religious persecution while maintaining principles of equality and non-discrimination?
- Inclusive Dialogue: The Middle Path approach encourages open and respectful dialogue among different viewpoints, potentially offering a way forward in the polarized CAA debate.

The Citizenship Amendment Act of 2019 presents a complex set of challenges and opportunities when viewed through the lens of Buddhist principles and experiences. While the Act offers potential relief to persecuted Buddhist minorities from specific countries, it also raises important questions about the nature of compassion, equality, and social harmony in contemporary India.

The diverse perspectives within the Buddhist community reflect the multifaceted nature of the CAA debate. From the practical concerns of Buddhist refugees to the philosophical reflections on compassion and interdependence, Buddhism offers valuable insights into the ethical dimensions of citizenship and belonging.

As India continues to grapple with the implementation and implications of the CAA, the Buddhist emphasis on the Middle Path may provide a valuable approach to navigating the complex terrain of religious identity, human rights, and national policy. By encouraging dialogue, compassion, and a nuanced understanding of interdependence, Buddhist principles can contribute to a more inclusive and harmonious resolution to the challenges posed by the CAA.

Ultimately, the intersection of Buddhism and the CAA highlights the ongoing relevance of ancient wisdom in addressing contemporary social and political issues. As India and the world continue to face complex questions of citizenship, migration, and religious freedom, the Buddhist perspective offers a unique and valuable contribution to these crucial discussions.

References

1. Supreme Court Observer. (n.d.). Citizenship Amendment Act - Supreme Court Observer. https://www.scobserver.in/cases/constitutionality-of-the-citizenship-amendment-act-2019-caa/
2. Wikipedia. (2024). Citizenship (Amendment) Act, 2019. https://en.wikipedia.org/wiki/Citizenship_(Amendment)_Act,_2019
3. Wikipedia. (2024). Tibetan Buddhism. https://en.wikipedia.org/wiki/Tibetan_Buddhism
4. Polar Journal. (2020, September 7). India's Citizenship Amendment Act (CAA). https://polarjournal.org/2020/09/07/indias-citizenship-amendment-act-caa-citizenship-and-belonging-in-india/
5. Amnesty International. (2024, March). India:

Citizenship Amendment Act is a blow to Indian constitutional values and international standards. https://www.amnesty.org/en/latest/news/2024/03/india-citizenship-amendment-act-is-a-blow-to-indian-constitutional-values-and-international-standards/

6. Vajira IAS Academy. (2024, December 10). Citizenship Amendment Act (CAA) 2019 - Latest Rules. https://vajiramandravi.com/quest-upsc-notes/citizenship-amendment-act/

CHAPTER 8: JAINISM AND THE CITIZENSHIP QUESTION

The Citizenship Amendment Act (CAA) of 2019 has sparked significant debate and discussion across India, including within the Jain community. This chapter explores the multifaceted relationship between Jainism and the citizenship question, examining the Jain community's response to the CAA, the application of the ahimsa principle in the context of refugee acceptance, the potential impact on Jain business communities, and Jain perspectives on national security and compassion.

Jain Community's Response to the CAA

The Jain community's response to the Citizenship Amendment Act has been largely supportive, aligning with the broader acceptance from various religious minority groups in India. Religious leaders from the Jain community, along with those from Sikh and other communities have expressed their support for the CAA, viewing it as a positive step towards addressing the plight of persecuted minorities from neighbouring countries.

The CAA, which amends the Citizenship Act of 1955, provides an accelerated pathway to Indian citizenship for persecuted religious minorities from Afghanistan, Bangladesh, and Pakistan who entered India on or before December 31, 2014. The act specifically mentions six religious communities: Hindus, Sikhs, Buddhists, Jains, Parsis, and Christians.

Reasons for Support

1. Protection of Persecuted Minorities: Many Jain leaders view

the CAA as a necessary measure to protect and provide refuge to persecuted religious minorities from neighbouring countries. This aligns with the Jain principle of compassion and the duty to help those in need.

2. Historical Context: The support for the CAA among Jains can be understood in the context of India's partition and the subsequent treatment of minorities in neighbouring countries. The act is seen as a means to address the historical injustices faced by these communities.

3. Preservation of Cultural Heritage: As a minority community themselves, Jains may see the CAA as a way to preserve and protect the cultural and religious heritage of persecuted groups, which resonates with their own experiences and concerns.

Voices of Support

Prominent Jain religious leaders have publicly endorsed the CAA, emphasizing its importance in addressing the needs of persecuted minorities. For instance, Dasturji Khurshed Dastoor, the high priest of the Udvada temple, stated, "The initiative taken by Modi ji should be welcomed but the opposition lacks the vision. We see it as a welcome step for the country and our community. It will be helpful for the people of our community to get citizenship in this holy land".

Concerns and Criticisms

While there is significant support for the CAA within the Jain community, it is important to note that opinions are not monolithic. Some members of the community have expressed concerns about the act's potential to create divisions and its perceived discriminatory nature, particularly its exclusion of Muslim refugees.

Ahimsa Principle in the Context of Refugee Acceptance

The principle of ahimsa, or non-violence, is a cornerstone of Jain philosophy and ethics. In the context of refugee acceptance and the CAA, the application of ahimsa presents both support for and challenges to the act.

Ahimsa as Support for Refugee Acceptance

1. Compassion for the Persecuted: The Jain concept of ahimsa extends beyond mere non-violence to encompass active compassion for all living beings. In this light, providing refuge to persecuted minorities can be seen as an expression of ahimsa, as it aims to alleviate suffering and protect vulnerable populations.

2. Protection of Life: Jainism places supreme importance on the protection of life, considering it the highest form of charity (abhayadānam). By offering citizenship to those fleeing religious persecution, the CAA can be viewed as aligned with this aspect of ahimsa.

3. Minimizing Harm: From a Jain perspective, the CAA could be seen as a means to minimize harm by providing a safe haven for those who have faced violence and discrimination in their home countries.

Challenges to Ahimsa in the CAA

1. Selective Application: The exclusion of certain groups, particularly Muslims, from the CAA's provisions could be seen as conflicting with the universal application of ahimsa. Jain philosophy emphasizes compassion for all living beings, regardless of religious affiliation.

2. Potential for Social Conflict: The implementation of the CAA has led to protests and social unrest in parts of India. From an ahimsa perspective, any policy that leads to violence or social discord could be viewed as problematic.

3. Discrimination Concerns: The principle of ahimsa is closely

tied to the concept of equality and respect for all life. The CAA's differentiation based on religion might be seen as inconsistent with this aspect of ahimsa.

Impact on Jain Business Communities

The Jain community has historically been associated with business and commerce, often avoiding occupations that could potentially cause harm to living beings. The implementation of the CAA could have various impacts on Jain business communities:

Potential Positive Impacts

1. Expanded Labor Pool: The influx of skilled and unskilled workers from the communities granted citizenship under the CAA could provide Jain businesses with a larger labor pool, potentially benefiting industries where Jains are prominently involved.

2. New Market Opportunities: The integration of new citizens could create new market segments and business opportunities, particularly in sectors catering to the specific needs of these communities.

3. Enhanced International Relations: If the CAA leads to improved relations with neighbouring countries, it could potentially open up new avenues for international trade and business expansion for Jain entrepreneurs.

Potential Challenges

1. Social Unrest and Economic Instability: The protests and social tensions surrounding the CAA implementation could lead to economic instability, affecting businesses across the board, including those owned by Jains.

2. Ethical Dilemmas: Jain business owners might face ethical dilemmas if their business practices or employment policies are perceived as conflicting with the principles of equality and

non-discrimination, especially in light of the CAA's selective approach.

3. Reputational Risks: Businesses associated with communities supporting the CAA might face reputational risks in regions or markets where the act is viewed unfavourably.

Jain Perspectives on National Security and Compassion

The CAA brings to the forefront the complex interplay between national security concerns and the principle of compassion, both of which are relevant to Jain perspectives.

Balancing Security and Compassion

1. National Security Considerations: While Jainism emphasizes non-violence and compassion, it also recognizes the need for societal order and protection. Some Jains may view the CAA as a necessary measure to address potential security threats posed by illegal immigration.

2. Compassionate Approach to Security: The Jain approach to national security would likely emphasize non-violent methods and solutions that minimize harm to all parties involved. This could include supporting measures that address the root causes of refugee crises and illegal immigration.

3. Selective Compassion vs. Universal Compassion: The CAA's selective approach to granting citizenship based on religion presents a dilemma when viewed through the lens of Jain universal compassion. While it extends compassion to certain persecuted groups, it potentially excludes others who may be equally in need.

Jain Ethical Framework in Policy Evaluation

1. Anekantavada (Many-Sidedness): This Jain principle of multiple viewpoints could be applied to understand the complex issues surrounding citizenship and immigration,

encouraging a nuanced approach that considers various perspectives.

2. Aparigraha (Non-Possessiveness): This principle might inspire a more open approach to sharing resources and opportunities with refugees and immigrants, potentially supporting policies that are more inclusive than the current CAA.

3. Satya (Truthfulness): The Jain emphasis on truth could be relevant in evaluating the implementation and effects of the CAA, encouraging transparency and honest assessment of its impacts.

Reconciling Tradition and Contemporary Challenges

1. Adapting Ancient Principles: Jain leaders and scholars face the challenge of interpreting and applying ancient ethical principles to contemporary issues like citizenship and immigration.

2. Engaging in Public Discourse: The CAA debate provides an opportunity for the Jain community to engage in broader public discussions on ethics, governance, and social responsibility.

3. Promoting Non-Violent Solutions: Jain perspectives could contribute to developing non-violent approaches to addressing the complex issues of refugee rights, national security, and social integration.

In conclusion, the Citizenship Amendment Act of 2019 presents a complex set of issues when viewed through the lens of Jainism. While there is significant support for the act within the Jain community, particularly from religious leaders who see it as a compassionate response to the plight of persecuted minorities, the CAA also raises challenging questions about the application of core Jain principles like ahimsa and universal compassion in the context of modern governance and national security.

The Jain community's response to the CAA reflects the broader debates within Indian society about identity, security, and the nature of citizenship. As the implementation of the act continues and its long-term impacts become clearer, it will be interesting to observe how Jain perspectives on these issues evolve and contribute to the on-going national dialogue on citizenship and social inclusion.

References:

1. Amnesty International. (2024, March). India: Citizenship Amendment Act is a blow to Indian constitutional values and international standards.
2. Chhajed, S. (2022, February). Jain Perspective of Compassion in current times. Jainavenue.
3. Economic Times. (2024, December 28). CAA notification: Religious leaders from Jain, Sikh and other communities support Citizenship Amendment Act, say opposition lacks the vision.
4. Press Information Bureau, Government of India. (2019). Parliament passes the Citizenship (Amendment) Bill 2019.
5. Supreme Court Observer. (n.d.). Citizenship Amendment Act.
6. Wikipedia. (2024, November 15). Citizenship (Amendment) Act, 2019.
7. Wikipedia. (2024, October 13). Ahimsa in Jainism.
8. Wikipedia. (2024, October 5). Refugees in India.

CHAPTER 9: ZOROASTRIANISM: A UNIQUE PERSPECTIVE

The Parsi community, adherents of Zoroastrianism in India, offers a unique perspective on religious migration, cultural preservation, and demographic challenges. This chapter explores the historical journey of Parsis to India, their views on contemporary legislation, demographic trends, and efforts to maintain their distinct identity in a rapidly changing world.

Parsi Community's Historical Migration to India

The story of the Parsi community in India is one of religious persecution, migration, and cultural adaptation. Following the Arab-Islamic conquest of Iran in the 7th century CE, Zoroastrians faced increasing pressure to convert to Islam. This led to a significant exodus of Zoroastrians from their Persian homeland to the Indian subcontinent, where they sought refuge and religious freedom.

The exact timeline of this migration is subject to debate among historians. While traditional accounts, such as the Qissa-i Sanjan written in 1599, place the arrival of Zoroastrians in India around the 8th century CE, recent scholarship suggests a more complex picture. Archaeological evidence points to the early-to-mid-eighth century as the most likely period for the initial wave of Zoroastrian immigrants to India.

Upon their arrival in India, the Zoroastrian refugees, who would come to be known as Parsis, settled primarily in the Gujarat region? A popular folktale recounts their reception by the local ruler, Jadi Rana. According to this legend, when presented with a full glass of milk symbolizing that there was no room for newcomers, the Zoroastrian leaders added a spoonful of sugar to the milk. This gesture cleverly illustrated their intention to blend into Indian society while enhancing it, without causing disruption.

The Parsis were allowed to settle under certain conditions, which included adopting the local language (Gujarati), wearing local attire, and explaining their religion to the ruler. These conditions set the stage for the unique cultural synthesis that would characterize the Parsi community in India over the centuries to come.

It's important to note that the migration of Zoroastrians to India was not a single event but occurred in successive waves during the Islamic period. Some scholars, like Andre Wink, suggest that many of these early immigrants were merchants, with religious experts and priests joining them later. This theory aligns with the historical evidence of long-standing trade relations between Iran and India predating the Islamic conquest.

The Parsis initially settled in Sanjan, Gujarat, naming their new home after their hometown in Iran. Over time, they spread to other parts of Gujarat and eventually to other regions of India, particularly to what would become the city of Mumbai (formerly Bombay). The Parsi community played a significant role in the development of Mumbai as a major commercial center during the British colonial period.

Zoroastrian Views on the CAA

The Citizenship Amendment Act (CAA) of 2019 has sparked intense debate in India, and the Parsi community, as one of the religious groups mentioned in the Act, finds itself in a unique position. The CAA aims to provide a pathway to Indian citizenship for persecuted religious minorities from Afghanistan, Bangladesh, and Pakistan, including Hindus, Sikhs, Buddhists, Jains, Parsis, and Christians.

While the CAA explicitly includes Parsis as one of the beneficiary groups, the Zoroastrian community's response to the legislation has been nuanced. As a minority group that has historically benefited from India's tradition of providing refuge to persecuted communities, many Parsis may view the CAA as an extension of this humanitarian principle.

However, the Parsi community's perspective on the CAA is not monolithic. Some members of the community, along with other civil society groups, have expressed concerns about the Act's potential implications for India's secular fabric. The exclusion of certain religious groups, particularly Muslims, from the CAA's provisions has been a point of contention.

Organizations like Amnesty International have criticized the CAA, arguing that it discriminates on the basis of religion and is incompatible with India's international human rights obligations. This criticism extends to concerns about the potential weaponization of the CAA, in conjunction with other proposed measures like the National Register of Citizens (NRC), against minority communities in India.

For the Parsi community, which has long prided itself on its contributions to India's pluralistic society, these debates present a complex challenge. On one hand, the recognition of Parsis in the CAA acknowledges their historical persecution and their status as a religious minority. On the other hand, the community's commitment to secularism and equal treatment of all religions, which has been a hallmark of Parsi integration in India, may lead some to question the exclusionary aspects of the Act.

It's worth noting that the Parsi community's small size and its demographic challenges (discussed in the next section) mean that the practical impact of the CAA on Parsi immigration to India is likely to be limited. However, the Act and the debates surrounding it touch on fundamental questions of religious identity, citizenship, and the nature of Indian secularism – issues that are of great significance to the Parsi community given its unique historical experience in India.

Impact on Parsi Demographics in India

The Parsi community in India faces significant demographic challenges that threaten its long-term survival. Despite their cultural and economic influence, Parsis have experienced a steady decline in population over the past several decades.

In 1941, the Parsi population in India numbered around 114,000[8]. By 2011, this number had dropped dramatically to approximately 50,000, according to the latest census data. This represents a decline of over 50% in just 70 years. The trend shows no signs of reversing, with projections suggesting that the Parsi population could plummet to as low as 23,000 in the near future.

Several factors contribute to this demographic decline:

1. Low Fertility Rates: Parsi fertility rates have fallen below viable levels. Only one in nine wholly Parsi families has a child under the age of 10[7]. In 2013, there were 735 deaths in the community but only 174 births, representing a 13.43% drop from the previous year.

2. Late Marriages and Non-Marriage: One in every 10 Parsi women and one in every five Parsi men remains unmarried by age 50. This high rate of non-marriage significantly impacts the community's birth rate.

3. Intermarriage: There has been a rising trend of marriages outside the community. In 1991, 19% of all Parsi marriages in Mumbai were to non-Parsis. By 2010, this figure had risen to 38%. Traditionally, children of Parsi women who marry outside the community are not accepted as Parsis, further contributing to the population decline.

4. Migration: Many young Parsis have migrated overseas for education and employment opportunities, reducing the number of Parsis of reproductive age in India.

5. Community Practices: The Parsi community's strict endogamy and non-acceptance of converts have limited the potential for population growth.

The demographic decline of the Parsi community has raised serious concerns about its future viability. If current trends continue, the community faces the risk of becoming demographically unsustainable, potentially leading to the loss of a unique cultural and religious tradition.

In response to these challenges, both the Parsi community and the Indian government have initiated efforts to address the population decline. The government launched the "Jiyo Parsi" (Long Live Parsi) scheme in 2013, which includes a series of initiatives aimed at encouraging marriages within the community and promoting childbirth. These efforts include holiday programs for Parsi youth, cultural events to facilitate socializing among young Parsis, and even an online dating platform specifically for the Parsi community.

However, these initiatives face significant challenges. The community's high levels of education and urbanization, coupled with changing social norms, make it difficult to reverse long-standing demographic trends. Additionally, there are ongoing debates within the community about issues such as accepting children of inter-faith marriages, which could potentially expand the community but also raise questions about preserving traditional Parsi identity.

The demographic challenges faced by the Parsi community highlight the complex interplay between cultural preservation, religious identity, and modern social trends. As the community grapples with these issues, it faces the fundamental question of how to ensure its survival while adapting to the realities of contemporary Indian society.

Preserving Zoroastrian Identity in Changing Times

In the face of demographic decline and rapid social change, the Parsi community has been engaged in ongoing efforts to preserve its unique Zoroastrian identity. These efforts span various domains, from cultural and religious practices to tangible and intangible heritage preservation.

One of the key initiatives in this regard is the UNESCO Parzor Project, which aims to preserve and promote Parsi Zoroastrian heritage. The project has undertaken extensive documentation of Parsi cultural practices, rituals, and traditions across India. This includes recording oral histories, documenting traditional skills such as incense making and embroidery, and preserving artifacts and manuscripts.

The Parzor Project has also focused on recording the intangible aspects of Parsi-Zoroastrian heritage, recognizing that much of this knowledge is held by elderly members of the community. This work has involved documenting the practices of priests, musicians, artists, and traditional medical practitioners, among others.

In addition to these preservation efforts, the Parsi community has been grappling with questions of identity and adaptation in the modern world. This includes debates about the acceptance of children from inter-faith marriages, the role of women in religious practices, and how to maintain cultural distinctiveness while fully participating in broader Indian society.

The community's efforts to preserve its identity are complicated by its small size and dispersed nature. Many of the smaller Parsi settlements, particularly in interior regions of India, are in danger of disappearing. This has led to increased efforts to document and preserve the diverse lifestyles and practices found across different Parsi communities in India.

Another aspect of identity preservation relates to the community's connections with its Iranian roots. Some Parsis have been migrating back to Iran, strengthening ties between the Indian and Iranian Zoroastrian communities. This connection to Iran serves as a reminder of the community's ancient heritage and has played a role in shaping Parsi identity in India.

The Parsi community's efforts to preserve its identity also extend to the realm of public perception and representation. Parsis have long been known for their contributions to Indian business, science, and culture, and maintaining this legacy of achievement is seen as an important aspect of community identity.

However, these efforts at preservation and adaptation are not without challenges. The community faces tensions between traditionalists who advocate for strict adherence to historical practices and those who argue for more flexibility in defining Parsi identity. These debates touch on fundamental questions of who can be considered a Parsi and how the community can ensure its survival without losing its distinctive character.

In conclusion, the Parsi community in India presents a unique case study in religious migration, cultural adaptation, and the challenges of preserving minority identities in a rapidly changing world. From their historical journey to India centuries ago to their current efforts to address demographic decline and maintain cultural distinctiveness, the Parsis exemplify the complex interplay between tradition and modernity, between preservation and adaptation.

The community's experience raises important questions about the nature of religious and ethnic identity in pluralistic societies, the challenges faced by minority groups in maintaining their traditions, and the role of cultural heritage in shaping community cohesion. As the Parsi community continues to navigate these challenges, its journey offers valuable insights into the broader issues of cultural preservation, religious freedom, and demographic change in contemporary India and beyond.

References:

1. https://en.wikipedia.org/wiki/Zoroastrianism_in_India
2. https://pluralism.org/zoroastrians-in-india-and-iran
3. https://www.hinduamerican.org/press/india-citizenship-amendment-bill
4. https://www.demographic-research.org/volumes/vol25/17/25-17.pdf
5. https://www.bbc.com/news/world-asia-india-35219331
6. https://www.dw.com/en/how-can-india-turn-around-the-parsi-communitys-dwindling-demographics/a-62822568
7. https://en.wikipedia.org/wiki/Parsi
8. https://www.unescoparzor.com/heritage-cultural-studies
9. https://journals.sagepub.com/doi/full/10.1177/02627280221120336
10. https://www.opindia.com/2022/07/the-persecution-of-parsis-by-muslims-and-their-migration-to-india/
11. https://www.amnesty.org/en/latest/news/2024/03/india-citizenship-amendment-act-is-a-blow-to-indian-constitutional-values-and-international-standards/

CHAPTER 10: TRIBAL RELIGIONS AND THE CAA

The Citizenship Amendment Act (CAA) of 2019 has sparked widespread debate and controversy across India, particularly regarding its impact on tribal communities and their religious practices. This chapter explores the multifaceted implications of the CAA on indigenous faiths, citizenship issues for tribal populations, its influence on tribal migration patterns, and the challenges of preserving tribal religious identities in light of this legislation.

Impact on Indigenous Faiths and Practices

The CAA's focus on providing citizenship to persecuted religious minorities from Afghanistan, Bangladesh, and Pakistan has raised concerns about its impact on indigenous faiths and practices in India, particularly in the northeastern states.

Threat to Cultural and Religious Diversity

The CAA's emphasis on specific religious groups (Hindus, Sikhs, Buddhists, Jains, Parsis, and Christians) overlooks the rich tapestry of indigenous faiths practiced by many tribal communities. This oversight potentially marginalizes these communities and their unique religious practices, which often do not fit neatly into the categories recognized by the Act.

Erosion of Traditional Belief Systems

There are growing concerns that the influx of migrants facilitated by the CAA could lead to the erosion of traditional tribal belief systems. As new populations settle in tribal areas, there is a risk of cultural dilution and the gradual disappearance of indigenous religious practices. This threat is particularly acute in regions where tribal populations are already minorities within their ancestral lands.

Challenges to Sacred Spaces

Many tribal religions are deeply connected to specific geographical locations, including sacred groves, mountains, and water bodies. The potential demographic changes resulting from the CAA could lead to encroachment on these sacred spaces, disrupting religious practices and rituals that are integral to tribal identities.

Citizenship Issues for Tribal Communities

The implementation of the CAA, especially when considered alongside the proposed National Register of Citizens (NRC), presents significant challenges for tribal communities in establishing their citizenship.

Documentation Challenges

One of the primary issues facing tribal communities is the lack of documentation required to prove citizenship. Many forest-dwelling and nomadic tribes do not possess the necessary papers due to their traditional lifestyles and historical displacement. This puts them at risk of being declared non-citizens, despite their deep-rooted presence in the country.

Historical Displacement and Its Consequences

Tribal communities have faced a long history of displacement due to development projects, mining activities, and other factors. This displacement has often resulted in the disappearance of entire villages, making it extremely difficult for displaced individuals to provide proof of residence or lineage. The CAA and NRC processes do not adequately account for this historical context, potentially rendering many tribal people stateless.

Exclusion from Citizenship Benefits

There are concerns that the CAA's provisions may inadvertently exclude certain tribal communities from citizenship benefits. For instance, some tribal groups who have migrated across borders due to historical reasons or traditional practices may find themselves ineligible for citizenship under the new rules.

CAA's Influence on Tribal Migration Patterns

The implementation of the CAA is likely to have significant effects on tribal migration patterns, both within India and across international borders.

Internal Displacement

The fear of being unable to prove citizenship may lead to internal displacement of tribal communities. Some may be forced to leave their traditional lands in search of areas where they can more easily establish their citizenship status or find safety in numbers.

Cross-Border Movement

The CAA's focus on religious persecution in neighbouring countries may inadvertently encourage cross-border movement of certain tribal groups seeking to benefit from the Act's provisions. This could lead to complex situations where tribal communities are split across international borders, further complicating their citizenship status.

Resettlement Concerns

There are apprehensions that tribal lands may be used as "dumping grounds" for refugees and migrants granted citizenship under the CAA. This could lead to significant demographic changes in tribal areas, altering traditional migration patterns and potentially causing conflicts over land and resources.

Preserving Tribal Religious Identities

In the face of these challenges, preserving tribal religious identities becomes a critical concern. Several factors come into play when considering the preservation of these unique cultural and religious practices.

Legal Protections and Their Limitations

While India has constitutional provisions and laws designed to protect tribal rights, such as the Forest Rights Act, their implementation in the context of the CAA remains uncertain. There is a need for stronger legal frameworks that specifically address the preservation of tribal religious identities in light of potential demographic changes.

Cultural Assimilation vs. Preservation

The influx of new populations into tribal areas may accelerate cultural assimilation processes. While some degree of cultural exchange is inevitable, there are concerns that dominant religious practices may overshadow indigenous faiths. Balancing integration with the preservation of unique tribal religious identities presents a significant challenge.

Education and Awareness

Preserving tribal religious identities requires increased education and awareness, both within tribal communities and in the broader Indian society. Efforts to document and promote understanding of indigenous religious practices can play a crucial role in their preservation.

Autonomy and Self-Governance

Strengthening tribal autonomy and self-governance mechanisms could be key to preserving religious identities. This includes empowering tribal councils and traditional governance structures to have a greater say in matters affecting their communities, including those related to citizenship and religious practices.

In conclusion, the Citizenship Amendment Act of 2019 poses significant challenges to tribal religions and communities in India. Its implementation has far-reaching implications for indigenous faiths, citizenship status of tribal populations, migration patterns, and the preservation of unique religious identities. Addressing these issues requires a nuanced approach that respects the historical context, cultural diversity, and rights of tribal communities while navigating the complex landscape of national citizenship laws.

References:

1. Baruah, S., Gohain, H., & Bhaumik, S. (n.d.). Studies on demographic change and indigenous cultures in northeastern India.
2. Cultural Survival. (n.d.). Citizenship Amendment Bill's impact on Indigenous Peoples in Northeast India.
3. Das, S. (2007). Tribal rights and land issues in Northeast India.
4. Fernandes, W. (2018). Migration and displacement in Northeast India.
5. Hazarika, S. (2004). Land, conflict and refugees in India's North-East.
6. Kujur, A. (2019). Interview on displacement and documentation issues for tribal communities.
7. Laishram, S. (2019). Interview on the impact of CAB on indigenous peoples of the northeast.
8. Sharma, B. K. (2001). Tribal migration in India.

CHAPTER 11: ATHEISM AND SECULARISM IN THE CAA ERA

The Citizenship Amendment Act (CAA) of 2019 has sparked intense debate and controversy in India, raising critical questions about the country's commitment to secularism and the rights of religious minorities. This chapter examines the CAA through the lens of atheism and secularism, exploring rationalist perspectives on the law, the challenges it poses to India's secular fabric, atheist movements' responses to religion-based citizenship, and the delicate balance between national security concerns and secular values.

Rationalist Perspectives on the CAA

From a rationalist standpoint, the CAA represents a troubling departure from the principles of secularism and equality enshrined in the Indian Constitution. The act introduces religion as a criterion for citizenship, granting expedited citizenship to non-Muslim minorities from Afghanistan, Bangladesh, and Pakistan while excluding Muslims from this provision. This selective approach to citizenship based on religious identity runs counter to the rationalist ideal of a society governed by reason and evidence rather than religious belief.

Rationalists argue that the CAA's religious classification is arbitrary and lacks a logical foundation. The act's purported aim of protecting persecuted minorities from neighbouring countries is undermined by its exclusion of other persecuted groups, such as Rohingya Muslims from Myanmar or Tamil Hindus from Sri Lanka. This selective application of humanitarian concern raises questions about the true motivations behind the law.

Furthermore, rationalists point out the inherent contradiction in using religious identity as a basis for citizenship in a supposedly secular state. The CAA effectively creates a hierarchy of religions, privileging certain faiths over others in the realm of citizenship rights. This approach not only violates the principle of state neutrality in matters of religion but also sets a dangerous precedent for further discrimination based on religious identity.

The rationalist critique of the CAA extends to its potential long-term consequences for Indian society. By institutionalizing religious discrimination in citizenship laws, the act may exacerbate existing communal tensions and reinforce divisive ideologies. Rationalists argue that a truly secular and progressive society should move towards eliminating religious considerations from governance, rather than enshrining them in law.

Challenges to the Secular Fabric of India

The CAA poses significant challenges to India's secular fabric, threatening to erode the foundational principles of religious neutrality and equal treatment under the law. India's constitution establishes the country as a secular democracy, guaranteeing equal rights and protections to all citizens regardless of their religious affiliation. The CAA, however, introduces a religious test for citizenship, marking a departure from this secular tradition.

One of the primary challenges posed by the CAA is its potential to alter the demographic and social landscape of India. By providing a path to citizenship for non-Muslim immigrants while excluding Muslims, the act could lead to significant shifts in the religious composition of certain regions, particularly in border areas. This demographic change may, in turn, fuel social tensions and communal conflicts.

The CAA also raises concerns about the erosion of

constitutional protections for religious minorities. By singling out Muslims for exclusion, the act sends a troubling message about the status of India's largest religious minority. Critics argue that this exclusion, coupled with other government policies and rhetoric, contributes to a growing sense of marginalization and insecurity among Indian Muslims.

Furthermore, the CAA challenges the principle of equality before the law, a cornerstone of secular governance. Article 14 of the Indian Constitution guarantees equal protection of the laws to all persons within the territory of India. By creating different standards for citizenship based on religious identity, the CAA appears to violate this fundamental principle. Legal scholars argue that this religious classification fails to meet the test of reasonable classification required under Article 14, as it bears no rational relation to the purported objective of protecting persecuted minorities.

The implementation of the CAA, particularly when considered alongside the proposed National Register of Citizens (NRC), raises additional concerns about the potential for widespread disenfranchisement and statelessness. The combination of these policies could create a situation where individuals, particularly Muslims, may be required to prove their citizenship or risk losing their rights and status within the country.

Atheist Movements' Responses to Religious-Based Citizenship

Atheist and rationalist movements in India have been vocal in their opposition to the CAA, viewing it as a dangerous conflation of religion and citizenship that threatens the secular foundations of the state. These movements have responded to the CAA through various means, including public protests, legal challenges, and advocacy for a more inclusive and secular approach to citizenship.

Many atheist organizations have participated in the widespread protests against the CAA, joining forces with secular civil society groups, students, and concerned citizens. These protests have emphasized the importance of maintaining India's secular character and rejecting any form of religious discrimination in matters of citizenship. Atheist groups have used these platforms to advocate for a rationalist approach to governance that prioritizes evidence-based policymaking over religious considerations.

Atheist movements have also been active in challenging the constitutional validity of the CAA through legal means. They argue that the act violates the basic structure of the Indian Constitution, particularly its commitment to secularism and equality before the law. By supporting legal challenges to the CAA, atheist groups aim to uphold the secular principles enshrined in the constitution and prevent the erosion of India's democratic foundations.

In response to the religious-based citizenship criteria introduced by the CAA, atheist movements have called for a more inclusive and secular approach to citizenship. They advocate for citizenship laws based on universal human rights principles rather than religious identity. This approach would extend protection to all persecuted individuals, regardless of their religious affiliation, and maintain the state's neutrality in matters of faith.

Atheist and rationalist groups have also used the CAA controversy as an opportunity to promote broader discussions about the role of religion in public life and governance. They argue that the CAA exemplifies the dangers of allowing religious considerations to influence state policy, advocating instead for a strict separation of religion and state.

Furthermore, atheist movements have highlighted the potential consequences of the CAA for freedom of belief and non-belief in India. They argue that by privileging certain religious identities in citizenship laws, the act implicitly discriminates against atheists, agnostics, and those who choose not to identify with any religion. This criticism underscores the importance of maintaining a truly secular state that respects the rights of believers and non-believers alike.

Balancing National Security and Secular Values

The CAA has been defended by its proponents as a necessary measure to address national security concerns, particularly with regard to illegal immigration and the protection of persecuted minorities from neighbouring countries. However, critics argue that these security objectives can and should be achieved without compromising India's secular values and constitutional principles.

The challenge of balancing national security and secular values is not unique to India, but the CAA brings this tension into sharp focus. On one hand, the government argues that the act is necessary to provide sanctuary to religious minorities facing persecution in neighbouring Muslim-majority countries. This humanitarian justification is framed within the context of national security, with the implication that these persecuted minorities pose less of a threat to India's security than other immigrant groups.

On the other hand, secular critics and rationalists contend that true national security is best achieved through the consistent application of secular principles and the equal treatment of all individuals, regardless of their religious background. They argue that discriminatory policies like the CAA may actually undermine national security by exacerbating social tensions, alienating minority communities, and providing fuel for extremist ideologies.

The debate surrounding the CAA highlights the need for a

more nuanced and inclusive approach to national security that does not compromise fundamental constitutional values. A truly secure nation, critics argue, is one that upholds the rights and dignity of all its residents, fosters social cohesion, and addresses the root causes of conflict and extremism.

One proposed alternative to the CAA's religion-based approach is the adoption of a refugee policy based on international humanitarian standards. Such a policy would provide protection to persecuted individuals based on their specific circumstances and the dangers they face, rather than their religious identity. This approach would align more closely with India's secular traditions while still addressing legitimate security concerns.

Another important consideration in balancing national security and secular values is the role of the judiciary in safeguarding constitutional principles. The Indian Supreme Court has historically played a crucial role in interpreting and upholding the constitution's secular character. As legal challenges to the CAA make their way through the courts, the judiciary's response will be critical in determining how the balance between security concerns and secular values is struck.

The CAA controversy also raises broader questions about the relationship between secularism and national identity in India. While the country's constitution establishes a secular state, there have been ongoing debates about the role of religion in public life and national culture. The CAA represents a significant shift towards a more explicitly religious conception of Indian citizenship, challenging the longstanding ideal of unity in diversity.

Rationalists and secular advocates argue that true national security is best served by reinforcing India's commitment to pluralism and diversity. They contend that policies that divide citizens along religious lines or create hierarchies of belonging ultimately weaken the social fabric and make the country more vulnerable to internal and external threats.

In conclusion, the Citizenship Amendment Act of 2019 presents significant challenges to India's secular traditions and constitutional principles. From a rationalist perspective, the act's religion-based approach to citizenship is arbitrary, discriminatory, and contrary to the ideals of a secular democracy. The CAA poses serious threats to India's secular fabric, potentially altering the country's demographic landscape and eroding constitutional protections for religious minorities.

Atheist and rationalist movements have responded to the CAA with vocal opposition, participating in protests, supporting legal challenges, and advocating for a more inclusive and secular approach to citizenship. These movements emphasize the importance of maintaining a strict separation between religion and state, and warn of the dangers of allowing religious considerations to influence public policy.

The debate surrounding the CAA highlights the complex challenge of balancing national security concerns with secular values. While proponents argue that the act is necessary to address specific security issues, critics contend that true national security is best achieved through the consistent application of secular principles and the equal treatment of all individuals.

As India grapples with the implications of the CAA, it faces a critical juncture in its history as a secular democracy. The resolution of this controversy will have far-reaching consequences for the country's constitutional values, social cohesion, and national identity. Ultimately, the challenge lies in finding a path forward that addresses legitimate security concerns while upholding the principles of secularism, equality, and justice that have long been central to India's democratic ethos.

References:

1. Amnesty International. (2024). India: Citizenship Amendment Act is a blow to Indian constitutional values and international standards. Retrieved from [1]

2. Chatterji, A. P. (2020). Shaheen Bagh and the Politics of Protest in the Anti-CAA Movement in India. Lectito Publishing. Retrieved from [8]

3. Dutta, D., Roy, S., & Sanganeria, V. (2024). India's Citizenship Amendment Act: Bigotry Triumphs Over Empathy. Routed Magazine. Retrieved from [9]

4. Jaffrelot, C. (2021). Modi's India: Hindu Nationalism and the Rise of Ethnic Democracy. Princeton University Press.

5. Jamal, E. O. (2024). CAA and its effects on Indian secularism and regional stability. The Daily Star. Retrieved from [5]

6. Nagarwal, N. (2024). CAA Rules go against Equality, Federalism, and India's Constitution. Vajira IAS Academy. Retrieved from [4]

7. Patel, A. (2024). India: Citizenship Amendment Act is a blow to Indian constitutional values and international standards. Amnesty International. Retrieved from [1]

8. Suresh, M. (2020). Why the CAA Violates the Constitution. The India Forum. Retrieved from [3]

9. The Amikus Qriae. (2024). The Impact of the Citizenship Amendment Act on Indian Secularism and Citizenship Laws. Retrieved from [6]

10. The Probe. (2024). Is India's Citizenship Amendment Act Eroding the Nation's Secular Fabric? Retrieved from [10]

11. UPSC Daily Current Affairs. (2024). CAA Rules go against Equality, Federalism, and India's Constitution. Vajira IAS Academy. Retrieved from [4]

CHAPTER 12: INTERFAITH MARRIAGES AND THE CAA

Interfaith marriages have long been a topic of discussion and debate in India's diverse religious landscape. With the introduction of the Citizenship Amendment Act (CAA) in 2019, new concerns have arisen regarding the impact on mixed-religion families, citizenship issues for interfaith couples, social acceptance, and legal implications for children born to such unions. This chapter explores these complex intersections between interfaith marriages and the CAA in detail.

Impact on Mixed-Religion Families

The CAA has introduced new complexities for mixed-religion families in India, particularly those involving Muslim and non-Muslim partners. The Act provides expedited citizenship for persecuted religious minorities from Afghanistan, Bangladesh, and Pakistan, specifically mentioning Hindus, Sikhs, Buddhists, Jains, Parsis, and Christians. However, it notably excludes Muslims from this provision.

For interfaith couples where one partner is Muslim and the other belongs to one of the specified religions, the CAA creates an uneven playing field in terms of citizenship rights. This disparity can lead to significant challenges within families:

- Unequal Access to Citizenship: In cases where both partners are immigrants, the non-Muslim partner may have an easier path to citizenship under the CAA, while the Muslim partner faces a more complex process. This inequality can strain relationships and create legal uncertainties for the family unit.

- Impact on Children: Children born to interfaith couples may face confusion regarding their citizenship status, especially if one parent's citizenship is in question. This can lead to emotional stress and identity issues for the children as they grow up.
- Family Separation Concerns: In extreme cases, there are fears that the CAA could potentially lead to family separations if one partner faces deportation while the other is granted citizenship. While the government has stated that the CAA does not affect existing citizens, the anxiety around such possibilities remains a concern for many interfaith families.

The impact of the CAA on mixed-religion families extends beyond legal considerations. It also affects the social and psychological well-being of these families:

- Increased Scrutiny: Interfaith couples, especially those involving Muslim partners, may face increased scrutiny from authorities and society at large. This can lead to feelings of insecurity and marginalization.
- Emotional Stress: The uncertainty surrounding citizenship status can create significant emotional stress for family members, affecting their mental health and overall well-being.
- Community Relations: The CAA's perceived bias against Muslims may strain relationships between interfaith couples and their extended families or communities, potentially leading to isolation or conflict.

Citizenship Concerns for Interfaith Couples

The CAA has raised several citizenship concerns specifically for interfaith couples, particularly in cases where one partner is Muslim. These concerns stem from the Act's focus on religious identity as a criterion for expedited citizenship:

- Unequal Citizenship Pathways: Under the CAA, a Hindu individual married to a Muslim partner from Pakistan, Bangladesh, or Afghanistan would have a faster route to citizenship compared to their spouse. This creates a disparity within the marriage, potentially leading to legal and personal complications.
- Documentation Challenges:Interfaith couples may face additional scrutiny when proving their citizenship or applying for citizenship for their children. The requirement for extensive documentation can be particularly challenging for couples where one partner's religious identity is questioned or disputed.
- Residency Requirements: The CAA's provisions regarding residency requirements for citizenship may create complications for interfaith couples who have moved between countries or have complex migration histories.
- Fear of Statelessness: In extreme cases, there are concerns that Muslim partners in interfaith marriages could face the risk of statelessness if they are unable to prove their citizenship under increasingly stringent requirements.

The citizenship concerns extend beyond legal status to affect various aspects of life for interfaith couples:

- Employment and Education: Uncertainty about citizenship status can impact access to employment opportunities and educational institutions for both partners and their children.

- Property Rights: Questions about citizenship may affect property ownership rights, especially in areas with restrictions on land ownership by non-citizens.
- Travel Restrictions: Couples with unresolved citizenship issues may face difficulties in international travel, affecting their personal and professional lives.

To address these concerns, legal experts and advocacy groups have called for clearer guidelines and protections for interfaith couples under the CAA. Some suggestions include:

- Extending the CAA's provisions to include all persecuted minorities, regardless of religion.
- Implementing specific protections for interfaith couples to ensure equal citizenship rights.
- Providing clear pathways for citizenship for children of interfaith marriages, regardless of their parents' religious backgrounds.

CAA's Influence on Social Acceptance of Interfaith Unions

The introduction of the CAA has had a significant impact on the social perception and acceptance of interfaith marriages in India. While interfaith unions have always faced challenges in the country's diverse religious landscape, the CAA has intensified existing tensions and created new obstacles:

- Increased Polarization: The CAA's focus on religious identity has contributed to increased religious polarization in society. This heightened tension has made it more challenging for interfaith couples to gain acceptance from their families and communities.
- Stigmatization: There is a growing concern that the CAA's perceived bias against Muslims has led to increased stigmatization of interfaith marriages

involving Muslim partners. This stigma can manifest in various forms, from social ostracism to more severe forms of discrimination.

- Legal Scrutiny: The increased focus on religious identity for citizenship purposes has led to greater legal scrutiny of interfaith marriages. Some states have introduced or proposed laws against "forced conversion" through marriage, which critics argue are targeted at interfaith unions.
- Media Representation: The debate surrounding the CAA has influenced media representation of interfaith marriages, often portraying them in a controversial light. This negative portrayal can shape public opinion and further complicate social acceptance.

The CAA's influence on social acceptance of interfaith unions is not uniform across India. Urban areas and more cosmopolitan regions generally show greater acceptance, while rural and more conservative areas may exhibit stronger resistance. Factors influencing social acceptance include:

- Education and Awareness: Higher levels of education and exposure to diverse cultures tend to correlate with greater acceptance of interfaith marriages.
- Regional Variations: Different states in India have varying levels of religious diversity and historical interfaith relations, which affect the acceptance of interfaith unions.
- Generational Differences: Younger generations often show more openness to interfaith marriages compared to older generations, reflecting changing social attitudes.

To counter the negative influence of the CAA on social acceptance of interfaith unions, various initiatives have been undertaken:

- Advocacy Groups: Organizations promoting interfaith harmony and secular values have increased their efforts to support interfaith couples and raise awareness about their rights.
- Legal Support: Legal aid organizations have stepped up to provide support and guidance to interfaith couples facing discrimination or legal challenges.
- Community Building: Support networks and communities for interfaith couples have emerged, providing a safe space for sharing experiences and resources.
- Educational Initiatives: Programs aimed at promoting religious tolerance and understanding in schools and communities have gained importance in light of the CAA debate.

Legal Implications for Children of Interfaith Marriages: The legal status of children born to interfaith couples has always been a complex issue in India, and the introduction of the CAA has added new dimensions to this complexity. The legal implications for these children span various aspects of their lives, from citizenship rights to inheritance laws:

- Citizenship Status: Under the Special Marriage Act (SMA), children born to interfaith couples are considered legitimate and have full inheritance rights from both parents. However, the CAA's focus on religious identity raises questions about how citizenship might be determined for children of interfaith marriages, especially if one parent's citizenship status is in question.
- Religious Identity: In India, a child's religious identity often follows that of the father. However, in interfaith marriages, this can lead to complications, especially when it comes to personal laws governing

marriage, divorce, and inheritance.

- Inheritance Rights: While the SMA provides for equal inheritance rights, the personal laws of different religions may come into play, potentially creating conflicts in inheritance matters for children of interfaith marriages.
- Educational and Employment Opportunities: The religious identity of children from interfaith marriages can affect their access to certain educational institutions or job opportunities that have religion-based reservations or preferences.

The legal landscape for children of interfaith marriages is further complicated by several factors:

- Lack of Uniform Civil Code: India's lack of a Uniform Civil Code means that personal laws based on religious identity continue to play a significant role in matters of marriage, divorce, and inheritance. This can create confusion and legal challenges for children of interfaith marriages.
- State-Specific Laws: Different states in India have varying laws regarding interfaith marriages and the status of children born to such unions. This lack of uniformity can lead to legal ambiguities and challenges.
- Documentation Issues: Children of interfaith marriages may face challenges in obtaining necessary documentation, such as birth certificates or school admission papers, due to confusion over their religious identity or citizenship status.

To address these legal implications, several measures have been proposed or implemented:

- Judicial Interventions: The Indian judiciary has played a crucial role in clarifying the rights of children born to interfaith couples. Several landmark judgments have emphasized the need to protect the interests of these children.

- Legal Reforms: There have been calls for legal reforms to provide clearer guidelines on the status and rights of children born to interfaith couples, especially in light of the CAA.
- Awareness Campaigns: Legal aid organizations and advocacy groups have launched awareness campaigns to educate interfaith couples about their rights and the legal status of their children.
- Streamlined Documentation Processes: Some states have taken steps to simplify documentation processes for children of interfaith marriages, recognizing the unique challenges they face.

In conclusion, the intersection of interfaith marriages and the CAA presents a complex landscape of legal, social, and personal challenges. The impact on mixed-religion families, citizenship concerns for interfaith couples, the CAA's influence on social acceptance, and the legal implications for children born to such unions are all critical aspects that require careful consideration and balanced policy approaches. As India continues to navigate its diverse religious landscape, addressing these issues will be crucial for maintaining social harmony and ensuring equal rights for all citizens, regardless of their religious backgrounds or family structures.

References

1. Aishwarya Sandeep. (n.d.). Rights of children born to couples under the Special Marriage Act. Retrieved from https://aishwaryasandeep.in/rights-of-children-born-to-couples-under-the-special-marriage-act-legal-protections/
2. Drishti IAS. (2020, November 16). The Concerns

over Interfaith Marriages. Retrieved from https://www.drishtiias.com/daily-news-editorials/the-concerns-over-interfaith-marriages

3. Forever Families - BYU. (n.d.). Strengthening Interfaith Marriage. Retrieved from https://foreverfamilies.byu.edu/strengthening-interfaith-marriage

4. Hindus for Human Rights. (n.d.). The Exclusionary Nature of India's Citizenship Amendment Act. Retrieved from https://www.hindusforhumanrights.org/en/blog/the-exclusionary-nature-of-indias-citizenship-amendment-act

5. IQRA IAS. (n.d.). Citizenship Evolution in Democracies and the Impact of CAA, 2019. Retrieved from https://www.iqraias.com/citizenship-evolution-in-democracies-and-the-impact-of-caa-2019/

6. NDTV. (2024, March 19). "Deeply Concerned About Impact Of CAA On Muslims In India": US Senator. Retrieved from https://www.ndtv.com/india-news/deeply-concerned-about-impact-of-caa-on-muslims-in-india-us-senator-5267318

7. Psych Central. (n.d.). The Emotional Challenges of Interfaith Marriage. Retrieved from https://psychcentral.com/lib/the-emotional-challenges-of-interfaith-marriage

8. ScholarWorks. (n.d.). The Challenges of Interfaith Relationships. Retrieved from https://scholarworks.calstate.edu/downloads/j098zd635

9. The Legal Crusader. (2024, August 31). Interfaith Marriages In India: Legal Aspects & Solution. Retrieved from https://thelegalcrusader.in/interfaith-marriages-in-india/

10. The Legal Quorum. (n.d.). Interfaith Marriages in India: Legal Framework, Challenges, and Societal

Perspectives. Retrieved from https://
thelegalquorum.com/interfaith-marriages-in-
india-legal-framework-challenges-and-societal-
perspectives/

11. Times of India. (n.d.). CAA rules decoded: Full
details about criteria, clauses and procedures for
citizenship. Retrieved from https://
timesofindia.indiatimes.com/india/caa-rules-
decoded-full-details-about-criteria-clauses-and-
procedures-for-citizenship/
articleshow/108397559.cms

12. University of 17 August 1945 Semarang. (n.d.).
Interfaith Marriage And Its Legal Consequences
For Children Born According To Islamic Law.
Retrieved from https://ijersc.org/index.php/go/
article/download/303/290/2072

CHAPTER 13: RELIGIOUS MINORITIES FROM NEIGHBOURING COUNTRIES

The South Asian region has long been characterized by complex religious dynamics, with minority groups often facing persecution and discrimination in their home countries. This chapter examines the experiences of religious minority refugees from Pakistan, Bangladesh, and Sri Lanka who have sought safety in neighbouring countries, particularly India. We will explore the challenges these groups face both in their countries of origin and in their efforts to integrate into new societies.

Experiences of Hindu and Sikh Refugees from Pakistan

The partition of India in 1947 led to one of the largest mass migrations in human history, with millions of people crossing newly formed borders based on their religious identities. While this event occurred over 70 years ago, its repercussions continue to be felt today, particularly for religious minorities in Pakistan.

Ongoing Persecution and Exodus

Despite the passage of time, Hindus and Sikhs in Pakistan continue to face significant challenges and discrimination. Many have been forced to flee their homes due to persistent threats, violence, and economic marginalization. The plight of these communities has been described as a "little-known human rights crisis" by activists working to support Pakistani refugees in India.

Hindu Singh Sodha, a prominent advocate for Pakistani

minorities living in India, provides insight into the factors driving this ongoing exodus:

"From the very beginning Pakistan wrote that the government would be known as the 'Islamic Republic of Pakistan' so it is very clear how the non-Muslim people will be treated, in particular the Hindu minority."

This constitutional framework has created an environment where religious minorities often feel like second-class citizens, vulnerable to discrimination and violence.

Forced Conversions and Abductions

One of the most disturbing aspects of the persecution faced by Hindus and Sikhs in Pakistan is the issue of forced conversions, particularly affecting young women and girls. According to a 2018 report by the Movement for Solidarity and Peace in Pakistan, at least 1,000 girls belonging to Christian and Hindu communities are forced to marry Muslim men every year. This practice not only violates the rights of these individuals but also serves to further diminish the size and influence of minority communities.

The emotional toll of these abductions is evident in the account of a Hindu father's public distress after his daughters were abducted and forcibly converted:

"The recent viral video of a Hindu father crying and beating himself up in front of a police station after his daughters were abducted, forcibly converted and married is perhaps the most moving evidence of the sheer helplessness of the Hindus in Pakistan."

Economic and Social Marginalization

Beyond the threat of violence and forced conversions, Hindu and Sikh communities in Pakistan often face economic and social barriers that make daily life increasingly difficult. Many refugees report struggling to access education, employment, and basic services due to their religious identity. This systemic discrimination has led many to conclude that they have no future in Pakistan, despite deep ancestral ties to the region.

Challenges in Seeking Refuge

For those who make the difficult decision to leave Pakistan, the journey to safety is often fraught with danger and uncertainty. Many refugees arrive in India with few possessions and limited resources, having left everything behind. Upon arrival, they face a new set of challenges as they attempt to navigate complex legal systems and establish new lives.

Sodha describes the precarious situation of many Pakistani Hindu migrants in India:

"Until now, there have been no legal mechanisms to ensure the safety and security of these migrants."

Without formal recognition as refugees, many individuals find themselves in a legal limbo, unable to access basic rights and services in their new home.

Christian Refugees from Bangladesh

While Bangladesh was founded on principles of secularism, the country has experienced growing religious tensions in recent years, leading some members of the Christian minority to seek refuge elsewhere.

Persecution and Violence

Christians in Bangladesh, particularly those from Muslim backgrounds, often face significant persecution from both state and non-state actors. This can include discrimination, social ostracism, and in some cases, violent attacks. The situation has been exacerbated by the rise of extremist groups and increasing political instability.

A teenage Christian from Bangladesh named Shakib describes his experiences of bullying and discrimination:

"During Ramadan, they wouldn't sit with me. They said if they sit beside me, it will be 'sinful' and their fasting won't be accepted by Allah. They mocked me and laughed at me because I didn't fast or do Muslim prayers with them."

Such experiences of social exclusion and harassment are common among Christian minorities in Bangladesh, contributing to a sense of insecurity and alienation.

Challenges for Converts

Converts to Christianity from Islam face particularly acute challenges in Bangladesh. Many are forced to practice their faith in secret due to fears of reprisal from family members or the broader community. This lack of religious freedom can have profound psychological impacts and may ultimately drive some individuals to seek asylum in other countries.

Rohingya Christian Refugees

The situation is even more complex for Christian converts among the Rohingya refugee population in Bangladesh. These individuals face a double layer of persecution – first as members of the stateless Rohingya minority, and second as Christians within a predominantly Muslim refugee community.

Arman, a young Rohingya Christian leader, describes the dangers faced by his community:

"There are seventy-eight families who are followers of Jesus, and we (my family and me) are taking care of them. They have all converted from Islam to Christianity. They are mostly my relatives and neighbours from Myanmar. Even though they escaped Myanmar, they are not safe because a terrorist group, Al Yakin, has formed within the Rohingya and has targeted the

Christians, my uncle specifically."

This account highlights the ongoing vulnerability of Christian converts even within refugee settings, where they might reasonably expect to find safety.

Buddhist Refugees from Sri Lanka

Sri Lanka's long-running civil war, which ended in 2009, led to significant displacement both within the country and to neighbouring nations. While the conflict was primarily ethnic in nature, it had religious dimensions that continue to impact inter-community relations today.

Post-War Religious Nationalism

Contrary to hopes for reconciliation following the end of the civil war, Sri Lanka has seen a rise in Sinhala-Buddhist nationalism that has created an increasingly hostile environment for religious minorities, including some Buddhists who do not align with nationalist ideologies.

This resurgent nationalism has manifested in various forms of discrimination and violence:

"Buddhist nationalist groups like Bodo Bala Sena, Ravana Balava, Sinhala Ravana, and the Sinhale Jathika Balamuluwa have launched massive campaigns, both online and on the ground, to restrict Sri Lanka's religious pluralism."

These campaigns have targeted not only other religious groups but also Buddhists who advocate for a more inclusive and pluralistic vision of Sri Lankan society.

Displacement and Seeking Refuge

While less common than Hindu or Christian refugees from other South Asian countries, some Sri Lankan Buddhists have sought asylum abroad due to political persecution or fears of violence. These individuals often face unique challenges, as they may not fit traditional conceptions of religious refugees.

The experience of Buddhist refugees highlights the complex intersections of religion, ethnicity, and politics in the region. Their stories serve as a reminder that persecution can occur even within nominally Buddhist-majority countries and that assumption about the relationship between majority religions and refugee status may not always hold true.

Challenges in Integration and Acceptance

Refugees from religious minority backgrounds face numerous obstacles as they attempt to integrate into new societies, whether in neighbouring South Asian countries or further afield.

Legal Limbo and Lack of Recognition

One of the primary challenges for many religious minority refugees is their lack of legal status. In India, for example, many Pakistani Hindu migrants find themselves in a precarious position:

"Basically, the Pakistani Hindu migrants have neither identity nor a country to call their own even though they regard India as their natural homeland."

Without formal refugee status or a clear path to citizenship, these individuals often struggle to access basic services, find employment, or build stable lives in their new communities.

Social and Cultural Adjustment

Adapting to life in a new country can be particularly challenging for religious minorities who may have distinct cultural practices or beliefs. Even when relocating to countries with similar majority religions, refugees often find that local customs and social norms differ significantly from those in their home communities.

For Christian refugees from Bangladesh or Pakistan, integrating into predominantly Hindu or secular societies can present unique challenges. Similarly, Hindu refugees from Pakistan may struggle to adapt to the specific cultural contexts of Indian states that differ from their ancestral regions.

Economic Hardship

Many religious minority refugees arrive in their host countries with few resources, having left behind property and livelihoods in their haste to escape persecution. Finding employment and establishing financial stability can be extremely difficult, particularly when compounded by language barriers, lack of recognized qualifications, and discrimination.

Ongoing Security Concerns

Even after relocating, many refugees continue to fear for their safety. This is particularly true for those who have fled to neighbouring countries where extremist ideologies may still pose a threat. The attack on Sri Lankan refugees in India following the 2019 Easter bombings illustrates how quickly sentiment can turn against vulnerable populations:

"Targeted by mobs who blame them for the 21 April attacks that killed more than 250 people at three churches and three hotels, the refugees and asylum-seekers – many belonging to persecuted religious minorities from Afghanistan, Iran and Pakistan – say they are reliving the horrors that forced them to originally flee their own countries."

Such incidents underscore the precarious position of religious minority refugees and the ongoing need for protection and support.

Psychological Trauma and Mental Health

The experiences of persecution, displacement, and the

challenges of rebuilding lives in new environments can have severe psychological impacts on refugees. Many struggle with trauma, anxiety, and depression, often without access to adequate mental health support.

Shakib, the young Christian from Bangladesh, describes the emotional toll of constant discrimination:

"When I had to leave my house in Negombo, I cried a lot. It reminded me of the harsh reality of our situation that we are neither safe in our country nor here. I feel vulnerable and insignificant."

Addressing these mental health needs is crucial for successful integration and the long-term well-being of refugee communities.

The experiences of religious minority refugees from Pakistan, Bangladesh, and Sri Lanka highlight the ongoing challenges to pluralism and religious freedom in South Asia. These individuals' stories of persecution, flight, and struggle for acceptance serve as a powerful reminder of the human cost of religious intolerance and the importance of protecting minority rights.

As the region continues to grapple with issues of religious nationalism, extremism, and inter-community tensions, the plight of religious minority refugee's demands greater attention and more comprehensive solutions. Addressing this crisis will require concerted efforts to promote religious tolerance, reform discriminatory laws and practices, and develop more robust systems for protecting and integrating refugees.

Ultimately, the ability of South Asian nations to embrace religious diversity and ensure the rights of all communities will be crucial in stemming the tide of displacement and creating more stable, inclusive societies. The experiences of these refugees underscore the urgent need for such transformations and the potential consequences of failing to address the root causes of religious persecution in the region.

References:

1. Hinduamerican.org. (n.d.). An interview with Pakistani refugee advocate Hindu Singh Sodha. Retrieved from https://www.hinduamerican.org/blog/hindu-singh-sodha-pakistan-refugees-1

2. Swarajyamag.com. (n.d.). Pakistani Hindu Refugees In Rajasthan: A Journey Through Tears, Trial and Triumph. Retrieved from https://swarajyamag.com/politics/pakistani-hindu-refugees-in-rajasthan-a-journey-through-tears-trial-and-triumph

3. Irenees.net. (n.d.). Pakistan : Conflict, Migration and Peace. Retrieved from https://www.irenees.net/bdf_fiche-analyse-648_en.html

4. Opendoorsuk.org. (n.d.). Bangladesh : World Watch List. Retrieved from https://www.opendoorsuk.org/countries-watch/bangladesh/

5. Cambridge.org. (n.d.). Taking refuge in religion: Buddhist-oriented coping following late-life immigration. Retrieved from https://www.cambridge.org/core/services/aop-cambridge-core/content/view/A7970C83758EDAE5E2E052C5F22F127B/S0714980821000684a.pdf/taking-refuge-in-religion-buddhist-oriented-coping-following-late-life-immigration.pdf

6. Gsdrc.org. (2020). Challenges Religious Minorities Face in Accessing Humanitarian Assistance. Retrieved from https://gsdrc.org/publications/challenges-religious-minorities-face-in-accessing-humanitarian-assistance/

7. USCIRF. (2022). 2022 Factsheet - Refugees Fleeing Religious Persecution Globally. Retrieved from https://www.uscirf.gov/sites/default/files/2022-05/2022%20Factsheet%20-%20Refugees%20Fleeing%20Religious%20Persecution%20Globally.pdf

8. YouTube. (n.d.). Sikh Refugees From Pakistan Shares His Experiences. Retrieved from https://www.youtube.com/watch?v=dIX0PaCf1CE

9. Indianexpress.com. (2022). A history of Sri Lankan refugees in India. Retrieved from https://indianexpress.com/article/research/a-history-of-sri-lankan-refugees-in-india-7858886/

CHAPTER 14: THE NORTHEAST INDIA CONUNDRUM

The Northeast region of India presents a complex tapestry of ethnic, cultural, and religious diversity that sets it apart from the rest of the country. This unique composition, coupled with historical, geographical, and political factors, has created a delicate balance that is now being challenged by national policies like the Citizenship Amendment Act (CAA). This chapter explores the intricate religious and ethnic landscape of Northeast India, the fears surrounding demographic changes, the potential impact on indigenous cultures and religions, and the challenge of reconciling national policies with regional sensitivities.

Unique Religious and Ethnic Composition of the Northeast

The Northeast region of India is characterized by a rich mosaic of ethnic groups, languages, and religious practices that reflect its historical and geographical context. This diversity is not only a source of cultural richness but also a complex factor in the region's socio-political dynamics.

Religious Landscape

The religious composition of Northeast India differs significantly from the national average, with Christianity and indigenous tribal religions playing a more prominent role alongside Hinduism and Islam. According to the 2011 Census, while Hinduism remains the most populous religion in the region at 54%, this is significantly lower than the national average of 79.80%. Christianity, on the other hand, represents 17.34% of the region's population, compared to just 2.30% nationally.

The distribution of religious groups varies widely across the Northeastern states:

- Nagaland has the highest proportion of Christians at 87.93%, followed closely by Mizoram at 87.16%.
- Meghalaya has a Christian majority of 74.59%.
- Tripura has the highest proportion of Hindus at 83.40%, followed by Assam at 61.47%.
- Assam has a significant Muslim population at 34.22%, the highest in the region.

This religious diversity is further enriched by the presence of Buddhism, particularly in Arunachal Pradesh (11.77%) and Mizoram (8.51%). Sikhism and Jainism also have small but notable presences in certain states.

Ethnic Diversity: The ethnic landscape of Northeast India is equally diverse, with numerous indigenous tribes and communities contributing to the region's cultural tapestry. Each state has its own unique ethnic composition:

- Arunachal Pradesh is home to various tribal groups with distinct religious practices such as Donyi-Polo, Wancho, and Nocte.
- Assam has significant populations of Karbis and Bodos, many of whom identify with "unclassified religions".
- Meghalaya features tribal religions like Songsarek, Niamtre, and Bhoi.
- Manipur and Nagaland are known for their Naga and Kuki tribal religions.

This ethnic diversity is reflected in the multitude of languages spoken across the region, with each community often having its own distinct dialect or language.

Historical Context: The unique religious and ethnic composition of Northeast India is the result of centuries of migration, cultural exchange, and historical events. The region has been influenced by various factors:

1. Ancient tribal settlements and migrations from neighbouring regions.

2. The spread of Hinduism and Buddhism through trade and royal patronage.

3. The arrival of Islam through conquest and trade.

4. The significant impact of Christian missionaries during the colonial period.

5. British colonial policies that encouraged migration for economic purposes.

These historical processes have created a complex social fabric where traditional tribal beliefs coexist with major world religions, often resulting in syncretic practices and beliefs.

Fears of Demographic Change Due to CAA

The introduction of the Citizenship Amendment Act (CAA) in 2019 has reignited long-standing concerns about demographic changes in Northeast India. The CAA, which aims to provide citizenship to persecuted minorities from Afghanistan, Bangladesh, and Pakistan, has been met with significant resistance in the region.

Historical Context of Migration: The Northeast's concerns about demographic change are rooted in historical experiences:

1. British colonial policies encouraged migration into Assam and Bengal for agricultural development.

2. The partition of India in 1947 led to significant population movements.

3. The Bangladesh Liberation War in 1971 resulted in a large

influx of refugees.

These historical events have shaped the region's perception of migration and its impact on local demographics.

Specific Concerns Related to CAA: The CAA has sparked several specific fears among the indigenous populations of Northeast India:

1. Alteration of Demographic Balance: There are concerns that the CAA could lead to a significant influx of new citizens, potentially altering the delicate demographic balance in the region.

2. Strain on Resources: The potential influx of new citizens is seen as a threat to limited local resources, including land, employment opportunities, and public services.

3. Cultural Dilution: Indigenous communities fear that large-scale migration could lead to the erosion of their distinct cultural identities and practices.

4. Political Representation: Changes in demographics could impact political representation, potentially marginalizing indigenous voices in local and state governance.

5. Economic Competition: There are concerns about increased competition for jobs and economic opportunities in a region already facing development challenges.

Regional Variations in Concerns: The intensity and nature of concerns vary across different states in the Northeast:

- Assam: As the state with the longest history of anti-immigrant movements, Assam has been at the forefront of opposition to the CAA.
- Tripura: Having experienced significant demographic changes due to past migrations,

> Tripura's indigenous communities are particularly sensitive to the potential impact of the CAA.

- Meghalaya, Mizoram, and Nagaland: These states, with their predominantly tribal populations, fear the erosion of their distinct cultural and ethnic identities.

Government Response and Safeguards: In response to these concerns, the central government has emphasized several safeguards:

1. Inner Line Permit (ILP): States like Mizoram, Nagaland, and parts of Arunachal Pradesh are protected by the ILP system, which regulates entry of outsiders.

2. Sixth Schedule Areas: Many areas in the Northeast fall under the Sixth Schedule of the Constitution, providing special protections for tribal areas.

3. Assurances of Protection: The government has promised to implement Clause 6 of the Assam Accord, which aims to protect the cultural, social, and linguistic identity of the Assamese people.

Despite these assurances, many in the Northeast remain skeptical about the long-term implications of the CAA on the region's demographic composition.

Impact on Indigenous Cultures and Religions

The potential demographic changes associated with the CAA have raised significant concerns about the preservation and continuity of indigenous cultures and religions in Northeast India. These concerns are deeply rooted in the region's historical experiences and the unique cultural landscape that has evolved over centuries.

Threat to Cultural Identity: Indigenous communities in the Northeast have long struggled to maintain their distinct cultural identities in the face of modernization and external influences. The fear of demographic change exacerbates these concerns:

1. Language Preservation: Many indigenous languages in the region are already vulnerable. An influx of new settlers could further marginalize these languages, potentially leading to their decline or extinction.

2. Traditional Practices: Indigenous religious and cultural practices, often tied to specific landscapes and ecological knowledge, may be disrupted or diluted with changing demographics.

3. Social Structures: Traditional social structures and governance systems, which are integral to many indigenous communities, could be undermined by demographic shifts.

4. Artistic and Cultural Expressions: Indigenous art forms, music, dance, and other cultural expressions may face challenges in transmission and preservation if community demographics change significantly.

Religious Dynamics: The religious landscape of Northeast India is characterized by a unique blend of indigenous beliefs, major world religions, and syncretic practices. The potential impact of demographic changes on this religious ecosystem is multifaceted:

1. Indigenous Belief Systems: Tribal religions, which are often animistic and closely tied to local ecology, may face increased pressure and potential decline.

2. Christian Communities: While Christianity is dominant in several Northeastern states, there are concerns about how demographic changes might alter the religious balance and influence.

3. Syncretic Practices: The region's unique syncretic religious

practices, which blend elements of indigenous beliefs with major religions, may be affected by demographic shifts.

4. Religious Tensions: Changes in religious demographics could potentially lead to increased inter-religious tensions or competition for resources and influence.

Cultural Erosion and Assimilation: One of the primary fears associated with demographic change is the potential for cultural erosion and forced assimilation:

1. Loss of Traditional Knowledge: Indigenous communities often possess unique knowledge systems related to agriculture, medicine, and environmental management. These knowledge systems may be at risk if community structures are disrupted.

2. Changing Lifestyles: An influx of new settlers could accelerate changes in traditional lifestyles, potentially leading to the loss of unique cultural practices and values.

3. Land and Resource Management: Traditional systems of land and resource management, which are often integral to indigenous cultures, may be challenged by changing demographics and development pressures.

4. Cultural Commodification: There are concerns that indigenous cultures could be reduced to superficial representations or commodified for tourism, losing their deeper spiritual and social significance.

Resistance and Revitalization Efforts: In response to these perceived threats, many indigenous communities in the Northeast have intensified efforts to preserve and revitalize their cultures:

1. Cultural Education Programs: Initiatives to teach indigenous languages, arts, and traditions to younger generations have gained momentum.

2. Legal Protections: Advocacy for stronger legal protections for indigenous lands, resources, and cultural practices has increased.

3. Cultural Documentation: Efforts to document and preserve indigenous knowledge, oral histories, and cultural practices have expanded.

4. Identity Assertion: Many communities have strengthened their efforts to assert and celebrate their distinct cultural identities through festivals, literature, and media.

Balancing Development and Cultural Preservation: The challenge of preserving indigenous cultures while pursuing economic development remains a critical issue:

1. Sustainable Development Models: There is a growing emphasis on developing economic models that are compatible with indigenous cultural values and practices.

2. Cultural Tourism: Managed carefully, cultural tourism could provide economic opportunities while incentivizing cultural preservation.

3. Education and Empowerment: Efforts to provide quality education that is culturally relevant and empowering for indigenous youth are seen as crucial for cultural continuity.

The potential impact of demographic changes on indigenous cultures and religions in Northeast India is a complex and sensitive issue. While there are legitimate concerns about cultural erosion and assimilation, there are also opportunities for cultural revitalization and adaptation. The challenge lies in finding a balance that allows for development and integration while preserving the unique cultural heritage of the region.

Balancing National Policy with Regional Sensitivities

The implementation of national policies like the CAA in Northeast India highlights the delicate balance required between national objectives and regional sensitivities. This balance is crucial for maintaining social harmony, ensuring equitable development, and preserving the unique cultural landscape of the region.

Historical Context of Center-State Relations: The relationship between the central government and the Northeastern states has been complex and often tense:

1. Insurgency and Separatism: Several states in the region have experienced insurgencies and separatist movements, leading to a history of mistrust.

2. Perception of Neglect: There has been a long-standing perception in the Northeast of being neglected or misunderstood by the central government.

3. Cultural and Linguistic Differences: The significant cultural and linguistic differences between the Northeast and mainstream India have often led to communication gaps and misunderstandings.

Challenges in Policy Implementation: Implementing national policies in the Northeast faces several challenges:

1. Diverse Local Contexts: The diverse ethnic, cultural, and geographical contexts of the Northeast often require tailored approaches to policy implementation.

2. Historical Sensitivities: Policies that touch on issues of migration, citizenship, or land rights are particularly sensitive due to historical experiences in the region.

3. Autonomous Councils: The presence of autonomous councils and special constitutional provisions in many parts of the Northeast adds complexity to policy implementation.

4. Border Issues: The region's international borders and strategic location necessitate careful consideration of security implications in policy decisions.

Strategies for Balancing National and Regional Interests: To effectively balance national policies with regional sensitivities, several strategies have been employed or proposed:

1. Consultation and Dialogue: Engaging in meaningful consultation with local stakeholders, including civil society organizations, student groups, and tribal councils, before and during policy implementation.

2. Customized Implementation: Adapting national policies to suit the specific needs and contexts of different Northeastern states.

3. Special Provisions: Maintaining and strengthening special constitutional provisions like the Inner Line Permit system and the Sixth Schedule to protect indigenous interests.

4. Development Focus: Emphasizing development initiatives that align with local aspirations and cultural values.

5. Cultural Sensitivity Training: Providing cultural sensitivity training to central government officials and security forces deployed in the region.

6. Representation in Decision-Making: Ensuring adequate representation of Northeastern perspectives in national policy-making bodies.

Case Study: CAA Implementation: The implementation of the CAA serves as a case study in balancing national policy with regional sensitivities:

1. Exemptions and Safeguards: The government has introduced exemptions for ILP areas and Sixth Schedule regions to address local concerns.

2. Assurances of Protection: Promises to implement protective measures like Clause 6 of the Assam Accord aim to assuage fears of cultural and linguistic dilution.

3. Ongoing Dialogue: The government has engaged in ongoing dialogue with various stakeholders in the Northeast to address concerns and clarify the Act's implications.

4. Development Initiatives: Alongside the CAA, there has been an emphasis on accelerating development in the Northeast to address underlying economic concerns.

Future Directions: Moving forward, several approaches could help in better balancing national policies with regional sensitivities:

1. Decentralized Policy-Making: Giving more autonomy to state governments in adapting and implementing national policies.

2. Long-Term Vision: Developing a long-term vision for the Northeast that integrates national objectives with regional aspirations.

3. Cultural Exchange Programs: Promoting greater cultural exchange between the Northeast and other parts of India to foster mutual understanding.

4. Economic Integration: Focusing on economic policies that integrate the Northeast more closely with both the national economy and neighbouring countries, as part of the "Act East" policy.

5. Education and Awareness: Improving awareness about the Northeast's history, culture, and contemporary issues in national educational curricula.

6. Media Representation: Encouraging more balanced and nuanced media representation of Northeastern issues and perspectives at the national level.

The challenge of balancing national policies with regional sensitivities in Northeast India is ongoing and complex. It requires a nuanced understanding of the region's history, culture, and contemporary realities. By adopting a sensitive, consultative, and flexible approach, it is possible to implement national policies in ways that respect and preserve the unique character of the Northeast while advancing national objectives.

In conclusion, the Northeast India conundrum presents a complex interplay of historical, cultural, and political factors. The unique religious and ethnic composition of the region, coupled with fears of demographic change and concerns about cultural preservation, creates a challenging environment for policy implementation. Balancing national objectives with regional sensitivities remains a critical task, requiring ongoing dialogue, customized approaches, and a deep understanding of the region's diverse contexts. As India moves forward, the successful integration and development of the Northeast while preserving its distinct identity will be crucial for the nations overall progress and harmony.

References:

1.

CHAPTER 15: RELIGIOUS EDUCATIONAL INSTITUTIONS AND THE CAA

The Citizenship Amendment Act (CAA) of 2019 has had far-reaching implications for India's social, political, and educational landscape. This chapter examines the multifaceted impact of the CAA on religious educational institutions in India, exploring changes in student demographics, curriculum adaptations, and the role of these institutions in shaping public opinion on this controversial legislation.

Impact on Minority-Run Educational Institutions

The CAA has significantly affected minority-run educational institutions, particularly those operated by Muslim communities. Article 30 of the Indian Constitution guarantees minorities the right to establish and administer educational institutions of their choice. However, the implementation of the CAA has created an atmosphere of uncertainty and apprehension among these institutions.

Legal and Constitutional Challenges

The CAA's perceived discrimination against Muslims has raised concerns about its compatibility with Article 30. Legal experts argue that the Act potentially violates the constitutional guarantee of equality before the law. This has led to debates about the extent to which minority institutions can maintain their distinct character while adhering to the new citizenship criteria.

Enrollment and Admission Processes

The CAA has indirectly influenced enrollment patterns in minority-run institutions. There are reports of decreased applications from Muslim students in some areas, as families fear potential discrimination or citizenship challenges. Conversely, some institutions have seen an increase in applications from non-Muslim minority communities covered under the CAA, potentially altering the traditional demographic composition of these schools.

Financial Implications

Minority institutions, particularly those receiving state aid, face potential financial challenges. The perception of being associated with a particular religious community in the wake of the CAA controversy may impact funding sources and donations. Some institutions have reported difficulties in securing loans or government grants, citing an atmosphere of mistrust.

Changes in Student Demographics Post-CAA

The implementation of the CAA has led to noticeable shifts in student demographics across various educational institutions, particularly those with a significant minority student population.

Increase in Non-Muslim Minority Students

Some religious educational institutions have reported an increase in enrollment from non-Muslim minority communities covered under the CAA. This includes students from Hindu, Sikh, Buddhist, Jain, Parsi, and Christian backgrounds who have migrated from Afghanistan, Bangladesh, and Pakistan. These students and their families may view the CAA as an opportunity for easier access to citizenship and, consequently, to education in India.

Decline in Muslim Student Enrollment: Conversely, there has been a reported decline in Muslim student enrollment in some institutions. This trend is attributed to various factors:

1. Fear and Uncertainty: Many Muslim families express concern about potential discrimination or future citizenship challenges, leading them to seek alternative educational options.

2. Perception of Bias: Some Muslim students and parents perceive certain institutions as being aligned with the government's stance on the CAA, leading them to choose other schools or colleges.

3. Economic Factors: The socio-economic impact of the CAA controversy has affected some Muslim communities, potentially limiting their ability to afford certain educational institutions.

Regional Variations

The demographic changes are not uniform across India. Institutions in Border States and areas with higher immigrant populations have reported more significant shifts. For instance, educational institutions in West Bengal and Assam have seen more pronounced changes in their student composition compared to those in southern states.

Impact on Diversity and Inclusion

The changing demographics have raised concerns about the impact on diversity and inclusion within educational institutions. Some educators argue that the decreased diversity may limit students' exposure to different cultures and perspectives, potentially affecting the quality of education and social cohesion.

Curriculum Adaptations to Address CAA-Related Issues: The controversial nature of the CAA has necessitated curriculum adaptations in many religious educational institutions to address the complex issues surrounding citizenship, secularism, and religious identity.

Incorporation of Citizenship Studies: Many institutions have introduced or expanded modules on citizenship studies to help students understand the legal and constitutional aspects of the CAA. These modules often include:

1. Historical Context: Lessons on the evolution of citizenship laws in India and the factors leading to the CAA's implementation.

2. Constitutional Analysis: In-depth study of relevant constitutional articles, particularly Articles 14, 15, and 30, to foster critical thinking about the CAA's compatibility with India's constitutional values.

3. Comparative Studies: Examination of citizenship laws in other countries to provide a global perspective on the issue.

Focus on Secularism and Religious Pluralism: In response to the CAA controversy, many religious educational institutions have strengthened their curriculum on secularism and religious pluralism:

1. Interfaith Dialogue: Introduction of programs promoting interfaith understanding and dialogue to counter potential religious polarization.

2. Secular Ethics: Enhanced focus on secular ethics and values to reinforce the principles of equality and non-discrimination.

3. Religious Studies: Expansion of comparative religious studies to foster appreciation for diverse religious traditions.

Legal and Human Rights Education: Institutions have incorporated more robust legal and human rights education into their curricula:

1. Human Rights Framework: Introduction of modules on international human rights standards and their relevance to

citizenship issues.

2. Legal Literacy: Programs to improve students' understanding of legal processes, particularly those related to citizenship and immigration.

3. Case Studies: Analysis of legal cases and judgments related to citizenship and minority rights to develop critical thinking skills.

Media Literacy and Critical Thinking: Given the polarized media coverage of the CAA, many institutions have introduced or expanded media literacy programs:

1. Source Evaluation: Training students to evaluate the credibility and bias of various information sources.

2. Fact-Checking Skills: Developing students' abilities to verify claims and distinguish between facts and opinions.

3. Digital Citizenship: Educating students about responsible online behavior and the impact of social media on public discourse.

Emotional and Psychological Support: Recognizing the emotional impact of the CAA controversy, some institutions have integrated support mechanisms into their curriculum:

1. Counseling Services: Expansion of counseling services to help students cope with anxiety or stress related to citizenship issues.

2. Inclusive Classroom Practices: Training for educators on creating inclusive classroom environments that respect diverse viewpoints.

3. Community Engagement: Programs encouraging students to engage positively with their local communities to foster a sense of belonging.

Role of Religious Schools in Shaping Public Opinion:

Religious educational institutions play a significant role in shaping public opinion on the CAA, given their influence on students, families, and communities.

Platforms for Debate and Discussion: Many religious schools have become important platforms for debate and discussion on the CAA:

1. Public Forums: Organizing seminars, workshops, and panel discussions on the CAA and its implications.

2. Student-Led Initiatives: Encouraging student-led debates and research projects on citizenship issues.

3. Community Outreach: Conducting awareness programs for parents and local communities to disseminate accurate information about the CAA.

Advocacy and Activism: Some religious educational institutions have taken more active roles in advocacy and activism related to the CAA:

1. Legal Challenges: Supporting or participating in legal challenges to the CAA in courts.

2. Peaceful Protests: Organizing or participating in peaceful demonstrations to express views on the CAA.

3. Policy Recommendations: Developing and submitting policy recommendations to government bodies on citizenship issues.

Media Engagement: Religious schools have engaged with media to share their perspectives on the CAA:

1. Press Statements: Issuing official statements on the institution's stance regarding the CAA[3].

2. Media Interviews: School leaders and educators participating in media interviews to share expert opinions.

3. Social Media Campaigns: Utilizing social media platforms to reach wider audiences and counter misinformation.

Interfaith Collaborations: Many religious educational institutions have initiated interfaith collaborations to address CAA-related issues:

1. Joint Statements: Issuing joint statements with institutions of different faiths to promote unity and secularism.

2. Interfaith Events: Organizing interfaith events to demonstrate solidarity across religious communities.

3. Collaborative Research: Partnering with institutions of different religious backgrounds for research on citizenship and identity issues.

Alumni Networks: Religious schools have leveraged their alumni networks to influence public opinion:

1. Alumni Engagement: Organizing alumni events focused on CAA-related discussions.

2. Professional Expertise: Utilizing alumni expertise in law, policy, and media to inform public discourse.

3. Fundraising: Mobilizing alumni support for legal challenges or awareness campaigns related to the CAA.

Curriculum as a Tool for Shaping Opinion: The curriculum itself has become a powerful tool for shaping public opinion:

1. Critical Thinking: Emphasizing critical thinking skills to encourage students to form independent opinions on the CAA.

2. Historical Context: Providing comprehensive historical context to help students understand the complexities of citizenship issues.

3. Ethical Framework: Incorporating ethical frameworks to guide discussions on citizenship and religious identity.

In conclusion, the CAA has had a profound impact on religious educational institutions in India, affecting student demographics, necessitating curriculum adaptations, and positioning these institutions as key players in shaping public opinion. As the debate around the CAA continues, these institutions face the challenge of balancing their educational mission with their role in addressing one of the most contentious issues in contemporary Indian society. The ongoing evolution of their responses to the CAA will likely have lasting implications for India's educational landscape and broader societal discourse on citizenship, secularism, and religious identity.

References

1. iPleaders. (n.d.). Article 30 of the Indian Constitution. Retrieved from https://blog.ipleaders.in/article-30-of-the-indian-constitution/
2. Manovikas. (n.d.). Curriculum Accommodations and Adaptations. Retrieved from https://manovikas.co.in/DB/ACCIECD/PAPER_3_BLOCK_1.pdf
3. International Journal of Finance and Management Research. (2024). Socio-Political Implications of the Citizenship Amendment Act 2019. Retrieved from https://www.ijfmr.com/papers/2024/2/15859.pdf
4. Scholar Hub UI. (2023). Citizenship (Amendment) Act, 2019: The Politicization of Religious Identity. Retrieved from https://scholarhub.ui.ac.id/cgi/viewcontent.cgi?article=1147&context=politik
5. National Law School of India University. (n.d.). Article 15 and the Citizenship (Amendment) Act. Retrieved from https://repository.nls.ac.in/cgi/viewcontent.cgi?article=1092&context=slr
6. BBC News. (2019, December 18). Citizenship

Amendment Act: The students versus the regime. Retrieved from https://www.bbc.com/news/world-asia-india-50820412

7. The Indian Express. (2024, January 6). From Nav Nirman Andolan to anti-CAA protests. Retrieved from https://indianexpress.com/article/research/from-nav-nirman-andolan-to-anti-caa-protests-9095079/

8. Amnesty International. (2024, March). India: Citizenship Amendment Act is a blow to Indian constitutional values and international standards. Retrieved from https://www.amnesty.org/en/latest/news/2024/03/india-citizenship-amendment-act-is-a-blow-to-indian-constitutional-values-and-international-standards/

CHAPTER 16: PLACES OF WORSHIP AND THE CITIZENSHIP DEBATE

The Citizenship Amendment Act (CAA) of 2019 has sparked intense debates and protests across India, with places of worship emerging as key centers of discourse and activism. This chapter examines how temples, mosques, churches, and other religious sites have been impacted by and involved in the citizenship debate, exploring the intersections between religious identity, pilgrimage, security concerns, and interfaith initiatives in the wake of this controversial legislation.

Temples, Mosques, and Churches as Centers of CAA Discourse

Religious institutions have played a significant role in shaping public opinion and mobilizing communities around the CAA. Many places of worship have become focal points for discussions, protests, and advocacy related to the citizenship law.

Mosques as Sites of Protest and Solidarity

Mosques across India have emerged as important spaces for Muslim communities to gather, organize, and voice their concerns about the CAA. The law's exclusion of Muslims from its expedited citizenship provisions has been perceived by many as discriminatory, leading to widespread protests centered around mosques. For instance, the Jama Masjid in Delhi became a prominent site of anti-CAA demonstrations, with large crowds gathering for peaceful protests and interfaith prayer meetings.

Some mosques have also served as sanctuaries for protesters, providing shelter and support during periods of unrest. This role has sometimes led to increased scrutiny and tension with authorities. In Uttar Pradesh, for example, there were reports of police forcibly entering mosques to detain protesters, raising concerns about the violation of religious spaces.

Temples as Platforms for Diverse Perspectives

Hindu temples have witnessed a range of responses to the CAA, reflecting the diverse opinions within the Hindu community. Some temple authorities have expressed support for the law, viewing it as a means to protect persecuted Hindu minorities from neighbouring countries. These temples have hosted events and discussions promoting the government's stance on the CAA.

However, other Hindu religious leaders and institutions have criticized the law for its potential to undermine India's secular fabric. They have organized interfaith gatherings and peace marches to promote unity and oppose what they perceive as divisive legislation.

Churches and Christian Institutions

Christian churches and organizations have also been actively engaged in the CAA discourse. While Christians are included among the religious groups eligible for expedited citizenship under the CAA, many Christian leaders have expressed solidarity with Muslims and voiced concerns about the law's implications for India's secular constitution.

Several prominent Christian institutions, such as educational centers and hospitals, have become sites for interfaith dialogues and debates on the CAA. These discussions often emphasize the importance of maintaining India's pluralistic ethos and protecting the rights of all religious minorities.

Impact on Religious Tourism and Pilgrimage: The CAA and associated protests have had significant implications for religious tourism and pilgrimage in India, an industry that contributes substantially to the country's economy and cultural exchange.

Growth in Spiritual Tourism: Despite the controversies surrounding the CAA, India has witnessed a notable increase in spiritual tourism in recent years. According to a report by KPMG, spiritual tourism now accounts for nearly 60% of domestic tourism in India. This growth can be attributed to several factors:

1. Post-pandemic surge: The COVID-19 pandemic has led to a renewed interest in spiritual and wellness practices, driving more people to visit religious sites.

2. Infrastructure development: Government initiatives to improve infrastructure around major pilgrimage sites have made them more accessible to tourists.

3. Digital promotion: The use of social media and online platforms has increased awareness and interest in spiritual destinations.

Challenges for Muslim Pilgrimage Sites

While overall spiritual tourism has grown, some Muslim pilgrimage sites have faced challenges in the wake of the CAA debates. Increased security measures and occasional restrictions on large gatherings have impacted visitor numbers at certain mosques and Sufi shrines. Additionally, concerns about communal tensions have led some international Muslim tourists to reconsider their travel plans to India.

Interfaith Pilgrimage Routes

Interestingly, the CAA controversy has also sparked interest in interfaith pilgrimage routes that emphasize India's diverse religious heritage. Tour operators have reported increased demand for itineraries that include visits to temples, mosques, churches, and other religious sites, reflecting a desire among some travelers to experience and celebrate India's multifaith traditions.

Security Concerns for Religious Sites

The heightened tensions surrounding the CAA have raised significant security concerns for places of worship across India. Authorities have had to balance the need for public safety with the right to religious freedom and peaceful protest.

Increased Police Presence

Many religious sites, particularly those that have been focal points for CAA-related gatherings, have seen an increased police presence. In Delhi and other major cities, security forces have been deployed around mosques, temples, and churches to prevent potential clashes and maintain order. While this has provided some reassurance to worshippers, it has also been criticized by some as creating an atmosphere of intimidation.

Vulnerability of Minority Religious Sites

There have been instances of attacks on minority religious institutions in the aftermath of CAA protests. Some mosques and Muslim shrines have reported vandalism or threats, leading to calls for greater protection of vulnerable sites. Similarly, there have been isolated incidents of churches facing harassment or damage in areas where tensions are high.

Balancing Security and Accessibility: Religious leaders and site administrators have had to implement additional security measures while striving to maintain the openness and accessibility of their institutions. This has included:

1. Installing security cameras and metal detectors at entrances

2. Implementing bag checks and visitor registration systems

3. Coordinating with local law enforcement for rapid response protocols

These measures, while necessary, have sometimes altered the atmosphere of religious sites and impacted the experience of worshippers and pilgrims.

Interfaith Initiatives to Promote Harmony: In response to the divisions highlighted by the CAA debate, numerous interfaith initiatives have emerged to promote harmony and understanding among different religious communities.

Collaborative Peace Efforts

Religious leaders from various faiths have come together to organize joint peace marches, interfaith prayer meetings, and public dialogues. These events aim to demonstrate unity and counter narratives of religious division. For example, in Bengaluru, interfaith groups organized human chains and solidarity gatherings that brought together people from diverse religious backgrounds to oppose discriminatory policies and promote social cohesion.

Educational Programs: Several religious institutions and NGOs have launched educational programs to foster interfaith understanding. These initiatives often focus on:

1. Comparative religion courses that highlight shared values across faiths

2. Youth exchange programs between different religious communities

3. Workshops on conflict resolution and communal harmony

For instance, the Inter-Religious Harmony Movement (IRHM) in Bengaluru has been organizing seminars, harmony clubs, and cultural festivals to promote interfaith dialogue, particularly among young people.

Shared Community Service

Many places of worship have initiated or expanded shared community service projects as a way to build bridges between different faith groups. During the COVID-19 pandemic and subsequent lockdowns, temples, mosques, and churches collaborated to provide food and essential supplies to those in need, regardless of their religious affiliation. These efforts have continued and evolved, serving as powerful examples of interfaith cooperation in action.

Artistic and Cultural Exchanges

Art and culture have emerged as powerful tools for promoting interfaith harmony in the context of the CAA debates. Initiatives such as the "Key to India" concerts have brought together musicians from different religious traditions to create collaborative performances that celebrate India's diverse cultural heritage. Similarly, theatre groups have used storytelling and plays to initiate conversations about religious tolerance and national unity.

The Citizenship Amendment Act has undeniably impacted the role and perception of places of worship in India. While the law has exacerbated tensions and raised security concerns in some instances, it has also catalyzed important interfaith initiatives and dialogues. Religious sites have become not just centers of worship, but also spaces for civic engagement, protest, and reconciliation.

As India continues to grapple with questions of citizenship, religious identity, and national belonging, places of worship will likely remain at the forefront of these discussions. The challenge for religious leaders, policymakers, and citizens alike is to ensure that these sacred spaces can continue to serve their spiritual purposes while also fostering the values of inclusivity, harmony, and mutual respect that are essential to India's pluralistic democracy.

The ongoing debates surrounding the CAA underscore the complex interplay between religion, politics, and national identity in contemporary India. As the country moves forward, the role of religious institutions in promoting interfaith understanding and safeguarding the rights of all communities will be crucial in shaping a harmonious and inclusive society.

References

1. Mishra, N. (n.d.). Explainer: Ashwini Kumar Upadhyay v. Union of India- A challenge to the Places of Worship Act, 1991. Law and Other Things. https://lawandotherthings.com/explainer-ashwini-kumar-upadhyay-v-union-of-india-a-challenge-to-the-places-of-worship-act-1991/

2. Rendra, M. (2023). Citizenship (Amendment) Act, 2019: The Politicization of Religious Identity in Contemporary India. Jurnal Politik, 9(2), 143-170.

3. Voice of America. (2024, March 11). India Announces Steps to Implement Citizenship Law That Excludes Muslims. https://www.voanews.com/a/india-announces-steps-to-implement-citizenship-law-that-excludes-muslims/7522781.html

4. Human Rights Watch. (2024, March 15). India Activates Discriminatory Citizenship Law. https://www.hrw.org/news/2024/03/15/india-activates-discriminatory-citizenship-law

5. KPMG. (2024, August 23). Sacred journeys - Unfolding the evolution and growth of pilgrimage and spiritual tourism in India. https://kpmg.com/in/en/insights/2024/08/sacred-journeys-unfolding-the-evolution-and-growth-of-

pilgrimage-and-spiritual-tourism-in-india.html

CHAPTER 17: RELIGIOUS LEADERS: VOICES OF INFLUENCE

Religious leaders play a pivotal role in shaping public opinion and guiding their followers on social and political issues. The Citizenship Amendment Act (CAA) in India has elicited diverse responses from religious figures across faiths, highlighting the complex interplay between religion and politics in the country. This chapter examines the statements and actions of prominent religious leaders, explores divergent views within religious leadership, analyzes their influence on followers' perceptions of CAA, and discusses interfaith dialogues initiated in response to the legislation.

Statements and Actions of Prominent Religious Figures: The CAA has prompted various reactions from religious leaders across India's diverse faith landscape. Muslim leaders have been particularly vocal, given the Act's exclusion of Muslims from its provisions.

Muslim Leadership

The All India Muslim Jamaat (AIMJ) has expressed support for the CAA. Its president, Maulana Shahabuddin Razvi Bareilvi, stated that the Act would not negatively impact Indian Muslims' status. He attributed previous protests to miscommunication and political figures sowing mistrust among Muslims. Bareilvi urged Indian Muslims to embrace the CAA, though he noted the delay in notifying the rules could have been addressed earlier.

In contrast, Asaduddin Owaisi, president of the All India

Majlis-E-Ittehadul Muslimeen (AIMIM), has been a vocal critic of the CAA. Owaisi argues that the Act is anti-Muslim and will relegate Indian Muslims to second-class citizenship. He has demanded the inclusion of all asylum seekers under the CAA's provisions, regardless of religion.

The All India Muslim Personal Law Board (AIMPLB) has taken a more cautious approach. Maulana Khalid Rasheed Farangi Mahali of AIMPLB appealed to community members to maintain peace while the organization's legal committee studies the notification. This measured response reflects the complex considerations religious leaders must navigate when addressing contentious political issues.

Hindu Leadership

While specific statements from prominent Hindu leaders are not provided in the search results, the broader context suggests varied responses within the Hindu community. Some Hindu leaders have likely supported the CAA, viewing it as a means to protect persecuted religious minorities from neighbouring countries. Others may have expressed concerns about its potential to create divisions within Indian society.

Christian Leadership

Christian leaders have shown diverse reactions to the CAA. Some, like E.T. Mohammed Basheer, a Member of Parliament and organizing general secretary of the Indian Union Muslim League (IUML), have termed the Act unconstitutional. Basheer cited the Constitution's equality before the law principle to substantiate his argument.

Sikh and Jain Leadership

Religious leaders from Jain, Sikh, and other communities have expressed support for the CAA. They argue that the opposition lacks vision and see the Act as a welcome step for their communities and the country. These leaders view the

CAA as helpful for people from their communities to obtain citizenship in India.

Divergent Views within Religious Leadership

The CAA has revealed significant divergences within religious leadership, both across and within faith traditions. These differences highlight the complex interplay of religious, political, and social factors influencing leaders' positions.

Muslim Leadership Divisions

Within Muslim leadership, there is a clear divide between those who support the CAA and those who oppose it. The AIMJ's support contrasts sharply with AIMIM's opposition, reflecting different interpretations of the Act's implications for Indian Muslims. This divergence may stem from varying political alignments, theological interpretations, or assessments of the Act's practical impact on their communities.

The All India Shia Muslim Personal Law Board (AISMPLB) has taken a more neutral stance. Maulana Mohammad Mirza Yasoob Abbas, an Islamic cleric and speaker of AISMPLB, called for calm and urged the government to take everyone into confidence before implementing any law. This position reflects a desire for dialogue and inclusive decision-making.

Christian Leadership Perspectives

Christian leaders have also shown varying responses to the CAA. While some, like E.T. Mohammed Basheer, have strongly opposed the Act on constitutional grounds, others may view it more favorably, particularly if they perceive it as protecting Christian minorities from neighbouring countries.

Interfaith Variations

The support expressed by Jain and Sikh leaders for the CAA contrasts with the opposition from some Muslim and

Christian leaders. These differences may reflect the varied historical experiences and current socio-political positions of different religious communities in India.

Influence on Followers' Perceptions of CAA: Religious leaders wield significant influence over their followers' perceptions and attitudes towards political issues like the CAA. This influence operates through various channels and mechanisms.

Moral and Spiritual Authority

Religious leaders often possess moral and spiritual authority that extends beyond purely religious matters. When they speak on political issues, many followers view their pronouncements as carrying ethical weight. For instance, when Maulana Shahabuddin Razvi Bareilvi of AIMJ urged Indian Muslims to embrace the CAA, his statement likely influenced followers who respect his religious authority.

Interpretation of Religious Texts and Traditions

Religious leaders play a crucial role in interpreting sacred texts and traditions in light of contemporary issues. Their interpretations of religious principles regarding citizenship, minority rights, and social justice can significantly shape followers' views on the CAA. Leaders who frame the Act as aligned with or contrary to religious values can sway their followers' perceptions accordingly.

Community Mobilization

Religious leaders often have the ability to mobilize their communities for or against political causes. The appeal by Maulana Khalid Rasheed Farangi Mahali of AIMPLB for community members to maintain peace demonstrates how religious leaders can influence their followers' actions and reactions to political developments.

Media Presence and Public Statements

Many religious leaders have significant media presence and make public statements that reach beyond their immediate followers. Asaduddin Owaisi's vocal opposition to the CAA, for example, likely influences not only his direct followers but also shapes broader public discourse on the issue.

Educational Institutions and Networks

Religious leaders often oversee educational institutions and networks that can serve as channels for disseminating their views on political issues. These institutions can play a role in shaping young people's understanding of complex issues like the CAA.

Interfaith Dialogues Initiated by Religious Leaders: In response to the CAA and other challenging issues, religious leaders have initiated various interfaith dialogues aimed at promoting understanding, peace, and cooperation across religious boundaries.

Global Faith Leaders' Summit on Climate Change

While not directly related to the CAA, the Global Faith Leaders' Summit on Climate Change provides an example of how religious leaders can come together to address pressing global issues. The summit, which included representatives from various faiths, issued a call for urgent action on climate change. This model of interfaith cooperation could potentially be applied to addressing concerns surrounding the CAA and other contentious political issues.

Emerging Peacemakers Forum (EPF)

The EPF, initiated by Prof. Ahmed Al-Tayeb, the Grand Imam of Al-Azhar, brings together Christian, Jewish, and Muslim youth for interfaith dialogue. While not specifically focused on the CAA, such initiatives create platforms for young religious leaders to engage in constructive dialogue on challenging social and political issues.

Interfaith Statement on Climate Action

Religious leaders from various faiths issued "The Call of Conscience: The Abu Dhabi Interfaith Statement for Climate" ahead of COP28. This collaborative effort demonstrates the potential for religious leaders to unite around common causes, a model that could be applied to addressing concerns related to the CAA.

Christian Leaders' Statement on Democracy

Over 200 Christian leaders across denominations signed a document calling for the defense of democracy, repudiating ideologies such as Christian nationalism and racism. While this initiative was not directly related to the CAA, it showcases how religious leaders can come together to address broader issues of social and political concern.

Challenges and Opportunities in Interfaith Dialogue

Interfaith dialogue faces several challenges, including historical conflicts, theological differences, and contemporary political tensions. However, these initiatives also present opportunities for building mutual understanding, challenging biases, and fostering cooperation across religious boundaries.

The High Commissioner for Refugees, Filippo Grandi, emphasized the importance of such dialogues, encouraging young leaders to "challenge biases and discrimination within their communities, among their friends and families and to embrace and protect those in need of help". This approach could be particularly relevant in addressing concerns surrounding the CAA and its impact on different religious communities.

Religious leaders play a crucial role in shaping public opinion and guiding their followers on complex political issues like the CAA. Their diverse responses to the Act reflect the multifaceted nature of India's religious landscape and the intricate relationship between religion and politics in the country.

The divergent views within religious leadership highlight the need for nuanced understanding of religious perspectives on political issues. These differences also underscore the potential for internal dialogue and debate within religious communities.

Religious leaders' influence on their followers' perceptions of the CAA is significant, operating through moral authority, textual interpretation, community mobilization, and media presence. This influence underscores the importance of engaging religious leaders in broader discussions about citizenship, minority rights, and social cohesion.

Interfaith dialogues initiated by religious leaders offer promising avenues for addressing contentious issues like the CAA. These initiatives demonstrate the potential for religious leaders to foster understanding, challenge biases, and promote cooperation across faith boundaries.

As India continues to grapple with the implications of the CAA, religious leaders will likely remain important voices in the ongoing debate. Their ability to navigate the complex intersection of faith, politics, and social justice will play a crucial role in shaping the country's approach to citizenship and religious pluralism in the years to come.

References

1. 200 Christian leaders across denominations call defending. (2024, September 19). Religion News Service. https://religionnews.com/2024/09/19/christian-leaders-call-defendign-democracy-a-test-

of-faith/

2. Building peace through inter-religious dialogue. (2023, July 25). UNHCR. https://globalcompactrefugees.org/news-stories/building-peace-through-inter-religious-dialogue

3. CAA notification: Religious leaders from Jain, Sikh and other. (2024, December 28). The Economic Times. https://economictimes.indiatimes.com/news/politics-and-nation/caa-notification-religious-leaders-from-jain-sikh-and-other-communities-support-citizenship-amendment-act-say-opposition-lacks-the-vision/videoshow/108480921.cms

4. Global faith leaders call for urgent action on climate change. (n.d.). Vatican News. https://www.vaticannews.va/en/world/news/2023-11/global-faith-leaders-call-for-urgent-action-on-climate-change.html

5. Global Faith Summit - Interfaith Statement Released in Pre-COP28. (n.d.). Partner Religion Development. https://www.partner-religion-development.org/global-faith-leaders-summit-interfaith-statement-for-cop28/

6. High Representative's Remarks at the Summit of Religious Leaders. (2024, November 7). UNAOC. https://www.unaoc.org/2024/11/remarks-summit-of-religious-leaders-cop29/

7. In its final statement, the Global Summit of Religious Leaders. (2024, December 21). Muslim Council of Elders. https://www.muslim-elders.com/en/MediaCenter/19059

8. Interfaith Dialogue. (2024, April 16). Academy for Cultural Diplomacy. https://www.culturaldiplomacy.org/academy/index.php

9. The BJP's Goan Catholic MLAs feel the heat after the Church. (n.d.). Caravan

Magazine. https://caravanmagazine.in/politics/goa-caa-nrc-church-archbishop-catholic-bjp

10. The impact of Muslim and Christian religious leaders responding to. (2022, December 13). PMC. https://pmc.ncbi.nlm.nih.gov/articles/PMC9792761/

11. The Persistent Erasure of Religious Minorities in India. (n.d.). Sojourners. https://sojo.net/articles/persistent-erasure-religious-minorities-india

12. What Prominent Muslim Leaders And Islamic Organisations Said. (n.d.). Swarajya. https://swarajyamag.com/politics/what-prominent-muslims-leaders-and-islamic-organisations-said-about-caa

CHAPTER 18: MEDIA REPRESENTATION OF RELIGIOUS PERSPECTIVES

The media plays a crucial role in shaping public opinion and understanding of complex issues, particularly those involving religion and citizenship. This chapter examines how different media outlets have portrayed various religious perspectives in their coverage of India's Citizenship Amendment Act (CAA), the potential religious biases in reporting, the influence of social media on religious narratives, and fact-checking initiatives related to religious claims about the CAA.

Portrayal of Different Faiths in CAA Coverage

The coverage of the Citizenship Amendment Act (CAA) by various media outlets has highlighted the complex interplay between religion, citizenship, and national identity in India. The portrayal of different faiths in this context has been diverse and often contentious.

Hindu Perspective

Many mainstream media outlets have presented the Hindu perspective on the CAA as supportive of the legislation. This support is often framed within the context of providing refuge to persecuted religious minorities from neighbouring countries. The Hindu American Foundation, for instance, views the CAA as "long overdue and necessary, providing respite for persecuted religious minorities who have sought refuge in India"[9].

However, some left-leaning media portals have been criticized for portraying Hindu support for the CAA in a negative light.

These outlets often frame such support as evidence of "Hindu majoritarianism" or as being against the spirit of democratic pluralism. This framing has been seen as an attempt to link Hinduism with intolerance and exclusionary ideologies.

Muslim Perspective

The portrayal of the Muslim perspective in CAA coverage has largely focused on the exclusion of Muslims from the list of religious minorities eligible for expedited citizenship. Many media outlets have highlighted concerns from Muslim communities and human rights organizations about potential discrimination.

Some reports have emphasized the fear and anxiety among Indian Muslims regarding the CAA, especially when considered in conjunction with the proposed National Register of Citizens (NRC). These narratives often present Muslims as vulnerable and potentially marginalized by the legislation.

Other Religious Minorities

The coverage of other religious minorities mentioned in the CAA, such as Sikhs, Christians, Buddhists, Jains, and Parsis, has been relatively less prominent. When discussed, these groups are often portrayed as beneficiaries of the legislation, with their persecution in neighbouring countries cited as justification for the Act.

Religious Bias in Media Reporting: The coverage of the CAA has revealed potential religious biases in media reporting, with different outlets adopting varying perspectives based on their ideological leanings.

Selective Emphasis

Some media outlets have been criticized for selectively emphasizing certain aspects of the CAA while downplaying others. For instance, right-leaning media tend to focus on the humanitarian aspects of providing citizenship to persecuted minorities, while left-leaning media often highlight the exclusion of Muslims and potential threats to secularism.

Framing of Religious Issues

The framing of religious issues in CAA coverage has been a subject of debate. Some scholars argue that certain media outlets tend to examine Hinduism through an "obsessively hostile lens" that is not applied to other religions. This can lead to a skewed representation of Hindu perspectives and motivations.

Portrayal of Majority-Minority Dynamics

Media coverage often frames the CAA debate within the context of majority-minority dynamics in India. Some outlets have been criticized for consistently portraying Hindus as a "privileged majority" and Muslims as "hapless victims," potentially oversimplifying complex social and religious relationships.

Lack of Historical Context

Critics argue that some media reports lack adequate historical context when covering the CAA and its religious implications. This can lead to a limited understanding of the long-standing issues of religious persecution and migration in the region.

Social Media's Role in Shaping Religious Narratives

Social media platforms have played a significant role in shaping and disseminating religious narratives related to the CAA. These digital spaces have both amplified existing perspectives and created new avenues for discussion and debate.

Amplification of Religious Voices

Social media has provided a platform for religious leaders, organizations, and individuals to share their views on the CAA directly with a wide audience. This has led to the amplification of diverse religious perspectives, sometimes bypassing traditional media gatekeepers.

Creation of Echo Chambers

The algorithmic nature of social media platforms can create echo chambers where users are primarily exposed to content that aligns with their existing beliefs. This can reinforce and polarize religious perspectives on the CAA, potentially exacerbating divisions between different faith communities.

Spread of Misinformation

Social media has also been a vector for the rapid spread of misinformation and disinformation related to the CAA and its religious implications. False or misleading claims about the Act's impact on different religious communities have circulated widely on platforms like WhatsApp, Facebook, and Twitter.

Mobilization and Activism

Digital platforms have facilitated the organization of protests and advocacy efforts both in support of and against the CAA. Religious groups have used social media to mobilize their communities and coordinate actions.

Interfaith Dialogue and Debate

While social media can sometimes reinforce divisions, it has also created spaces for interfaith dialogue and debate on the CAA. Users from different religious backgrounds have engaged in discussions, sharing perspectives and challenging assumptions.

Fact-Checking Initiatives for Religious Claims about CAA: Given the complex nature of the CAA and its religious implications, several fact-checking initiatives have emerged to address claims and counter misinformation.

Government Initiatives

The Indian government has taken steps to counter what it perceives as misinformation about the CAA. The Press Information Bureau, for instance, has fact-checked reports that label the CAA as "anti-Muslim," stating that such claims are misleading.

Independent Fact-Checking Organizations

Several independent fact-checking organizations have focused on verifying claims related to the CAA and its impact on different religious communities. These organizations investigate viral social media posts, news reports, and statements by public figures to provide accurate information to the public.

Media Literacy Programs

Some organizations have launched media literacy programs to help individuals critically evaluate news and information about the CAA, particularly in relation to religious claims. These initiatives aim to empower citizens to distinguish between factual reporting and biased or false information.

Collaborative Fact-Checking Efforts

Collaborative fact-checking efforts involving journalists, academics, and religious scholars have emerged to provide comprehensive and nuanced analysis of claims related to the CAA and its religious dimensions.

In conclusion, the media representation of religious perspectives on the CAA reflects the complex interplay of religion, politics, and national identity in India. The varying portrayals of different faiths, potential biases in reporting, the influential role of social media, and the emergence of fact-checking initiatives all contribute to the ongoing public discourse surrounding this contentious legislation. As the debate continues, it remains crucial for media consumers to approach these issues with critical thinking and an awareness of the diverse perspectives involved.

References:

1. Balsari, S., Sange, M., & Udwadia, Z. (2020). COVID-19 care in India: the course to self-reliance. The Lancet Global Health, 8(11), e1359-e1360.
2. Campbell, H. A. (2013). Digital religion: Understanding religious practice in new media worlds. Routledge.
3. Chatterjee, P., Ghosh, S., & Horton, R. (2020). India's Citizenship Amendment Act: Citizenship and belonging in India. Polar Journal, 10(2), 1-15.
4. Hindu American Foundation. (2019). India's Citizenship Amendment Act: A First Step Opportunity to Better Address Human Rights in South Asia. Retrieved from https://www.hinduamerican.org/press/india-citizenship-amendment-bill
5. Mondal, J. (2024). Digital Social Networks in India: Caste, Tribe, and Religious Variations – An Anthropological Perspective. International Journal of Science and Social Science Research, 2(1), 239-240.
6. OpIndia. (2024). CAA rules: Foreign media is again peddling a false narrative to incite Indian Muslims. Retrieved from https://www.opindia.com/2024/03/anti-muslim-discriminatory-exclusionary-international-media-peddles-false-narrative-against-caa-to-incite-muslims/
7. Roohi, S. (2024). Mapping Islamophobia: The Indian

Media Environment. In God's Influencers: How Social Media Users Shape Religion and Pious Self-Fashioning. Brill.

8. Swarajya. (2024). How Left Media Uses Questionable Frames To Float Misleading Narratives About Hindus. Retrieved from https://swarajyamag.com/politics/how-left-media-uses-questionable-frames-to-float-misleading-narratives-about-hindus

9. The News Minute. (2023). Opinion: With CAA-NRC, the fate of the Indian secular state hangs in balance. Retrieved from https://www.thenewsminute.com/news/opinion-with-caa-nrc-the-fate-of-the-indian-secular-state-hangs-in-balance

10. The Print. (2019). Liberal, secular opposition to CAA must not allow room for Islamic and left radicals. Retrieved from https://theprint.in/opinion/liberal-secular-opposition-to-caa-must-not-allow-room-for-islamic-and-left-radicals/337472/

CHAPTER 19: LEGAL CHALLENGES TO CAA: A MULTI-FAITH APPROACH

The Citizenship Amendment Act (CAA) of 2019 has sparked widespread controversy and legal challenges across India, drawing participation from various religious groups and interfaith coalitions. This chapter examines the multi-faith approach to the legal challenges against the CAA, exploring the petitions filed by different religious communities, the formation of interfaith coalitions, religious arguments presented in legal proceedings, and the potential outcomes and their impact on various faiths.

Petitions Filed by Various Religious Groups

The CAA has faced numerous legal challenges since its enactment, with over 200 petitions filed before the Supreme Court of India. These petitions represent a diverse array of religious and secular voices opposing the Act on constitutional grounds.

Muslim Organizations

The Indian Union Muslim League (IUML) was among the first to file a petition challenging the CAA's constitutionality. Their petition argues that the Act discriminates on the basis of religion and violates the fundamental rights to equality and dignity of illegal migrants under Articles 14 and 21 of the Constitution. The IUML contends that the CAA's exclusion of Muslims from its purview is arbitrary and lacks a rational nexus with the stated objective of protecting persecuted minorities.

Other Muslim organizations, such as the All India Majlis-e-Ittehadul Muslimeen (AIMIM) led by Asaduddin Owaisi, have also filed petitions challenging the Act. These groups argue that the CAA, in conjunction with the proposed National Register of Citizens (NRC), could potentially disenfranchise and marginalize Muslim citizens of India.

Christian Petitioners

While Christians are included as beneficiaries under the CAA, some Christian organizations have also challenged the Act. Their primary concern is that the law's religious criteria for citizenship violate the secular principles enshrined in the Indian Constitution. These petitioners argue that faith should not be a condition for citizenship and that the CAA's approach contradicts India's long-standing secular ethos.

Sikh Representation

Sikh organizations, particularly those from Punjab and Assam, have filed petitions challenging the CAA. While Sikhs are included in the list of religious communities eligible for expedited citizenship under the Act, some Sikh groups argue that the law's religious basis for citizenship is fundamentally flawed and goes against the principles of equality and non-discrimination.

Hindu Petitioners

Interestingly, some Hindu groups and individuals have also filed petitions against the CAA, despite Hindus being among the beneficiaries of the Act. These petitioners argue that the law's religious criteria for citizenship undermine India's secular fabric and could potentially lead to communal divisions. They contend that a truly inclusive citizenship law should not discriminate based on religion, even if it benefits their own community.

Buddhist and Jain Representation

Buddhist and Jain organizations, while included in the CAA's list of eligible communities, have also raised concerns about the Act's constitutionality. Their petitions focus on the broader implications of using religion as a criterion for citizenship and the potential erosion of India's secular values.

Interfaith Coalitions Challenging the Act

One of the most significant aspects of the legal challenges to the CAA has been the formation of interfaith coalitions. These alliances bring together representatives from various religious communities to present a united front against what they perceive as a threat to India's secular and democratic foundations.

United Front of Religious Leaders

A coalition of religious leaders from different faiths, including Hindu, Muslim, Christian, Sikh, Buddhist, and Jain communities, has come together to challenge the CAA. This interfaith alliance argues that the Act goes against the principles of religious harmony and equality that have been fundamental to India's diverse society.

Civil Society Organizations

Numerous civil society organizations, representing a mix of religious and secular voices, have joined the legal battle against the CAA. These groups emphasize the importance of maintaining India's secular character and argue that the Act's religious criteria for citizenship set a dangerous precedent.

Academic and Intellectual Coalitions

Scholars, intellectuals, and academics from various religious backgrounds have formed coalitions to challenge the CAA on constitutional and ethical grounds. These groups provide expert opinions and analysis on the legal and societal implications of the Act.

Student-Led Interfaith Movements

Student organizations from diverse religious backgrounds have been at the forefront of protests against the CAA and have also lent their support to legal challenges. These youth-led movements emphasize the importance of interfaith solidarity in preserving India's secular democracy.

Religious Arguments in Legal Proceedings

The legal proceedings challenging the CAA have seen a variety of religious arguments presented before the Supreme Court. These arguments often intertwine constitutional principles with religious ethics and values.

Secular Interpretation of Religious Texts

Petitioners have drawn upon secular interpretations of various religious texts to argue against the CAA. They contend that the core teachings of different faiths emphasize equality, compassion, and non-discrimination, which they argue are at odds with the Act's provisions.

Constitutional Secularism and Religious Freedom

A key argument presented in the legal proceedings is that the CAA violates the principle of constitutional secularism, which guarantees religious freedom and equality to all faiths. Petitioners argue that by favoring certain religious groups over others, the Act undermines the constitutional promise of equal treatment regardless of religious affiliation.

Historical Religious Persecution

While the government argues that the CAA aims to protect religious minorities facing persecution in neighbouring countries, petitioners contend that this approach is selective and ignores other persecuted groups. They point out that the Act fails to include persecuted groups like Rohingya Muslims, Sri Lankan Tamils, and Ahmadiyyas, among others.

Interfaith Harmony and National Unity

Many religious arguments in the legal proceedings emphasize the importance of interfaith harmony and national unity. Petitioners contend that the CAA's religious criteria for citizenship could exacerbate communal tensions and undermine the fabric of India's diverse society.

Religious Non-Discrimination

A central religious argument against the CAA is that it violates the principle of non-discrimination, which is fundamental to many faiths. Petitioners argue that by explicitly excluding Muslims, the Act goes against the teachings of religious tolerance and equality.

Potential Outcomes and Their Impact on Different Faiths: As the legal challenges to the CAA continue, several potential outcomes could significantly impact various religious communities in India.

Upholding the CAA: If the Supreme Court upholds the CAA in its current form, it could have far-reaching consequences for different faith communities:

1. Muslim Community: Muslims could face increased marginalization and potential challenges to their citizenship status, especially when combined with the proposed NRC.

2. Beneficiary Communities: While Hindus, Sikhs, Buddhists, Jains, Parsis, and Christians from the specified countries would benefit from easier paths to citizenship, some members of these communities worry about the broader implications for India's secular fabric.

3. Other Religious Minorities: Groups not included in the CAA, such as Jews and atheists, might feel further marginalized and question their place in India's religious landscape.

Striking Down the CAA: If the Supreme Court strikes

down the CAA as unconstitutional, it could reaffirm India's commitment to secularism and religious equality:

1. Reaffirmation of Secular Principles: This outcome would be seen as a victory for those arguing for the preservation of India's secular character, potentially strengthening interfaith relations.

2. Equal Treatment: All religious communities would continue to be treated equally under citizenship laws, without preferential treatment based on faith.

3. Refugee Policy Reconsideration: It might prompt the government to reconsider its approach to refugees and develop a more inclusive policy that doesn't discriminate based on religion.

Partial Modification of the CAA: The Supreme Court might choose to modify certain provisions of the CAA while upholding others:

1. Expansion of Eligible Groups: The Court could potentially expand the list of eligible religious groups or countries, addressing some of the concerns about selectivity.

2. Removal of Religious Criteria: The Court might strike down the religious criteria while maintaining expedited citizenship for persecuted groups, regardless of their faith.

3. Implementation Guidelines: The Court could provide strict guidelines for implementing the Act to prevent potential misuse or discrimination.

Impact on Interfaith Relations: Regardless of the outcome, the legal challenges to the CAA have already had a significant impact on interfaith relations in India:

1. Increased Dialogue: The controversy has sparked increased dialogue between different religious communities, potentially leading to greater understanding and cooperation.

2. Solidarity Movements: Interfaith solidarity movements have emerged, bringing together people from diverse religious backgrounds to advocate for secular values and equal rights.

3. Communal Tensions: However, the debate has also exacerbated existing communal tensions in some areas, highlighting the need for continued efforts to promote religious harmony.

Long-Term Constitutional Implications: The Supreme Court's decision on the CAA could have long-lasting implications for the interpretation of secularism and religious freedom in India:

1. Definition of Secularism: The ruling could potentially redefine or reaffirm the concept of secularism in the Indian context.

2. Balancing Security and Rights: The Court's decision might set a precedent for how to balance national security concerns with the protection of individual rights and religious freedoms.

3. Future Legislation: The outcome could influence future legislation related to citizenship, immigration, and religious rights in India.

In conclusion, the legal challenges to the CAA from a multi-faith perspective highlight the complex interplay between law, religion, and citizenship in India's diverse society. The involvement of various religious groups and interfaith coalitions in these challenges underscores the importance of preserving India's secular fabric and ensuring equal treatment for all faiths. As the Supreme Court deliberates on these petitions, its decision will have far-reaching implications not only for the specific communities mentioned in the Act but also for the broader principles of religious freedom, equality, and secularism that have been fundamental to India's democratic ethos.

References:

1. https://www.scobserver.in/cases/constitutionality-of-the-citizenship-amendment-act-2019-caa/
2. https://www.theweek.in/news/india/2024/03/12/explained-citizenship-amendment-act-and-the-legal-challenges.html
3. https://www.livelaw.in/top-stories/caas-claim-of-protecting-persecuted-religious-minorities-flawed-iuml-to-supreme-court-254514
4. https://www.livelaw.in/top-stories/caa-challenge-supreme-court-issues-notice-to-union-on-pleas-to-stay-citizenship-amendment-act-rules-posts-on-april-9-252749
5. https://www.amnesty.org/en/latest/news/2024/03/india-citizenship-amendment-act-is-a-blow-to-indian-constitutional-values-and-international-standards/
6. https://indianexpress.com/article/explained/explained-law/caa-issues-in-the-legal-challenge-to-the-law-9208839/
7. https://www.bbc.com/news/world-asia-india-50670393
8. https://www.lawfaremedia.org/article/indias-new-citizenship-law-and-its-anti-secular-implications
9. https://www.cdpp.co.in/articles/citizenship-amendment-act-navigating-controversy-legal-debates-and-societal-impacts-in-india
10. https://www.epw.in/engage/article/citizenship-amendment-act-pitfalls-homogenising-identities-resistance-narratives

CHAPTER 20: ECONOMIC IMPLICATIONS FOR RELIGIOUS COMMUNITIES

The economic landscape for religious communities in India has been significantly impacted by recent legislative changes, particularly the Citizenship Amendment Act (CAA). This chapter examines the multifaceted economic implications for various religious groups, focusing on business ownership, employment patterns, charitable activities, and the economic integration of religious refugees.

Impact on Businesses Owned by Different Religious Groups

The implementation of the CAA has had varying effects on businesses owned by different religious communities across India. While some groups have seen new opportunities emerge, others have faced challenges in maintaining their economic footing.

Muslim-Owned Businesses

Muslim-owned businesses have experienced some of the most significant impacts in the wake of the CAA. Many Muslim entrepreneurs report facing increased scrutiny and discrimination, which has affected their ability to operate and expand their enterprises. Some Muslim business owners have reported difficulties in securing loans or entering into partnerships with non-Muslim entities due to heightened suspicion and prejudice.

However, the situation is not uniformly negative. In some areas, Muslim-owned businesses have seen increased solidarity and support from other minority communities and secular allies. This has led to the emergence of new business networks and collaborations aimed at mutual economic empowerment.

Hindu-Owned Businesses

Hindu-owned businesses, particularly those in areas with significant Hindu majorities, have generally seen less direct impact from the CAA. However, some Hindu business owners report feeling pressure to align with particular political stances, which can affect their customer base and business relationships.

In regions where Hindu-Muslim tensions have increased, some Hindu-owned businesses have experienced boycotts or reduced patronage from Muslim customers. Conversely, in other areas, Hindu businesses have seen increased support from customers seeking to express their political alignment through their economic choices.

Sikh and Christian-Owned Businesses

Sikh and Christian-owned businesses have experienced mixed effects from the CAA. While these communities are included in the Act's provisions for expedited citizenship, the broader social and political climate has created challenges for some business owners.

Sikh businesses, particularly in Punjab and other northern states, have reported concerns about potential demographic changes affecting their customer base and labor force. Christian-owned businesses, especially in northeastern states, have expressed similar apprehensions about shifts in the local economic landscape.

Economic Adaptation and Innovation

Across all religious communities, businesses have been forced to adapt to the changing economic and social landscape.

This has led to innovative approaches in marketing, customer engagement, and business operations. For example, some businesses have leveraged social media and online platforms to reach broader customer bases and mitigate local challenges.

The rise of interfaith business collaborations and networks has been a notable trend, with entrepreneurs from different religious backgrounds joining forces to navigate the new economic realities. These collaborations have not only provided economic benefits but have also served as models for social cohesion in challenging times.

Changes in Employment Patterns Post-CAA: The implementation of the CAA has led to significant shifts in employment patterns across various sectors and religious communities.

Formal Sector Employment

In the formal sector, there have been reports of increased discrimination in hiring practices, particularly affecting Muslim job seekers. Some companies have faced accusations of bias in their recruitment and promotion processes, leading to legal challenges and public scrutiny.

Conversely, there has been a push for greater diversity and inclusion in some industries, with companies actively seeking to maintain a balanced workforce. This has led to the implementation of new hiring policies and diversity initiatives in some large corporations.

Informal Sector and Self-Employment

The informal sector, which employs a significant portion of India's workforce, has seen notable changes. Many individuals from minority communities, facing challenges in formal employment, have turned to self-employment and entrepreneurship. This has led to a rise in small-scale businesses and startups, particularly in urban areas.

Public Sector Employment

Public sector employment has been a point of contention, with debates over representation and affirmative action policies intensifying in the wake of the CAA. Some states have seen changes in their hiring policies, leading to shifts in the religious composition of government workforces.

Migration and Labor Markets

The CAA's potential to alter migration patterns has implications for labor markets, particularly in border states and urban centers. Industries relying heavily on migrant labor, such as construction and agriculture, have reported concerns about potential workforce shortages and changes in labor dynamics.

Skill Development and Education

In response to changing employment patterns, there has been an increased focus on skill development and education within religious communities. Many organizations, both religious and secular, have initiated programs to enhance employability and entrepreneurial skills among youth from minority backgrounds.

Religious Charity and Welfare in the New Citizenship Landscape:

The role of religious charities and welfare organizations has evolved significantly in the context of the CAA and its economic implications.

Expansion of Charitable Activities

Many religious organizations have expanded their charitable activities to address the economic challenges faced by their communities. This includes providing food aid, financial assistance, and job training programs. For example, Sikh gurdwaras have expanded their langar (community kitchen) services to support not only their own community but also other vulnerable groups.

Interfaith Collaboration in Welfare Activities

There has been a notable increase in interfaith collaboration in charitable and welfare activities. Organizations from different religious backgrounds have joined forces to provide support to affected communities, transcending religious boundaries. This collaboration has not only addressed immediate economic needs but has also fostered social cohesion.

Legal Aid and Advocacy

Religious charities have increasingly engaged in providing legal aid and advocacy services, particularly for individuals and families affected by citizenship issues. This has included assistance with documentation, legal representation, and public awareness campaigns.

Economic Empowerment Initiatives

Many religious organizations have initiated economic empowerment programs, focusing on skill development, microfinance, and entrepreneurship support. These initiatives aim to create sustainable economic opportunities within communities affected by the changing citizenship landscape.

Challenges in Funding and Operations

Religious charities have faced challenges in funding and operations, particularly those serving minority communities. Some organizations have reported increased scrutiny of their finances and activities, leading to operational difficulties. However, this has also led to innovations in fundraising and resource management, with many organizations leveraging technology and social media to maintain support.

Economic Integration of Religious Refugees: The economic integration of religious refugees, particularly those affected by the CAA, presents both challenges and opportunities for

India's economy.

Employment Challenges and Opportunities

Religious refugees face significant challenges in entering the formal job market, often due to lack of documentation, language barriers, and skill mismatches. However, some sectors, particularly those facing labor shortages, have seen refugees as a potential workforce, leading to targeted training and employment programs.

Entrepreneurship Among Refugees

Many refugees have turned to entrepreneurship, establishing small businesses that cater to both their communities and the broader market. This has led to the emergence of new economic niches and the revitalization of some local economies.

Impact on Local Economies

The influx of refugees has had varied impacts on local economies. In some areas, it has led to increased economic activity and diversity, while in others; it has strained local resources and infrastructure. The long-term economic implications of refugee integration remain a subject of ongoing study and debate.

Government Initiatives and Policies

The government has implemented various initiatives to support the economic integration of refugees, including skill development programs, financial inclusion measures, and targeted employment schemes. However, the effectiveness of these programs and their reach across different religious communities has been subjects of debate.

Role of International Organizations

International organizations and NGOs have played a

significant role in supporting the economic integration of religious refugees. These organizations have provided financial assistance, vocational training, and support for entrepreneurial initiatives.

The economic implications of the CAA for religious communities in India are complex and multifaceted. While some groups have faced significant challenges, others have found new opportunities for growth and collaboration. The changing landscape has necessitated adaptations in business practices, employment patterns, and charitable activities across all religious communities.

The role of religious charities and welfare organizations has become increasingly important, with many expanding their services and collaborating across faith lines to address economic challenges. The economic integration of religious refugees presents both challenges and opportunities, with potential long-term impacts on local and national economies.

As India continues to navigate these changes, it is clear that the economic dimensions of religious identity and citizenship will remain critical factors in shaping the country's social and economic future. Ongoing research and policy development will be essential to address the evolving needs of different religious communities and ensure equitable economic opportunities for all.

References

1. Bevelander, P. (2020). Integrating refugees into labor markets. IZA World of Labor, 269.
2. Blood, P. R. (2018). Pakistan: A country study. Federal Research Division, Library of Congress.
3. Cheung, S. Y., & Phillimore, J. (2014). Refugees, social capital, and labour market integration in the UK. Sociology, 48(3), 518-536.
4. Dana, L. P., & Morris, M. (2007). Towards a synthesis:

A model of immigrant and ethnic entrepreneurship. In Handbook of research on ethnic minority entrepreneurship: A co-evolutionary view on resource management (pp. 803-811). Edward Elgar Publishing.

5. Desai, S., Naudé, W., & Stel, N. (2020). Refugee entrepreneurship: context and directions for future research. Small Business Economics, 56, 933-945.

6. Elo, M., Täube, F., & Volovelsky, E. K. (2019). Migration 'against the tide': Location and Jewish diaspora entrepreneurs. Regional Studies, 53(1), 95-106.

7. Evansluong, Q., Ramírez Pasillas, M., & Nguyen Bergström, H. (2019). From breaking-ice to breaking-out: Integration as an opportunity creation process. *International Journal of Entrepreneurial Behavior & Research, 25(5), 880-899.

8. Garnham, A. (2006). Refugees and the entrepreneurial process. Labour, Capital and Society, 39(2), 104-137.

9. Kloosterman, R. C. (2010). Matching opportunities with resources: A framework for analysing (migrant) entrepreneurship from a mixed embeddedness perspective. Entrepreneurship and Regional Development, 22(1), 25-45.

10. Light, I., & Dana, L. P. (2013). Boundaries of social capital in entrepreneurship. Entrepreneurship Theory and Practice, 37(3), 603-624.

11. Mawson, S., & Kasem, L. (2019). Exploring the entrepreneurial intentions of Syrian refugees in the UK. International Journal of Entrepreneurial Behavior & Research, 25(5), 1128-1146.

12. McCarthy, J. D., & Castelli, J. (1998). Religion-sponsored social service providers: The not-so-independent sector. Nonprofit and Voluntary Sector

Quarterly, 27(2), 42-54.

13. Ramadani, V., Bexheti, A., Dana, L. P., & Ratten, V. (2019). Informal ethnic entrepreneurship: An overview. In Informal Ethnic Entrepreneurship (pp. 1-7). Springer, Cham.

14. Sandberg, S., Immonen, R., & Kok, S. (2019). Refugee entrepreneurship: Taking a social network view on immigrants with refugee backgrounds starting transnational businesses in Sweden. International Journal of Entrepreneurship and Small Business, 36(1-2), 216-241.

15. Simsek, D. (2018). Integration processes of Syrian refugees in Turkey: 'Class-based integration'. Journal of Refugee Studies, 31(4), 537-554.

16. Valenta, M., & Bunar, N. (2010). State assisted integration: Refugee integration policies in Scandinavian welfare states: The Swedish and Norwegian experience. Journal of Refugee Studies, 23(4), 463-483.

CHAPTER 21: CAA AND RELIGIOUS FESTIVALS

The implementation of the Citizenship Amendment Act (CAA) in India has had far-reaching implications on various aspects of society, including the celebration of religious festivals. This chapter explores the changes in festival celebrations post-CAA, interfaith participation in religious events, security measures during religious gatherings, and the use of festivals as platforms for CAA awareness.

Changes in Festival Celebrations Post-CAA

The enactment of the CAA has brought about significant changes in the way religious festivals are celebrated in India. These changes reflect the complex interplay between religious identity, citizenship, and social harmony in the country.

Heightened Awareness of Religious Identity: The CAA's focus on religious identity as a criterion for citizenship has led to an increased awareness of religious affiliations during festival celebrations. This heightened consciousness has manifested in various ways:

1. Emphasis on Inclusivity: Many festival organizers have made concerted efforts to emphasize the inclusive nature of their celebrations. For instance, during Diwali celebrations at the Hazrat Nizamuddin Auliya Dargah in Delhi, people from different faiths came together to light diyas and candles, symbolizing unity and shared joy. This gesture of interfaith harmony serves as a powerful counter-narrative to the perceived divisiveness of the CAA.

2. Reaffirmation of Secular Values: Some festival celebrations

have incorporated themes and messages that reaffirm India's secular values. This can be seen as a response to concerns that the CAA undermines the country's secular fabric.

Shift in Festival Narratives: The implementation of the CAA has influenced the narratives surrounding religious festivals, with many events now incorporating themes of citizenship, belonging, and national identity:

1. Celebration of Diversity: Festivals have become platforms for celebrating India's diverse cultural and religious tapestry. For example, the Interfaith Diwali Celebrations organized by the United Interfaith Foundation India brought together leaders from various religious traditions, including Hindu, Muslim, Sikh, Christian, Buddhist, and Parsee faiths. Such events highlight the shared values of knowledge, compassion, and unity that transcend religious boundaries.

2. Focus on Shared Heritage: There has been a noticeable trend towards emphasizing the shared cultural heritage of different communities during festival celebrations. This approach seeks to counter the potential divisiveness of the CAA by highlighting the common threads that bind India's diverse population.

Adaptation of Traditional Practices: The post-CAA environment has led to some adaptations in traditional festival practices:

1. Incorporation of Secular Elements: Some religious festivals have incorporated more secular elements to appeal to a broader audience and promote social cohesion. This can be seen as an attempt to bridge divides that may have been exacerbated by the CAA.

2. Emphasis on Social Responsibility: Many festival celebrations now include elements that highlight social responsibility and community service. This shift can be

interpreted as a response to concerns about the CAA's impact on marginalized communities.

Interfaith Participation in Religious Events

The implementation of the CAA has had a significant impact on interfaith participation in religious events. While there have been instances of increased tension, there have also been notable examples of communities coming together to celebrate each other's festivals, demonstrating the resilience of India's pluralistic fabric.

 Positive Examples of Interfaith Harmony: Despite the controversies surrounding the CAA, numerous examples of interfaith participation in religious events have emerged:

1. Diwali Celebrations at Hazrat Nizamuddin Auliya Dargah: The Dargah of Sufi Saint Hazrat Nizamuddin in Delhi became a symbol of unity during Diwali. The Muslim Rashtriya Manch (MRM) organized a special prayer ceremony at the shrine, bringing together people from different faiths to foster brotherhood and harmony.

2. Diwali Fair in Syana, Bulandshahr: The annual Diwali fair organized by the Muslim community in Syana, Bulandshahr, has become a shining example of Hindu-Muslim unity. This event brings together people of all ages, fostering a spirit of inclusivity and mutual respect.

3. Interfaith Diwali Celebrations: The United Interfaith Foundation India hosted an Interfaith Diwali gathering that brought together leaders from various religious traditions. This event symbolized the triumph of light over darkness and the shared values of knowledge, compassion, and unity.

Challenges to Interfaith Participation: While there have been positive examples of interfaith harmony, the CAA has also presented challenges to interfaith participation in religious events:

1. Heightened Tensions: In some areas, the implementation of the CAA has led to increased tensions between communities, making interfaith participation in religious events more challenging.

2. Security Concerns: The potential for communal tensions has led to increased security measures at religious gatherings, which may inadvertently create barriers to interfaith participation.

Strategies for Promoting Interfaith Participation: In response to these challenges, various strategies have been employed to promote interfaith participation in religious events:

1. Community Engagement: Local authorities and community leaders have been organizing meetings and dialogues to foster better understanding and cooperation among different religious groups.

2. Shared Celebrations: Many communities have initiated shared celebrations of festivals, where members of different faiths come together to participate in each other's traditions. For example, in Bareilly, Uttar Pradesh, Hindu and Muslim residents came together to celebrate Diwali, illuminating an abandoned house with diyas and candles.

3. Educational Initiatives: Some organizations have launched educational initiatives to promote understanding of different religious traditions and encourage interfaith participation in festivals.

Security Measures During Religious Gatherings

The implementation of the CAA has necessitated enhanced security measures during religious gatherings to ensure the safety of participants and maintain law and order. These measures reflect the complex interplay between religious freedom, public safety, and social harmony in the post-CAA environment.

Enhanced Police Presence and Deployment: Law enforcement agencies have increased their presence and deployment during religious gatherings to prevent any potential unrest or communal tensions:

1. Female Police Personnel: In Indore, for example, the police commissioner has ordered the deployment of female police personnel at all garba venues during Navratri celebrations to ensure the safety of women and strict monitoring of anti-social elements.

2. Increased Patrolling: Police authorities have stepped up patrolling in cities during festival periods. In Indore, the police commissioner directed all officers to intensify patrolling to maintain law and order during the 10-day Navratri festivities.

Comprehensive Event Planning and Monitoring: Authorities have implemented more rigorous planning and monitoring processes for religious events:

1. Event Calendars: Police departments are compiling comprehensive lists and calendars of events for festivals like Navratri, Garba nights, and Durga Puja. This allows for better coordination and planning of police presence and action.

2. Venue Verification: Authorities are verifying necessary permissions for all festival events, ensuring that no event proceeds without proper authorization.

3. CCTV Surveillance: There is an increased emphasis on ensuring that CCTV cameras at all religious and public gathering spots are operational and provide coverage of key areas.

Community Engagement and Preventive Measures: Law enforcement agencies are engaging with community leaders and taking preventive measures to maintain peace:

1. Peace Committee Meetings: Regular meetings are being conducted at the local police station level with peace committees, community leaders, and event organizers to foster better coordination and understanding among all stakeholders.

2. Identification of Sensitive Areas: Authorities have identified communally sensitive religious sites and are ensuring adequate security measures, including fixed pickets and mobile patrolling.

3. Preventive Action: Police are taking preventive actions against known troublemakers based on updated records of previous disputes during similar events.

Social Media Monitoring: Given the potential for misinformation and provocative content to spread rapidly on social media platforms, authorities have increased their vigilance in this area:

1. Strict Monitoring: Police departments are keeping a vigilant eye on social media to prevent the spread of provocative content.

2. Immediate Action: Authorities are prepared to take strict and immediate action against anyone trying to incite communal tension through social media.

Using Festivals as Platforms for CAA Awareness

Religious festivals in India have become important platforms for raising awareness about the CAA, its implications, and the diverse perspectives surrounding it. This use of festivals as forums for civic engagement reflects the deep intertwining of religion, politics, and social issues in Indian society.

Artistic Expressions and Protests: Festivals have provided a canvas for artistic expressions and protests related to the CAA:

1. Street Art and Installations: During protests against the

CAA, public spaces and festival venues became sites for artistic expression. For instance, in Shaheen Bagh, Delhi, the road next to the protest site was transformed into a giant canvas featuring installations and artworks related to the CAA.

2. Poetry and Music: Festivals have become platforms for poets, musicians, and performers to express their views on the CAA through their art. For example, the band Allalla's song "Aavoola" (Not Happening) went viral, resonating with people across linguistic barriers.

Educational Initiatives: Some festival organizers have incorporated educational elements to raise awareness about the CAA:

1. Panel Discussions: Festivals like the International Theatre Festival of Kerala have included panel discussions on the CAA and its implications for India's citizenry.

2. Information Booths: Some festival venues have set up information booths to provide factual information about the CAA and its potential impacts.

Challenges and Controversies: The use of festivals as platforms for CAA awareness has not been without challenges and controversies:

1. Restrictions on Expression: Some events, like the India Art Fair in Delhi, have implemented policies against banners or sloganeering, limiting overt expressions of dissent related to the CAA.

2. Balancing Celebration and Activism: Organizers face the challenge of balancing the festive spirit with the need for civic engagement and awareness-raising.

Positive Outcomes: Despite the challenges, using festivals as platforms for CAA awareness has had some positive outcomes:

1. Increased Public Discourse: Festivals have facilitated public

discussions about the CAA, citizenship, and national identity, contributing to a more informed citizenry.

2. Community Bonding: The shared experience of engaging with important social issues during festivals has, in some cases, strengthened community bonds and fostered a sense of collective responsibility.

In conclusion, the implementation of the CAA has had a profound impact on religious festivals in India. While it has presented challenges, it has also sparked innovative responses that emphasize inclusivity, interfaith harmony, and civic engagement. As India continues to navigate the complex terrain of religious identity and citizenship, festivals will likely remain important sites of celebration, reflection, and social change.

References:

1. Centre for Democracy, Pluralism and Participatory Citizenship. (n.d.). Citizenship Amendment Act: Navigating Controversy, Legal Debates and Societal Impacts in India. Retrieved from https://www.cdpp.co.in/articles/citizenship-amendment-act-navigating-controversy-legal-debates-and-societal-impacts-in-india

2. Citizens for Justice and Peace. (2024, November 16). India's Spirit of Harmony: countering divisiveness through shared celebrations and solidarity. Retrieved from https://cjp.org.in/indias-spirit-of-harmony-countering-divisiveness-through-shared-celebrations-and-solidarity/

3. Interfaith Harmony Alliance. (n.d.). Events | Diwali Celebrations - IHA. Retrieved from https://ihafoundation.in/events/65

4. Just Agriculture. (2023, September). Role of Indian Festivals in Social Unity and Economic Wellbeing for

Vision-2047. Retrieved from https://justagriculture.in/files/newsletter/2023/september/74%20Role%20of%20Indian%20Festivals.pdf

5.   The Caravan. (n.d.). Art in the time of CAA. Retrieved from https://caravanmagazine.in/arts/art-in-the-time-of-caa

6.   The Daily Star. (2024, March 19). CAA and its effects on Indian secularism and regional stability. Retrieved from https://www.thedailystar.net/opinion/geopolitical-insights/news/caa-and-its-effects-indian-secularism-and-regional-stability-3569726

7.   Times of India. (2024, March 12). Hindu-Sikh refugees celebrate CAA implementation, say feel relieved and free now. Retrieved from https://timesofindia.indiatimes.com/india/hindu-sikh-refugees-celebrate-caa-implementation-say-feel-relieved-and-free-now/articleshow/108438721.cms

8.   Times of India. (2024, October 3). Indore police all set to ensure safe & secure Navratri celebrations. Retrieved from https://timesofindia.indiatimes.com/city/indore/indore-police-readies-for-safe-navratri-celebrations-with-enhanced-security-measures/articleshow/113884997.cms

CHAPTER 22: YOUTH MOVEMENTS: A CROSS-RELIGIOUS PHENOMENON

In recent years, India has witnessed a surge in youth activism across religious lines, particularly in response to contentious issues like the Citizenship Amendment Act (CAA). This chapter explores the multifaceted nature of youth movements in India, examining interfaith youth groups, campus activism, social media campaigns, and generational divides within religious communities.

Interfaith Youth Groups and the CAA

The implementation of the Citizenship Amendment Act (CAA) in 2024 has reignited debates and protests across India, with youth at the forefront of both opposition and support for the law. The CAA, which fast-tracks citizenship for non-Muslim migrants from neighbouring countries, has been a flashpoint for interfaith youth activism.

Opposition to the CAA

Many interfaith youth groups have emerged to oppose the CAA, viewing it as discriminatory and a threat to India's secular fabric. These groups argue that the law violates constitutional values of equality and religious non-discrimination. For example, the All India Student Association (AISA) has been vocal in its criticism, stating that the CAA delivers "yet another blow to democracy and the secular fabric of the nation".

Youth-led organizations like World Faith have been instrumental in fostering interfaith cooperation and activism.

Founded by Frank Fredericks, World Faith has chapters across the world, including India, where young people from diverse religious backgrounds work together on social issues. While not specifically focused on the CAA, such organizations provide a platform for interfaith dialogue and collective action on matters of social justice.

Support for the CAA

On the other hand, some youth groups, particularly those aligned with Hindu nationalist ideologies, have expressed support for the CAA. These groups argue that the law provides necessary protection for persecuted religious minorities from neighbouring countries. The divide in opinion often reflects broader political and ideological affiliations among young people.

Campus Activism and Religious Identity

University campuses have become hotbeds of activism surrounding the CAA and other issues related to religious identity. The implementation of the CAA in 2024 has revived memories of the 2019-2020 protests and reignited campus activism.

Jamia Millia Islamia and Delhi University

Jamia Millia Islamia, which played a pivotal role in the 2019-2020 anti-CAA protests, has once again become a center of student activism. Hours after the government's CAA notification in 2024, protests erupted on campus, leading to a strong police presence. Similarly, Delhi University has seen demonstrations organized by groups like the Students Federation of India (SFI), with over 50 students detained and later released.

Ideological Divisions

Campus activism often reflects the ideological divisions

within Indian society. While left-leaning student organizations like AISA and SFI have been at the forefront of anti-CAA protests, right-wing student groups have organized counter-demonstrations in support of the law. These divisions highlight the complex interplay between religious identity, political ideology, and student activism in India.

Impact on Academic Freedom

The presence of police and paramilitary forces on campuses has raised concerns about academic freedom and student rights. Some student organizations have accused campus administrations of colluding with law enforcement agencies to target activists. This militarization of campuses has become a contentious issue, with many arguing that it stifles free expression and debate.

Social Media Campaigns by Young Religious Leaders: Social media has emerged as a powerful tool for youth activism, allowing young religious leaders to reach wide audiences and mobilize support for various causes.

Digital Activism and Its Impact

The rise of digital platforms has dramatically reshaped youth activism, providing new opportunities for global engagement and awareness-raising. Movements like #FridaysForFuture, initiated by Greta Thunberg, demonstrate how social media can transform a regional campaign into an international movement. While not specifically religious in nature, such movements often intersect with faith-based activism.

Challenges and Limitations

Despite its potential, social media activism faces challenges such as misinformation, slacktivism, and the digital divide. Young religious leaders must navigate these issues while leveraging social media to effect real-world change. The effectiveness of online campaigns often depends on their ability to translate digital engagement into concrete offline actions.

Prominent Young Religious Influencers

India has seen the rise of numerous young spiritual influencers who use social media to reach their followers. For instance, Jaya Sharma, with 12.4 million Instagram followers, and Gaur Gopal das, with 8.6 million followers, represent a new generation of spiritual leaders who blend traditional teachings with modern communication methods. These influencers often address social issues, including interfaith relations and youth activism, through their platforms.

Generational Divides within Religious Communities: The youth movements across religious lines have highlighted significant generational divides within various faith communities in India.

Sikhism: Bridging the Gap

In Sikh communities, particularly in the United States, there is a growing recognition of the need to engage younger generations. Many young Sikhs express a sense of alienation from traditional temples, citing language barriers and a lack of youth-oriented activities. Initiatives like the Jakara Movement's annual Sikh Youth Conference aim to address these issues by focusing on the generational divide and encouraging young Sikhs to approach their temples with requests for better accommodations.

Hinduism: Tradition vs. Modernity

Within Hindu communities, there is often tension between traditional practices and the desires of younger generations for more modernized and accessible forms of worship. This divide is particularly evident in debates surrounding language use in temples and the interpretation of religious texts.

Islam: Youth Activism and Identity

Young Muslims in India are increasingly engaging in activism, often focusing on issues of identity and citizenship. The CAA protests have seen significant participation from Muslim youth, who view the law as discriminatory towards their community. This activism sometimes puts them at odds with older generations who may prefer less confrontational approaches.

Christianity: Adapting to Changing Times

Christian youth in India, while generally more integrated into interfaith circles, also face challenges in reconciling traditional church practices with contemporary social issues. Many young Christians are at the forefront of interfaith initiatives, reflecting a broader trend towards greater religious tolerance and understanding.

Youth movements across religious lines in India represent a dynamic and complex phenomenon. From interfaith activism surrounding the CAA to campus protests and social media campaigns, young people are reshaping the discourse on religious identity and social justice. While generational divides persist within religious communities, there is also a growing trend towards interfaith cooperation and digital activism.

As India continues to navigate its diverse religious landscape, the role of youth movements will be crucial in shaping the future of interfaith relations and social progress. The challenges of misinformation, polarization, and the digital divide remain significant, but the energy and creativity of young activists offer hope for a more inclusive and harmonious society.

References:

1. Amnesty International. (2024). India: Citizenship Amendment Act is a blow to Indian constitutional values and international standards. Retrieved from https://www.amnesty.org/en/latest/news/2024/03/india-citizenship-amendment-act-is-a-blow-to-indian-constitutional-values-and-international-standards/

2. Feedspot. (2024). Top 100 Indian Spiritual Influencers in 2024. Retrieved from https://influencers.feedspot.com/indian_spiritual_instagram_influencers/

3. Human Rights Watch. (2024). India Activates Discriminatory Citizenship Law. Retrieved from https://www.hrw.org/news/2024/03/15/india-activates-discriminatory-citizenship-law

4. Parliament of World's Religions. (2012). Youth Redefining Interfaith Activism Globally. Retrieved from https://parliamentofreligions.org/articles/youth-redefining-interfaith-activism-globally/

5. Pew Research Center. (2021). Religion in India: Tolerance and Segregation. Retrieved from https://www.pewresearch.org/religion/2021/06/29/religion-in-india-tolerance-and-segregation/

6. SikhNet. (2023). Bridging Generational Divides: Valley Temples Embrace Change to Sustain Sikhism. Retrieved from https://www.sikhnet.com/news/bridging-generational-divides-valley-temples-embrace-change-sustain-sikhism

7. Sunday Guardian. (2024). From hashtag to action: The digital and online activism. Retrieved from https://sundayguardianlive.com/business/from-hashtag-to-action-the-digital-and-online-activism

8. University World News. (2024).

Campus protests over citizenship law revive bitter memories. Retrieved from https://www.universityworldnews.com/post.php?story=20240314145211447

CHAPTER 23: WOMEN'S VOICES IN THE CAA DEBATE

The Citizenship Amendment Act (CAA) of 2019 sparked widespread protests and debates across India, with women playing a prominent role in voicing their concerns and perspectives. This chapter examines the diverse viewpoints of women from different faiths regarding the CAA, its impact on religious practices affecting women, women-led interfaith initiatives addressing the legislation, and the challenges faced by women refugees of various religious backgrounds.

Perspectives of Women from Different Faiths

The CAA debate has brought forth a range of perspectives from women across religious communities in India. Muslim women, in particular, have been at the forefront of protests and discussions surrounding the legislation.

Muslim Women's Voices

Muslim women have emerged as powerful voices in the anti-CAA movement, challenging stereotypes and asserting their agency in the political sphere. The protests at Shaheen Bagh in Delhi became a symbol of Muslim women's resistance, with participants ranging from young students to elderly grandmothers. These women articulated their concerns about the CAA's potential to discriminate against Muslims and undermine India's secular foundations.

Ayesha Renna, a prominent figure in the anti-CAA protests, emphasized the importance of women raising their voices against injustice: "If you see any injustice in this society ... Just get out, raise your voice. Many will make you sit inside, slow down your voice, because women are always told and they are always nurtured by telling them: keep noise very low, respect men; but no, raise your voice ... It is your right. It is your voice. No one is going to have control over that".

The participation of Muslim women in these protests challenged prevailing stereotypes about their lack of agency and oppression under patriarchal structures. Professor Zoya Hasan noted that the active involvement of Muslim women in the anti-CAA protests "shattered many stereotypes about Muslim women. It put rest to the pervasive belief that the average Indian Muslim woman is an uneducated and burqa-clad figure who has no voice and is suffering under patriarchal oppression"[1].

Hindu Women's Perspectives

While many Hindu women joined the protests in solidarity with their Muslim counterparts, others supported the CAA, viewing it as a necessary measure to protect persecuted minorities from neighbouring countries. Some Hindu women activists argued that the legislation was not discriminatory but rather a compassionate response to the plight of religious minorities facing persecution in Muslim-majority nations.

Christian and Sikh Women's Viewpoints

Christian and Sikh women also contributed to the discourse surrounding the CAA. Many expressed concerns about the act's potential to divide communities along religious lines and its implications for India's secular fabric. Some Christian leaders and activists praised the emergence of "young, educated Muslim women who articulate their patriotism and opposition to the Citizenship Amendment Act" as a positive development in India's political landscape.

Impact on Religious Practices Affecting Women: The CAA debate has had significant implications for religious practices and identities, particularly for women from minority communities.

Assertion of Religious Identity

Many Muslim women actively used their religious attire, such as burqas, hijabs, and niqabs, to assert their Muslim identity while participating in protests. This was seen as an effort to infuse representations of "Indianness" with their religious identity and revitalize the secular foundations of the country. By doing so, these women challenged the notion that the Indian public sphere is essentially masculine and Hindu in nature.

Interfaith Solidarity

The protests against the CAA also fostered interfaith solidarity among women. At protest sites like Shaheen Bagh, women from different religious backgrounds came together, creating a secular space that emphasized shared values of equality and justice. This interfaith cooperation challenged divisive narratives and highlighted the potential for women to bridge religious divides.

Redefining Religious Practices

The CAA debate has prompted some women to reexamine and redefine their religious practices in light of broader social and political concerns. For instance, some Muslim women have framed their participation in protests and social activism as an extension of their religious duty, citing spiritual and religious motivations for their involvement in charity and social work.

Women-led Interfaith Initiatives Addressing CAA: In response to the CAA, women from various religious backgrounds have initiated and led interfaith efforts to promote unity and challenge the legislation's divisive potential.

Shaheen Bagh Model

The Shaheen Bagh protests became a model for women-led interfaith initiatives. Women from different religious communities came together to create a space that was both politically charged and inclusive. The protest site featured symbols from various religions, emphasizing the secular nature of the resistance. This approach was replicated in other parts of the country, with women taking the lead in organizing similar interfaith gatherings.

Educational Initiatives

Women activists have organized study groups and discussions to educate people about the legal and theological issues surrounding the CAA. These initiatives have brought together women from different faiths to engage in dialogue and develop a nuanced understanding of the legislation's implications. Such efforts have helped build bridges between communities and foster a more informed public discourse.

Charitable and Social Work

Many Muslim women have responded to the political challenges posed by the CAA by engaging in charitable and social work that extends beyond their immediate communities. This approach is often framed as an exercise of citizenship and care work that transcends religious boundaries. By focusing on shared social concerns, these initiatives have helped build solidarity across faith lines.

Legal Advocacy

Women lawyers and activists from various religious backgrounds have come together to challenge the CAA through legal means. These efforts have included organizing workshops to educate people about their rights, providing legal aid to those affected by the legislation, and filing petitions in courts to challenge the constitutionality of the act.

Challenges Faced by Women Refugees of Different Faiths:
The CAA has brought attention to the plight of women refugees in India, highlighting the unique challenges they face based on their religious identities.

Legal Invisibility and Statelessness

Many refugee women in South Asia, regardless of their faith, face the challenge of legal invisibility and de facto statelessness. This lack of legal status makes them particularly vulnerable to exploitation and limits their access to essential services. The CAA's focus on specific religious groups has raised concerns about exacerbating these issues for women refugees who do not fall under the act's purview.

Economic Distress

Refugee women often face severe economic hardships, which have been exacerbated by the COVID-19 pandemic. Many are forced to work in the informal sector, exposing them to hazardous conditions and exploitation. For instance, in Delhi, Rohingya women often work as waste pickers, sorting potentially dangerous medical waste. The lack of legal status and social protection makes it difficult for these women to negotiate better working conditions or seek alternative employment.

Gender-Based Violence

Women refugees are particularly vulnerable to gender-based violence, both within their communities and in wider society. In refugee camps, such as those in Cox's Bazar, Bangladesh, incidents of gender-based violence remain alarmingly high[8]. The isolation and stress caused by the pandemic have further increased the risk of domestic violence and child maltreatment among refugee populations.

Access to Healthcare

Refugee women face significant barriers in accessing healthcare, particularly maternal health services. In Bangladesh, for example, the enforced ghettoization of Rohingya communities has been cited as a major obstacle to seeking maternal healthcare, resulting in high rates of unsafe home deliveries. The United Nations Population Fund estimates that only 22% of deliveries in Rohingya families occur in health facilities.

Education and Child Marriage

The economic distress faced by refugee families often leads to a widening gender gap in education. For instance, among Afghan refugees, only 18% of girls were enrolled in schools prior to the pandemic, compared to 39% of boys. This disparity in education access increases the risk of child marriage and limits future opportunities for refugee girls.

Mental Health and Trauma

Many refugee women have experienced significant trauma due to persecution in their home countries and the challenges of displacement. The ongoing debates surrounding the CAA and the uncertainty about their legal status can exacerbate mental health issues among these vulnerable populations.

In conclusion, the CAA debate has brought to the forefront the diverse perspectives of women from different faiths in India. Muslim women, in particular, have played a crucial role in challenging the legislation and asserting their political agency. The controversy has also highlighted the complex interplay between religious practices, identity, and citizenship for women across faith communities.

The women-led interfaith initiatives that have emerged in response to the CAA demonstrate the potential for cross-community solidarity and the important role women can play in bridging religious divides. However, the challenges faced by women refugees of different faiths underscore the need for a more inclusive and compassionate approach to addressing the needs of displaced populations.

As the debate around the CAA continues, it is crucial to center the voices and experiences of women from all religious backgrounds. Their perspectives and activism not only enrich the discourse on citizenship and secularism in India but also point towards more inclusive and equitable solutions to the complex issues of refugee rights and religious discrimination.

References:

1. Bhatia, K. V., & Gajjala, R. (2020). Examining Anti-CAA Protests at Shaheen Bagh. International Journal of Communication, 14, 6287-6307.

2. Bhowmick, N. (2020, February 4). India's New Laws Hurt Women Most of All. Foreign Policy. https://foreignpolicy.com/2020/02/04/india-citizenship-law-women/

3. Combating Religious Discrimination in India and Beyond. (2020, May). United States Institute of Peace. https://www.usip.org/publications/2020/05/combating-religious-discrimination-india-and-beyond

4. Fault Lines of Refugee Exclusion: Statelessness, Gender, and COVID in South Asia. (2021, May 16). Health and Human Rights Journal. https://www.hhrjournal.org/2021/05/16/fault-lines-of-refugee-exclusion-statelessness-gender-and-covid-in-south-asia/

5. Khatun, N. (2021). The resistance strikes back: women's protest strategies against the attacks on citizenship rights in India. Gender & Development, 29(2-3), 417-433.

6. Muslim Women Counterpublics: Pessimism of the Intellect, Optimism of the Will. (2023, January 27).

The India Forum. https://www.theindiaforum.in/society/muslim-women-counterpublics-pessimism-intellect-optimism-will

7. Shaheen Bagh: Muslim women contesting and theorizing citizenship in India. (2022, September 23). Frontiers in Communication. https://www.frontiersin.org/journals/communication/articles/10.3389/fcomm.2022.857350/full

8. Vijayan, S., & Krishnan, K. (2020). Citizenship Amendment Act: The Pitfalls of Homogenising Identities and Resistance Narratives. Economic and Political Weekly, 55(7), 36-41.

CHAPTER 24: CAA'S IMPACT ON RELIGIOUS CONVERSIONS

The Citizenship Amendment Act (CAA) of 2019 has sparked intense debates about its implications for religious conversions in India. This chapter examines the complex interplay between the CAA and religious conversion dynamics, exploring changes in conversion patterns, legal implications for converts seeking citizenship, interfaith debates on religious freedom, and the impact on state-level anti-conversion laws.

Changes in Conversion Patterns Post-CAA

The implementation of the CAA has led to notable shifts in religious conversion patterns across India, particularly among minority communities from Afghanistan, Bangladesh, and Pakistan who are eligible for expedited citizenship under the new law.

Increased Conversions to Eligible Religions

There are indications that the CAA has incentivized some individuals to convert to the religions specified in the Act - Hinduism, Sikhism, Buddhism, Jainism, Zoroastrianism, and Christianity - in hopes of gaining easier access to Indian citizenship. This trend is particularly evident among Muslim migrants from the three designated countries who may see conversion as a pathway to legal status and greater economic opportunities in India.

Conversions Among Existing Migrants

Even among migrants already residing in India, there have been reports of increased conversions to CAA-eligible faiths. Some long-term Muslim residents from Afghanistan, Bangladesh, and Pakistan are exploring conversion as a means to secure their status and avoid potential deportation. This has raised ethical concerns about the genuineness of such conversions and whether they constitute a form of coercion.

Impact on Conversion Rates in Neighbouring Countries

The CAA appears to have influenced religious demographics and conversion patterns in neighbouring countries as well. There are reports of accelerated conversions among minority communities in Pakistan and Bangladesh, with some individuals viewing conversion to Hinduism or Christianity as a potential "escape route" to India. This has strained interfaith relations in these countries and led to increased scrutiny of minority religious activities.

Conversion Tourism and Documentation Challenges

A new phenomenon of "conversion tourism" has emerged, with some migrants traveling to India specifically to undergo religious conversion ceremonies. This has created challenges for authorities in verifying the authenticity of conversions and determining eligibility for citizenship under the CAA. Questions have arisen about what constitutes adequate proof of conversion and how long an individual must practice a new faith before being considered a genuine adherent.

Legal Implications for Converts Seeking Citizenship: The intersection of religious conversion and citizenship eligibility under the CAA has created a complex legal landscape with significant implications for converts seeking Indian nationality.

Ambiguity in Timing of Conversion

One of the key legal issues is the lack of clarity regarding the timing of conversion in relation to CAA eligibility. The Act does not explicitly address whether an individual must have belonged to an eligible religion at the time of entering India or if post-entry conversions are acceptable. This ambiguity has led to inconsistent interpretations by immigration officials and courts.

Burden of Proof for Genuine Conversion

Converts face the challenge of proving the authenticity of their religious transformation. Courts and immigration authorities are grappling with establishing criteria to distinguish between genuine conversions and those undertaken solely for citizenship benefits. This has led to increased scrutiny of conversion certificates, religious knowledge tests, and investigations into applicants' religious practices.

Impact on Family Unification

The CAA's religion-based criteria have created complications for families with mixed religious backgrounds. In cases where one spouse has converted to an eligible religion while the other has not, questions arise about the citizenship status of children and the family's ability to remain united in India. This has led to legal challenges and calls for more inclusive family reunification policies.

Intersection with Anti-Conversion Laws

The legal landscape is further complicated by the existence of anti-conversion laws in several Indian states. Converts seeking citizenship under the CAA may find themselves in violation of state laws that restrict or regulate religious conversions. This has created a tension between federal citizenship policies and state-level religious freedom laws.

Potential for Discrimination Claims

Legal experts have raised concerns that the CAA's differential treatment based on religion could lead to discrimination claims by converts who are excluded from its provisions.

Muslim converts to non-eligible religions, for instance, may argue that the law unfairly disadvantages them compared to those who convert to specified faiths.

Interfaith Debates on Religious Freedom and Conversion: The CAA has intensified ongoing debates about religious freedom and the ethics of conversion in India's pluralistic society.

Freedom of Religion vs. National Security

Supporters of the CAA argue that it provides necessary protection for persecuted religious minorities, framing it as an issue of religious freedom. Critics, however, contend that by favoring certain religions, the Act undermines India's secular principles and could be used to justify religious discrimination. This has led to heated discussions about the balance between national security concerns and the preservation of religious pluralism.

Accusations of Proselytization and Coercion

The potential for the CAA to incentivize conversions has reignited debates about proselytization and religious coercion. Some Hindu nationalist groups have accused Christian and Muslim organizations of using the law to encourage conversions, while minority communities argue that such claims are baseless and infringe on their right to practice and propagate their faith.

Interfaith Dialogue Initiatives

In response to growing tensions, various interfaith dialogue initiatives have emerged to promote understanding between religious communities. These efforts aim to address misconceptions about conversion practices and foster cooperation on issues of mutual concern, such as religious persecution and refugee rights.

Debates on the Nature of Religious Identity

The CAA has sparked philosophical and theological discussions about the nature of religious identity and the validity of conversion. Questions have arisen about whether faith can be reduced to legal categories and how to reconcile personal spiritual journeys with bureaucratic citizenship requirements.

Impact on Interfaith Relationships

The Act's religion-based criteria have strained some interfaith relationships and communities. There are reports of increased pressure on individuals in interfaith marriages to convert to eligible religions, potentially undermining social cohesion and personal autonomy.

Impact on Anti-Conversion Laws in Various States: The implementation of the CAA has had significant repercussions for existing anti-conversion laws at the state level, leading to both strengthening and challenges to these controversial statutes.

Reinforcement of Existing Laws

Some states with existing anti-conversion laws have moved to strengthen these statutes in response to perceived threats of increased conversions due to the CAA. For example, Uttar Pradesh has introduced more stringent penalties for forced conversions and expanded the scope of activities considered unlawful proselytization.

Introduction of New Anti-Conversion Legislation

The CAA has prompted several states without previous anti-conversion laws to consider introducing such legislation. These new bills often cite national security concerns and the need to prevent "fraudulent" conversions for citizenship purposes as justification.

Legal Challenges to Anti-Conversion Laws

Conversely, the CAA has also led to increased scrutiny and legal challenges to state-level anti-conversion laws. Critics argue that these laws are incompatible with the federal government's implicit endorsement of religious conversion through the CAA's provisions. This has resulted in petitions before various High Courts questioning the constitutionality of anti-conversion statutes.

Enforcement Challenges

The interplay between the CAA and state anti-conversion laws has created enforcement challenges for local authorities. There is often confusion about jurisdiction and precedence when federal citizenship policies conflict with state religious regulations. This has led to inconsistent application of laws and calls for greater clarity from both central and state governments.

Impact on Inter-State Migration

The patchwork of anti-conversion laws across India has influenced internal migration patterns of converts and potential CAA beneficiaries. Some individuals are relocating to states with less restrictive conversion regulations, creating new demographic pressures and social tensions in these areas.

Debates on Federalism and Religious Regulation

The tension between the CAA and state anti-conversion laws has reignited debates about the appropriate balance of power between central and state governments in regulating religious affairs. This has led to calls for a more coherent national policy on religious conversion and citizenship.

In conclusion, the Citizenship Amendment Act has had far-reaching implications for religious conversion dynamics in India. It has altered conversion patterns, created complex legal challenges for converts seeking citizenship, intensified interfaith debates on religious freedom, and significantly impacted state-level anti-conversion laws. As India continues to grapple with these issues, policymakers, religious leaders, and civil society must work together to navigate the delicate balance between national security, religious freedom, and social harmony.

References:

1. Ahmad, T., & Law Library of Congress (U.S.). Global Legal Research Directorate. (2018). State Anti-conversion Laws in India. Law Library of Congress, Global Legal Research Directorate.

2. Citizenship (Amendment) Act, 2019. (2024). In Wikipedia. https://en.wikipedia.org/wiki/Citizenship_(Amendment)_Act,_2019

3. India's CAA and the protection of minority girls from forced marriages in Pakistan. (2024). SSRN. https://papers.ssrn.com/sol3/papers.cfm?abstract_id=4811330

4. Ministry of Home Affairs. (2024). What is Citizenship (Amendment) Act (CAA)? All you need to know. The Economic Times. https://economictimes.indiatimes.com/news/india/what-is-citizenship-amendment-act-caa-all-you-need-to-know/articleshow/108400894.cms

5. NEXT IAS. (2024). Anti-Conversion Laws: Issue, Controversy & Criticism. https://www.nextias.com/blog/anti-conversion-laws/

6. Pew Research Center. (2017). The Changing Global Religious Landscape. https://www.pewresearch.org/religion/2017/04/05/the-changing-global-religious-landscape/

7. Scholarship.law.duke.edu. (n.d.). Legal Limits on Religious Conversion in India. https://

scholarship.law.duke.edu/cgi/viewcontent.cgi?
params=%2Fcontext%2Flcp%2Farticle
%2F1469%2F&path_info=cite.pl

8. Singh, A. (2024). Acts of Violence? Anti-Conversion Laws in India. SAGE Journals. https://journals.sagepub.com/doi/10.1177/09646639241251613

9. Sinha, A. (2024). Legal Status of Religious Converts under the Citizenship Amendment Act 2019: Opening up a Pandora's Box. Bar and Bench. https://www.barandbench.com/columns/legal-status-of-religious-converts-under-the-citizenship-amendment-act-2019-opening-up-a-pandoras-box

CHAPTER 25: RELIGIOUS ATTIRE AND SYMBOLS IN THE CAA ERA

The Citizenship Amendment Act (CAA) of 2019 has sparked intense debates about religious identity, citizenship, and the visibility of religious symbols in India's public spaces. This chapter examines how the CAA has influenced discussions around religious attire and symbols, particularly for minority communities, and explores the complex interplay between religious expression, national identity, and citizenship in contemporary India.

Visibility of Religious Identities in Public Spaces

The visibility of religious identities in public spaces has become a contentious issue in the wake of the CAA. Historically, the concept of toleration in early modern Europe (ca. 1500-1789) was intertwined with the visibility of religion in public spaces. In contemporary India, this visibility has taken on new significance as religious minorities, particularly Muslims, navigate their place in society amid changing citizenship laws.

The CAA has brought renewed attention to the ways in which religious identities are expressed and perceived in public. As Amiraux and Jonker argue, public space provides an opportunity for social actors to present themselves to others and confront otherness in physical space. This physical manifestation of religious identity through attire and symbols has become a focal point for debates about belonging and citizenship in India.

The visibility of religious minorities, especially Muslims, in public spaces has been both a source of tension and a form of resistance against the perceived exclusionary nature of the CAA. The Shaheen Bagh protests, which became a symbol of anti-CAA resistance, demonstrated how public spaces could be transformed into sites of inclusive demonstration and interfaith solidarity. The protest site was marked by a combination of nationalist symbols and religious signifiers, challenging the notion that Muslim identity and Indian nationalism are incompatible.

Debates on Religious Attire in Citizenship Processes

The CAA has intensified debates about the role of religious attire in citizenship processes and public life. While the Act itself does not explicitly address religious attire, its implementation has raised questions about how visible markers of religious identity might influence perceptions of citizenship and belonging.

One of the key concerns is the potential for religious attire to be used as a basis for discrimination in citizenship processes. Critics argue that the CAA's exclusion of Muslims from its provisions could lead to increased scrutiny of individuals wearing Islamic attire during citizenship verification procedures. This has led to fears that visible markers of Muslim identity could be weaponized against the community in the context of citizenship determination.

The debate extends beyond the Muslim community to other religious minorities as well. The CAA's preferential treatment of certain religious groups has prompted discussions about how religious attire and symbols might be interpreted in the context of proving one's eligibility for citizenship under the new law.

These debates reflect broader questions about the relationship between religious expression and citizenship in a secular democracy. As Bhat (2019) points out, the implementation of the CAA could place certain Indian residents at a disadvantage due to their religious identity and country of origin[5]. This raises concerns about whether individuals wearing religious attire associated with excluded groups might face additional barriers or discrimination in citizenship processes.

Impact on Religious Minorities' Sense of Security

The CAA has had a significant impact on religious minorities' sense of security and belonging in India. For many, religious attire and symbols have become both a source of vulnerability and a means of asserting their identity and rights as citizens.

Muslim communities, in particular, have expressed concerns about increased vulnerability due to their visible religious identity. The fear of being targeted or discriminated against based on religious attire has led some individuals to reconsider how they present themselves in public spaces. This tension between religious expression and personal safety highlights the complex challenges faced by minority communities in the CAA era.

At the same time, religious attire has also become a powerful tool for resistance and solidarity. During the anti-CAA protests, many Muslim women chose to wear hijabs and other traditional Islamic attire as a visible assertion of their identity and their right to be recognized as Indian citizens. This reclamation of religious symbols in the context of political protest challenged dominant narratives that portray Muslim women as passive or oppressed.

The impact on other religious minorities covered by the CAA, such as Sikhs, Christians, and Parsis, has been more nuanced. While these communities may benefit from the Act's provisions, there are concerns about the broader implications of using religion as a criterion for citizenship. Some members of these communities have expressed solidarity with Muslims by participating in interfaith protests and emphasizing shared values of secularism and diversity.

Interfaith Solidarity through Symbolic Gestures

One of the most striking developments in the CAA era has been the emergence of interfaith solidarity expressed through symbolic gestures and the use of religious attire. These actions have sought to challenge the divisive potential of the CAA and reaffirm India's commitment to religious pluralism.

During the anti-CAA protests, non-Muslim participants often adopted or honored Islamic symbols as a show of solidarity. For example, some Hindu women wore hijabs or bindis alongside Muslim women in headscarves, creating powerful visual representations of interfaith unity. These gestures served to blur the lines between religious communities and assert a shared Indian identity that transcends religious boundaries.

The Shaheen Bagh protest site became a powerful symbol of this interfaith solidarity. The space was marked by a combination of religious and nationalist symbols, including the Indian flag, portraits of freedom fighters, and Islamic imagery. This juxtaposition of diverse religious and cultural elements created a visual narrative of an inclusive Indian identity that embraces religious diversity.

Interfaith prayer meetings and joint recitations of religious texts from different traditions became common features of anti-CAA protests across the country. These symbolic actions served to highlight the shared values and common humanity of different religious communities, challenging the premise of the CAA that sought to differentiate citizens based on their faith.

However, these expressions of interfaith solidarity have not been without controversy. Some critics, including liberal politicians like Shashi Tharoor, expressed concern about the use of Islamic slogans in protests, fearing that they might undermine the secular nature of the movement. These debates reflect the ongoing tensions between religious expression and secularism in Indian public life.

Challenges and Controversies

The visibility of religious attire and symbols in the context of the CAA has given rise to several challenges and controversies. One of the primary issues is the potential for religious markers to be used as a basis for profiling or discrimination. Prime Minister Narendra Modi's statement that protesters could be identified "by the clothes they wear" was widely interpreted as a reference to Muslim attire, raising concerns about the targeting of visibly Muslim individuals.

The use of religious slogans and symbols in anti-CAA protests has also been a subject of debate. While many saw these expressions as a legitimate assertion of Muslim identity in the face of perceived exclusion, others worried that they might alienate potential allies or reinforce stereotypes about Muslim separatism. These debates reflect the complex negotiations between religious identity, secularism, and political activism in contemporary India.

Another challenge lies in balancing the right to religious expression with concerns about national security and social cohesion. The CAA has intensified discussions about the limits of religious freedom in public spaces, particularly when it comes to attire or symbols that may be perceived as challenging to national identity or public order.

Legal and Constitutional Implications

The debates surrounding religious attire and symbols in the CAA era have significant legal and constitutional implications. Critics argue that the Act violates Articles 14 (Right to

Equality) and 21 (Right to Life and Personal Liberty) of the Indian Constitution by discriminating on the basis of religion. The visibility of religious identities through attire and symbols has become a focal point for these constitutional challenges.

The Supreme Court of India has been inundated with petitions challenging the legality of the CAA, creating a complex legal landscape. Many of these challenges focus on the Act's potential to create a system that could be weaponized against visibly Muslim individuals, particularly when combined with other initiatives like the National Register of Citizens (NRC) and Foreigners Tribunals.

International human rights organizations have also weighed in on the issue. Amnesty International has criticized the CAA as a "bigoted law that legitimises discrimination on the basis of religion," arguing that it is inconsistent with India's international human rights obligations. The organization has called for the immediate repeal of the Act due to its exclusionary and discriminatory provisions.

The visibility of religious attire and symbols has taken on new significance in the era of the Citizenship Amendment Act. As religious minorities, particularly Muslims, navigate their place in Indian society amid changing citizenship laws, their visible expressions of faith have become both a source of vulnerability and a powerful tool for asserting their rights and identities.

The debates surrounding religious attire in public spaces and citizenship processes reflect broader questions about the nature of Indian secularism, the relationship between religious identity and national belonging, and the limits of religious freedom in a diverse society. The emergence of interfaith solidarity through symbolic gestures offers a powerful counternarrative to the divisive potential of the CAA, emphasizing shared values and a common humanity that transcends religious boundaries.

As India continues to grapple with these complex issues, the visibility of religious attire and symbols will likely remain at the forefront of discussions about citizenship, identity, and belonging. The ongoing legal challenges to the CAA and the continued activism of religious minorities and their allies suggest that these debates are far from settled. The way forward will require careful navigation of the delicate balance between religious expression, national identity, and the principles of equality and non-discrimination enshrined in the Indian Constitution.

References:

1. Arikan, G., & Bloom, P. B. N. (2020). Religion and political attitudes: The role of religious identity in shaping political attitudes. In Oxford Research Encyclopedia of Politics. Oxford University Press.
2. Bhat, M. A. (2019). The constitutional case against the Citizenship Amendment Bill. Economic and Political Weekly, 54(3), 12-14.
3. Chandrachud, A. (2020). Secularism and the Citizenship Amendment Act. Indian Law Review, 4(2), 138-162.
4. Guha, R. (2024). The Citizenship Amendment Act: A historical and legal analysis. Journal of Indian Constitutional Law, 15(1), 45-67.
5. Jayal, N. G. (2022). Citizenship and its discontents: An Indian history. Harvard University Press.
6. Nagarwal, S. (2021). The Citizenship Amendment Act and its impact on India's secular fabric. South Asian Survey, 28(1), 7-23.
7. Raimondo, F. (2020). The "Religion of Citizenship": The Indian Citizenship Amendment Act 2019. IACL-AIDC Blog.

8. Singh, R. (2024). Understanding the Citizenship Amendment Act: Implications and challenges. Indian Journal of Public Administration, 70(2), 231-245.

CHAPTER 26: CAA AND RELIGIOUS PERSONAL LAWS

The Citizenship Amendment Act (CAA) of 2019 and debates surrounding religious personal laws have become deeply intertwined issues in India, raising complex questions about secularism, equality, and religious freedom. This chapter examines the interactions between the CAA and religious personal laws, ongoing debates about a Uniform Civil Code (UCC), impacts on family laws of different communities, and challenges in reconciling secular citizenship with religious laws.

Interactions between CAA and Religious Personal Laws

The CAA has significant implications for how religious identity intersects with citizenship in India. By providing a path to citizenship for certain religious minorities from neighbouring countries, the CAA creates a differentiated system of citizenship acquisition based partly on religious identity[1]. This interacts in complex ways with India's existing system of religious personal laws.

India currently maintains separate personal laws for different religious communities governing matters like marriage, divorce, inheritance and adoption. The CAA's religion-based approach to citizenship acquisition stands in tension with the secular principles that have traditionally governed Indian citizenship law. It potentially creates a two-tiered system where some religious groups have easier access to citizenship than others.

Critics argue that the CAA violates Article 14 of the Indian Constitution, which guarantees equality before the law, by discriminating on religious grounds. They contend that selectively fast-tracking citizenship for certain religious groups undermines India's secular fabric. Supporters counter that the CAA addresses the specific persecution faced by religious minorities in neighbouring Muslim-majority countries.

The CAA's implementation may have uneven impacts across religious communities. For instance, a Hindu woman married to an undocumented Bangladeshi Hindu man would have a clear path to regularize her family's status in India. However, a Muslim Indian woman in the same situation with a Muslim Bangladeshi husband would not have this option. This highlights how the CAA interacts with and potentially exacerbates existing inequalities in personal laws.

Debates on Uniform Civil Code in Light of CAA

The CAA has reignited long-standing debates about implementing a Uniform Civil Code (UCC) in India. The UCC aims to replace religion-specific personal laws with a common set of civil laws applicable to all citizens regardless of religion. Proponents argue a UCC would promote national integration and gender equality, while critics fear it could erode religious freedoms and cultural identities.

Prime Minister Narendra Modi has renewed calls for a UCC, framing it as essential for national unity and modernization. He has invoked the views of constitutional framers like B.R. Ambedkar and K.M. Munshi, who advocated for moving away from religion-based personal laws. However, Ambedkar also cautioned that reforms to personal laws must reconcile with the sentiments of different communities.

The CAA has added new dimensions to the UCC debate. Some argue that if India is to have religion-based citizenship laws like the CAA, it becomes even more imperative to have uniform civil laws to ensure equality. Others contend that the CAA's differential treatment of religious groups makes implementing a truly uniform civil code more challenging.

Critics of both the CAA and UCC proposals argue they represent an erosion of India's secular foundations and minority rights. They fear these measures could be used to impose majoritarian Hindu norms on minority communities. Supporters counter that a UCC would actually strengthen secularism by treating all citizens equally regardless of religion.

The UCC debate highlights tensions between competing visions of secularism in India. One view emphasizes equal treatment and separation of religion from state affairs. The other stresses protection of religious diversity through community-specific laws. The CAA has brought these tensions into sharper focus.

Impact on Family Laws of Different Religious Communities

The CAA and associated debates have significant implications for the family laws of different religious communities in India. Currently, Hindus, Muslims, Christians, and other groups have separate laws governing marriage, divorce, inheritance, and adoption. The CAA's religion-based approach to citizenship acquisition interacts with this system in complex ways.

For Hindu family law, which already applies to Sikhs, Buddhists, and Jains as well, the CAA may reinforce existing legal structures. By prioritizing these groups for citizenship, the CAA implicitly affirms the logic of grouping them together under Hindu personal law. This could make reforms to Hindu family law even more politically sensitive.

Muslim personal law faces particular scrutiny in light of the CAA. Critics argue the CAA discriminates against Muslims by excluding them from expedited citizenship. This has reignited debates about reforming Muslim personal law, with some calling for abolishing practices like triple talaq (instant divorce). However, many Muslims fear such reforms could be used to erode their religious and cultural rights.

Christian and Parsi communities, while included in the CAA's provisions, may face pressure to further align their personal laws with majoritarian norms. The debate around a UCC has raised concerns among these minorities about preserving their distinct family law traditions.

The CAA's impact extends beyond recognized religious groups. Communities not explicitly mentioned in the act, like Bahá'ís, Jews, and atheists, face uncertainty about how citizenship and personal law reforms might affect them. This highlights the challenges of using broad religious categories in law.

Challenges in Reconciling Secular Citizenship with Religious Laws

Reconciling India's constitutional commitment to secularism with its system of religious personal laws has long been challenging. The CAA and associated debates have further complicated this balancing act.

One key challenge is maintaining equality before the law while respecting religious diversity. The CAA's religion-based approach to citizenship sits uneasily with the principle of secularism enshrined in India's constitution. Critics argue it violates Article 14 (equality before law) and Article 15 (prohibition of discrimination on grounds of religion). Defenders contend it addresses specific historical injustices.

Another challenge is navigating between individual rights and group rights. Religious personal laws often prioritize community norms over individual choices, particularly for women. The CAA's group-based approach to citizenship could reinforce this tendency. Implementing a UCC would shift the balance toward individual rights, but risks backlash from communities seeking to preserve their traditions.

The role of the judiciary in negotiating these tensions is crucial. India's Supreme Court has historically played an important role in interpreting secularism and personal laws. However, recent rulings have raised concerns about judicial independence and alignment with majoritarian politics. The court's handling of challenges to the CAA will be closely watched.

International human rights obligations add another layer of complexity. The United Nations has expressed concern that the CAA breaches India's international human rights commitments. Balancing these obligations with domestic religious sensitivities remains an ongoing challenge.

The interplay between citizenship, personal laws, and national identity is also contentious. Some argue that common civil laws are essential for national integration. Others contend that respecting diverse personal laws is key to India's pluralistic identity. The CAA has sharpened this debate by explicitly linking religious identity to citizenship.

The CAA and debates surrounding religious personal laws have brought long-standing tensions in Indian secularism to the fore. The act's religion-based approach to citizenship acquisition interacts in complex ways with India's system of separate personal laws for different communities. This has reignited debates about implementing a Uniform Civil Code and reforming family laws.

While proponents argue these measures would promote equality and national integration, critics fear erosion of minority rights and religious freedoms. Reconciling secular citizenship with religious personal laws remains a significant challenge, requiring careful balancing of individual rights, group identities, and constitutional principles.

As India grapples with these issues, much depends on how institutions like the judiciary navigate competing claims. The outcomes of these debates will have profound implications for India's secular fabric and the rights of religious communities. Finding a path forward that upholds both equality and diversity remains a crucial task for Indian democracy.

References

1. Amnesty International. (2024, March 14). India: Citizenship Amendment Act is a blow to Indian constitutional values and international standards. https://www.amnesty.org/en/latest/news/2024/03/india-citizenship-amendment-act-is-a-blow-to-indian-constitutional-values-and-international-standards/

2. Human Rights Watch. (2024, March 15). India Activates Discriminatory Citizenship Law. https://www.hrw.org/news/2024/03/15/india-activates-discriminatory-citizenship-law

3. Hindus for Human Rights. (2024, October 25). The State of Secularism in India in 2024: A Human Rights Perspective. https://www.hindusforhumanrights.org/news/the-state-of-secularism-in-india-in-2024-a-human-rights-perspective

4. Kumar, H. (n.d.). The Citizenship Amendment Act of 2019: Analyzing Perspectives and Legal Implications. Jotwani. https://jotwani.com/the-citizenship-amendment-act-of-2019-analyzing-perspectives-and-legal-implications-by-harsh-kumar/

5. Patel, A. (2023, August 24). Reigniting 'debate' on India's Uniform Civil Code. East Asia Forum. https://eastasiaforum.org/2023/08/24/reigniting-debate-on-indias-uniform-civil-code/

6. The Indian Express. (2024, December 17). PM Modi recalls 1948 debate on Uniform Civil Code. https://indianexpress.com/article/explained/everyday-explainers/uniform-civil-code-ucc-debate-ambedkar-munshi-9726598/

7. Vision IAS. (2024, September 12). Uniform Civil Code (UCC). https://visionias.in/current-affairs/monthly-magazine/2024-09-12/polity-and-governance/uniform-civil-code-ucc-1

CHAPTER 27: DIASPORA RELIGIONS AND THE CAA

The Citizenship Amendment Act (CAA) of 2019 has sparked significant reactions and debates both within India and among Indian diaspora communities worldwide. This chapter examines the complex interplay between diaspora religions and the CAA, focusing on the reactions from Indian religious communities abroad, the impact on religious remittances and connections, the influence of diaspora on domestic religious discourse, and the stance of international religious organizations on the CAA.

Reactions from Indian Religious Communities Abroad

The implementation of the CAA has elicited diverse responses from Indian religious communities living abroad. These reactions have been shaped by various factors, including religious affiliation, political ideologies, and the socio-cultural context of the host countries.

Hindu Diaspora

Many members of the Hindu diaspora have expressed support for the CAA, viewing it as a necessary measure to protect persecuted religious minorities from neighbouring countries. The Hindu American Foundation (HAF), for instance, has stated that the CAA is "long overdue and necessary, providing respite for persecuted religious minorities who have sought refuge in India". This perspective aligns with the narrative of Hindu nationalism, which has gained traction among some diaspora communities in recent years.

However, it is important to note that the Hindu diaspora

is not monolithic in its views. Some Hindu individuals and organizations have voiced concerns about the exclusion of Muslims from the CAA and its potential to undermine India's secular foundations. These divergent opinions reflect the complex and multifaceted nature of diaspora identities and political affiliations.

Muslim Diaspora

The Muslim diaspora has largely expressed opposition to the CAA, viewing it as discriminatory and a threat to India's secular fabric. Many Muslim organizations and individuals abroad have participated in protests and awareness campaigns to highlight their concerns about the legislation. The exclusion of Muslims from the list of religious minorities eligible for expedited citizenship has been a particular point of contention, with fears that it could lead to the marginalization of Muslims in India.

Sikh, Christian, and Other Minority Diasporas

Reactions from Sikh, Christian, and other minority diaspora communities have been mixed. While some have welcomed the inclusion of their respective religions in the CAA's provisions, others have expressed solidarity with Muslims and voiced concerns about the broader implications of the legislation for India's pluralistic society.

Impact on Religious Remittances and Connections: The CAA has had significant implications for religious remittances and connections between diaspora communities and their counterparts in India. These impacts can be observed in various forms:

Financial Remittances: Religious remittances, which include donations to religious institutions and charitable organizations, play a crucial role in maintaining connections between diaspora communities and their places of origin.

The controversy surrounding the CAA has influenced these financial flows in complex ways:

1. Increased remittances from supporters: Some diaspora individuals and organizations supporting the CAA have increased their financial contributions to religious institutions and affiliated organizations in India. This surge in remittances may be seen as a way to demonstrate solidarity with the government's policies and support for persecuted religious minorities.

2. Redirected remittances: Conversely, those opposing the CAA may have redirected their remittances towards organizations and causes that advocate for secularism and minority rights in India. This shift in financial support reflects the polarization of opinions within diaspora communities.

Cultural and Religious Exchanges: The CAA has also affected cultural and religious exchanges between diaspora communities and India:

1. Strengthened connections: For some diaspora groups, particularly those supporting the CAA, the legislation has strengthened their sense of connection to India as a homeland for persecuted religious minorities. This has led to increased participation in cultural and religious events that celebrate India's Hindu heritage.

2. Strained relationships: On the other hand, diaspora communities opposing the CAA may experience strained relationships with religious institutions and organizations in India that support the legislation. This tension could potentially lead to a decrease in cultural and religious exchanges for these groups.

Influence of Diaspora on Domestic Religious Discourse: The Indian diaspora has played a significant role in shaping domestic religious discourse surrounding the CAA. This influence is manifested in several ways:

Transnational Activism: Diaspora communities have engaged in transnational activism, using their global networks and resources to influence public opinion and policy-making in India:

1. Social media campaigns: Diaspora individuals and organizations have utilized social media platforms to disseminate information, organize protests, and mobilize support for or against the CAA. This digital activism has contributed to the global visibility of the issue and has influenced domestic debates in India.

2. Lobbying efforts: Some diaspora groups have lobbied their host country governments and international organizations to pressure India on the CAA issue. These efforts have contributed to the internationalization of the debate and have forced the Indian government to address concerns raised by the global community.

Shaping Religious Narratives: The diaspora has played a crucial role in shaping religious narratives surrounding the CAA, both within their host countries and in India:

1. Reinforcing Hindu nationalism: Some Hindu diaspora organizations have reinforced the narrative of Hindu nationalism, framing the CAA as a necessary measure to protect persecuted Hindus and other minorities from neighbouring countries. This narrative has resonated with certain sections of the population in India and has contributed to the polarization of public opinion.

2. Promoting secularism: Conversely, diaspora groups opposing the CAA have emphasized the importance of maintaining India's secular character and protecting the rights of all religious minorities, including Muslims. These voices have contributed to the counter-narrative challenging

the government's justification for the CAA.

Intellectual Contributions: Diaspora scholars, intellectuals, and religious leaders have made significant contributions to the academic and public discourse surrounding the CAA:

1. Academic analysis: Diaspora academics have produced scholarly works analyzing the legal, social, and religious implications of the CAA. These intellectual contributions have informed public debates and policy discussions both in India and abroad.

2. Religious interpretations: Diaspora religious leaders have offered various interpretations of religious texts and traditions to support or critique the CAA. These interpretations have influenced religious discourse within diaspora communities and have sometimes found their way into domestic debates in India.

International Religious Organizations' Stance on CAA: The CAA has drawn attention from various international religious organizations, each offering its perspective on the legislation's implications for religious freedom and minority rights in India.

United States Commission on International Religious Freedom (USCIRF)

The USCIRF has taken a strong stance against the CAA, expressing deep concern about its potential impact on religious minorities in India, particularly Muslims. In March 2024, a US senator, echoing the USCIRF's concerns, stated, "I am deeply concerned by the Indian government's decision to notify its controversial Citizenship Amendment Act, particularly the law's potential ramifications on India's Muslim community". The USCIRF's position has been influential in shaping the US government's response to the CAA and has contributed to diplomatic tensions between India and the United States.

Organization of Islamic Cooperation (OIC)

The OIC has expressed concern over the CAA, stating that it is "increasingly concerned" by the legislation due to its apparent discrimination against Indian Muslims. The OIC's stance reflects the broader concerns of Muslim-majority nations regarding the treatment of Muslims in India and has added to the international pressure on the Indian government to address these concerns.

Christian Organizations

Various international Christian organizations have offered mixed responses to the CAA. While some have welcomed the inclusion of persecuted Christians in the legislation's provisions, others have expressed solidarity with Muslims and voiced concerns about the broader implications for religious freedom in India.

Hindu Organizations

International Hindu organizations have generally been supportive of the CAA, viewing it as a necessary measure to protect persecuted Hindu minorities in neighbouring countries. The Hindu American Foundation, for example, has stated that the CAA is "a first step opportunity to better addresses human rights in South Asia"[8]. However, some Hindu organizations have also called for amendments to make the legislation more inclusive and aligned with international human rights norms.

Sikh Organizations

International Sikh organizations have expressed varied opinions on the CAA. While some have welcomed the inclusion of Sikhs in the legislation, others have raised concerns about its exclusionary nature and potential impact on India's secular fabric.

Human Rights Organizations

Although not strictly religious organizations, international human rights groups have played a significant role in shaping the global discourse on the CAA. Organizations such as Human Rights Watch and Amnesty International have criticized the legislation, arguing that it violates international human rights standards and discriminates against Muslims.

The Citizenship Amendment Act has had far-reaching implications for diaspora religions and their relationship with India. The diverse reactions from Indian religious communities abroad reflect the complex interplay of religious identity, political ideology, and transnational connections. The impact on religious remittances and connections has been significant, with some groups increasing their support for the legislation while others redirect their resources towards opposing it.

The influence of the diaspora on domestic religious discourse in India has been substantial, with diaspora communities playing a crucial role in shaping narratives, engaging in transnational activism, and contributing intellectual perspectives to the debate. This influence has both reinforced and challenged the government's justification for the CAA, contributing to the polarization of public opinion.

International religious organizations have taken varied stances on the CAA, with some expressing strong opposition while others offer qualified support. These diverse perspectives have added to the global scrutiny of India's citizenship policies and have implications for India's international relations and its image as a secular democracy.

As the implementation of the CAA continues to unfold, it is likely that diaspora religions will continue to play a significant role in shaping the discourse and influencing policy outcomes. The ongoing debate surrounding the legislation underscores the complex relationship between religion, citizenship, and national identity in an increasingly interconnected world.

References

1. Amnesty International. (2024, March 15). India: Citizenship Amendment Act is a blow to Indian constitutional values and international standards. https://www.amnesty.org/en/latest/news/2024/03/india-citizenship-amendment-act-is-a-blow-to-indian-constitutional-values-and-international-standards/

2. Hindu American Foundation. (n.d.). India's Citizenship Amendment Act: A First Step Opportunity to Better Address Human Rights in South Asia. https://www.hinduamerican.org/press/india-citizenship-amendment-bill

3. Human Rights Watch. (2024, March 15). India Activates Discriminatory Citizenship Law. https://www.hrw.org/news/2024/03/15/india-activates-discriminatory-citizenship-law

4. NDTV. (2024, March 19). "Deeply Concerned About Impact Of CAA On Muslims In India": US Senator. https://www.ndtv.com/india-news/deeply-concerned-about-impact-of-caa-on-muslims-in-india-us-senator-5267318

5. Observer Research Foundation. (n.d.). Analyzing global response to the controversial Citizenship Amendment Act. https://www.orfonline.org/expert-speak/analyzing-global-response-to-the-controversial-citizenship-amendment-act-59529/

6. Palit, A. (2019). The Citizenship Amendment Bill of India: Implications for South Asia. Institute of South Asian Studies.

7. Sahoo, A. K. (2018). Diaspora, Development, and the Indian State. In R. S. Hegde & A. K. Sahoo (Eds.), Routledge Handbook of the Indian Diaspora (pp. 99-113). Routledge.

8. Smart, N. (1999). The World's Religions. Cambridge University Press.

9. Therwath, I. (2012). Cyber-Hindutva: Hindu Nationalism, the Diaspora and the Web. Social Science Information, 51(4), 551-577.

10. United States Commission on International Religious Freedom. (2024). Annual Report 2024. USCIRF.

11. Zavos, J. (2015). Digital Media and Networks of Hindu Organizations in the UK. In S. D. Brunn (Ed.), The Changing World Religion Map (pp. 2291-2307). Springer.

CHAPTER 28: CAA'S INFLUENCE ON RELIGIOUS PHILANTHROPY

The Citizenship Amendment Act (CAA) of 2019 has had far-reaching implications on various aspects of Indian society, including religious philanthropy. This chapter explores the multifaceted impact of the CAA on donation patterns to religious institutions, cross-border religious charities, interfaith philanthropic initiatives, and the scrutiny of religious organizations' funding.

Changes in Donation Patterns to Religious Institutions

The implementation of the CAA has led to significant shifts in donation patterns to religious institutions across India. These changes can be attributed to several factors, including heightened religious tensions, changes in perceived religious affiliations, and alterations in the socio-economic landscape.

Increased Polarization and Its Effects

The CAA has contributed to increased religious polarization in India, which has had a direct impact on religious giving. Religious people are generally more likely to donate to charitable causes, with 91% of religious individuals donating money compared to 66% of secular individuals. However, the CAA's perceived favoritism towards certain religious groups has led to changes in donation patterns.

Some religious institutions, particularly those associated with minority groups not explicitly mentioned in the CAA, have reported a decrease in donations. This decline can be attributed to fears of increased scrutiny and potential discrimination. Conversely, institutions aligned with the religious groups mentioned in the CAA have seen an uptick in donations, as supporters seek to bolster these communities.

Shift Towards Secular Charities

The controversial nature of the CAA has led some donors to redirect their contributions from religious institutions to secular charities. This shift is particularly noticeable among younger, urban donors who may be more inclined to support causes that promote interfaith harmony and social cohesion in response to the perceived divisiveness of the CAA.

Impact on Religious Attendance and Giving

Religious attendance is strongly correlated with charitable giving. The CAA's implementation has affected religious attendance patterns in some communities, particularly among minority groups feeling marginalized by the act. This change in attendance has had a ripple effect on donations, as regular attendees typically give more than infrequent attendees.

Online Giving and Technology Adoption

The controversy surrounding the CAA, coupled with the global COVID-19 pandemic, has accelerated the adoption of online giving platforms by religious institutions. This shift has allowed donors to continue supporting their preferred religious organizations while maintaining social distancing and anonymity. The trend towards online giving may have long-lasting effects on religious philanthropy in India, potentially democratizing the donation process and making it more accessible to a wider range of donors.

Impact on Cross-Border Religious Charities

The CAA has had significant implications for cross-border religious charities, particularly those operating between India and its neighbouring countries mentioned in the act:

Afghanistan, Bangladesh, and Pakistan.

Increased Scrutiny of International Donations

The implementation of the CAA has led to increased scrutiny of international donations to religious organizations in India. This heightened oversight is partly due to concerns about foreign influence on religious institutions and potential misuse of funds for activities that could be perceived as undermining the spirit of the CAA.

Challenges for Minority Religious Charities

Cross-border religious charities associated with minority groups not explicitly mentioned in the CAA have faced increased challenges in their operations. These organizations have reported difficulties in transferring funds, obtaining necessary permits, and carrying out their charitable activities. The perceived exclusion of certain religious groups from the CAA's provisions has led to a climate of uncertainty for these charities.

Shift in Focus for International Religious Charities

Some international religious charities have shifted their focus in response to the CAA. Organizations that previously concentrated on providing general humanitarian aid are now allocating more resources to programs that specifically address issues of religious freedom, citizenship rights, and social integration. This shift reflects the changing needs of communities affected by the CAA and the evolving priorities of donors in light of the act's implementation.

Collaboration with Local Partners

To navigate the complex regulatory environment post-CAA, many cross-border religious charities have increased their collaboration with local partners. This approach allows them to continue their philanthropic work while ensuring compliance with new regulations and addressing potential concerns about foreign influence.

Interfaith Philanthropic Initiatives Post-CAA: The implementation of the CAA has paradoxically led to an increase in interfaith philanthropic initiatives, as various communities and organizations seek to counteract the perceived divisiveness of the act.

Rise of Grassroots Interfaith Movements

In response to the CAA, numerous grassroots interfaith movements have emerged across India. These initiatives often focus on promoting religious harmony, social cohesion, and mutual understanding between different faith communities. For example, during the protests against the CAA, there were instances of interfaith solidarity, such as Muslim youth forming human chains to protect Hindu temples.

Collaborative Philanthropic Projects

The post-CAA landscape has seen an increase in collaborative philanthropic projects that bring together donors and volunteers from different religious backgrounds. These initiatives often focus on addressing common social issues, such as poverty alleviation, education, and healthcare, while explicitly promoting interfaith cooperation.

Interfaith Dialogue and Education Programs

Organizations like the Inter-Religious Harmony Movement (IRHM) and the Bangalore Initiative of Religious Dialogue (BIRD) have intensified their efforts in promoting interfaith dialogue and understanding in the wake of the CAA. These programs often include seminars, cultural festivals, and educational initiatives that bring together people from diverse religious backgrounds.

Corporate Support for Interfaith Initiatives

Some corporate entities have increased their support for interfaith philanthropic initiatives as part of their corporate social responsibility (CSR) programs. This trend reflects a growing recognition of the importance of social cohesion and religious harmony in maintaining a stable business environment.

Scrutiny of Religious Organizations' Funding: The implementation of the CAA has led to increased scrutiny of religious organizations' funding, particularly for those associated with minority groups not explicitly mentioned in the act.

Enhanced Regulatory Oversight

Government agencies have intensified their oversight of religious organizations' financial activities in the post-CAA era. This increased scrutiny is aimed at ensuring compliance with existing regulations and preventing the potential misuse of funds for activities that could be perceived as undermining the spirit of the CAA.

Transparency Initiatives

In response to the heightened scrutiny, many religious organizations have implemented new transparency initiatives. These measures often include more detailed financial reporting, regular audits, and increased disclosure of funding sources. While these initiatives can help build trust with donors and regulatory bodies, they also place additional administrative burdens on religious charities.

Impact on Smaller Religious Organizations

The increased scrutiny has had a disproportionate impact on smaller religious organizations, which may lack the resources to comply with more stringent reporting requirements. This situation has led to concerns about the potential marginalization of grassroots religious charities that play crucial roles in their local communities.

Shift in Donor Behavior

The heightened scrutiny of religious organizations' funding has influenced donor behavior. Some donors have become more cautious about their contributions, seeking greater assurances about how their donations will be used. This trend has led to an increased emphasis on impact measurement and reporting among religious charities.

Challenges for International Funding

Religious organizations receiving funding from international sources have faced particular challenges in the post-CAA environment. The increased scrutiny of foreign contributions has led to delays in fund transfers and, in some cases, the freezing of accounts. This situation has prompted some organizations to seek alternative funding sources or to restructure their operations to rely more heavily on domestic donations.

The Citizenship Amendment Act has had a profound and multifaceted impact on religious philanthropy in India. While the act has contributed to increased polarization and scrutiny in some areas, it has also sparked new interfaith initiatives and collaborations. The long-term effects of these changes on India's rich tradition of religious giving remain to be seen, but it is clear that the philanthropic landscape has been significantly altered by the CAA's implementation.

As India continues to navigate the complex interplay between religion, citizenship, and philanthropy, it is crucial for policymakers, religious leaders, and civil society organizations to work together to ensure that the spirit of generosity and community support that has long characterized Indian society is preserved and strengthened. The challenges posed by the CAA to religious philanthropy also present opportunities for innovation, increased transparency, and greater interfaith cooperation, which could ultimately lead to a more robust and inclusive philanthropic ecosystem in India.

References

1. Brooks, A. C. (2006). Who really cares: The surprising truth about compassionate conservatism. Basic Books.
2. Chaves, M. (2004). Congregations in America. Harvard University Press.
3. Greeley, A. M., McCourt, K., & McCready, W. C. (1976). Catholic schools in a declining church. Sheed and Ward.
4. Hoge, D. R. (1994). The problem of understanding church giving. Review of Religious Research, 36(2), 101-110.
5. Hoge, D. R., & Polk, D. T. (1980). A test of theories of Protestant church participation and commitment. Review of Religious Research, 21(3), 315-329.
6. Iannaccone, L. R. (1994). Why strict churches are strong. American Journal of Sociology, 99(5), 1180-1211.
7. Inskeep, K. W. (1994). Giving trends in the Evangelical Lutheran Church in America. Review of Religious Research, 36(2), 238-244.
8. Krauser, E. (2007). Bequest giving: Revisiting donor motivation with dimensional qualitative research. Chicago, IL: Campbell & Company.
9. Reitsma, J., Scheepers, P., & Te Grotenhuis, M. (2006). Dimensions of individual religiosity and charity: Cross-national effect differences in European countries? Review of Religious Research, 47(4), 347-362.
10. Ronsvalle, J., & Ronsvalle, S. (2007). The state of church giving through 2005: Abolition of the

institutional enslavement of overseas missions. Empty Tomb.

11. Routley, C., Sargeant, A., & Scaife, W. (2007). Bequests to educational institutions: A review of the literature. International Journal of Educational Advancement, 7(3), 193-204.

12. Schervish, P. G. (2007). Is today's philanthropy failing beneficiaries? Always a risk, but not for the most part. Nonprofit and Voluntary Sector Quarterly, 36(2), 373-379.

13. Shariff, A. F., & Norenzayan, A. (2007). God is watching you: Priming God concepts increases prosocial behavior in an anonymous economic game. Psychological Science, 18(9), 803-809.

CHAPTER 29: RELIGIOUS ART AND LITERATURE IN RESPONSE TO CAA

The Citizenship Amendment Act (CAA) of 2019 sparked widespread protests and debates across India, triggering a surge of artistic and literary expressions that reflected the religious sentiments and societal tensions surrounding the controversial legislation. This chapter explores the diverse ways in which religious art and literature responded to the CAA, examining interfaith collaborations, censorship issues, and the role of creative works in shaping public opinion.

Artistic Expressions of Religious Sentiments about CAA

The CAA protests saw an outpouring of artistic expressions that conveyed religious sentiments and critiqued the perceived discriminatory nature of the legislation. Artists from various faiths used their creative skills to voice concerns and foster solidarity across religious lines.

One of the most prominent forms of artistic expression during the anti-CAA protests was the creation of protest art at demonstration sites. At Shaheen Bagh in Delhi, which became an iconic location for sustained peaceful protests, the road adjacent to the protest site transformed into a giant canvas for artistic expression. Installations appeared and disappeared over the course of two months, serving as powerful visual representations of the protesters' sentiments.

A notable example was the installation of paper boats by artist Arif Nayeem, featuring text from Faiz Ahmed Faiz's poem "Hum Dekhenge" (We Shall See). This installation symbolized hope and resilience, with the paper boats serving as metaphorical vessels carrying Faiz's words of defiance and unity to the gathered protesters. The choice of Faiz's poem, which has become an anthem of resistance across South Asia, underscored the interfaith nature of the protests, as it drew on Islamic imagery while resonating with people of all faiths.

Visual art played a crucial role in conveying complex ideas about citizenship, secularism, and religious identity. Murals and posters proliferated at protest sites, often featuring imagery that emphasized India's diverse religious heritage. One striking example was a giant mural that appeared almost overnight in Shaheen Bagh, created through a collaborative project led by artists like Shilo Shiv Suleman. The mural depicted women as falcons, drawing on a popular meme and symbolizing strength and freedom across religious boundaries.

Music and poetry emerged as powerful mediums for expressing religious sentiments about the CAA. Protest songs and poems went viral, with many incorporating religious themes and imagery to emphasize India's pluralistic traditions. The song "Hum Kagaz Nahin Dikhayenge" (We Won't Show Our Papers) became an anthem of resistance, its lyrics defying the potential requirement for citizens to prove their nationality through documentation. Another viral poem by Aamir Aziz, "Sab Yaad Rakha Jayega" (Everything Will Be Remembered), used poetic language to document the experiences of protesters and critique the government's actions.

Young women, in particular, found their artistic voices during the protests. Nabiya Khan, a university student, penned a poem with the refrain "the revolution will come wearing bangles, bindi and hijab," which went viral on social media. This poem reclaimed symbols often associated with women's oppression in different religious contexts, transforming them into emblems of strength and resistance. By incorporating both Hindu (bindi) and Muslim (hijab) symbols, the poem emphasized interfaith solidarity in the face of perceived discrimination.

Interfaith Collaborations in Creative Fields

The CAA controversy catalyzed numerous interfaith collaborations in the creative fields, as artists, writers, and performers sought to emphasize India's syncretic traditions and challenge the divisive narrative surrounding the legislation.

Theatre emerged as a powerful medium for fostering interfaith understanding and critiquing the CAA. In Bengaluru, theatre groups initiated conversations around interfaith tolerance through storytelling, plays, and improvisational performances. Zafer Mohiuddin, founder of the theatre group Kathputliya, prepared to stage Sayed Asghar Wajahat's acclaimed play on communal harmony, "Jis Lahore Nai Dekhaya," in 2021. The choice of this play, which explores the human cost of partition and the shared cultural heritage of Hindus and Muslims, served as a poignant commentary on the contemporary debates surrounding citizenship and religious identity.

Similarly, Bangalore Little Theatre (BLT), the city's oldest English language theatre group, also planned a production of Wajahat's play. These theatrical initiatives aimed to use art as a means of fostering empathy and understanding across religious divides, countering the polarizing rhetoric surrounding the CAA.

Music provided another avenue for interfaith collaboration and expression of solidarity. The Manav Ekta Mission promoted interfaith cooperation through its Key to India concerts in Bengaluru, Chennai, and Hyderabad. These concerts featured collaborations between artists from different religious backgrounds, such as classical pianist Anil Srinivasan and jazz pianist Sharik Hassan, merging diverse musical traditions to emphasize cultural unity.

During the anti-CAA protests, musical events at demonstration sites like Bilal Bagh in Bengaluru brought together performers from various faiths. These events not only entertained protesters but also served as powerful demonstrations of interfaith harmony and shared cultural heritage.

Literature played a crucial role in fostering interfaith understanding and critiquing the CAA. Writers from diverse religious backgrounds contributed to anthologies and online platforms, sharing stories that highlighted India's pluralistic traditions. One notable initiative was the India Love Project, which collated stories of interfaith couples to challenge divisive narratives and celebrate religious diversity.

Visual artists also engaged in interfaith collaborations to respond to the CAA. At protest sites like Shaheen Bagh, artists from different religious backgrounds worked together on murals, installations, and other visual art forms. These collaborative efforts often incorporated symbols and imagery from multiple religious traditions, emphasizing shared values and common humanity.

Censorship and Controversy Surrounding CAA-Related Art

The artistic responses to the CAA were not without controversy, and many artists faced censorship attempts or backlash for their work. These incidents highlighted the tensions between freedom of expression and political sensitivities in the context of the CAA debates.

One notable instance of censorship occurred at the India Art Fair in Delhi, where organizers put up a prohibitory sign stating, "We have a zero tolerance policy against banners or sloganeering at the art fair". This policy led to the removal of a project at the Italian Cultural Centre's booth, which featured a hijab-clad young woman doing calligraphy in Urdu. The project organizers and artists were told they had no permission for such activities, despite claiming they had announced it beforehand. This incident sparked debates about the limits of artistic expression in politically charged environments and the role of art fairs in fostering or suppressing dialogue on contentious issues.

The censorship attempts extended beyond formal art spaces to public demonstrations and protest art. In some cases, authorities removed or defaced murals and installations at protest sites, citing various reasons such as traffic obstruction or unauthorized use of public space. These actions were often seen by artists and protesters as attempts to suppress dissent and limit the visibility of anti-CAA sentiments.

Social media platforms became both a powerful tool for disseminating CAA-related art and a site of controversy and potential censorship. Many artists reported having their posts removed or accounts suspended after sharing artwork critical of the CAA or supportive of the protests. This raised concerns about digital censorship and the role of social media companies in moderating political speech.

The controversy surrounding CAA-related art also manifested in threats and intimidation directed at artists. Some artists reported receiving online harassment or threats of violence for their work, particularly if it was perceived as critical of the government or supportive of minority rights. This climate of fear led some artists to self-censor or withdraw from public engagement, impacting the diversity of artistic voices in the public sphere.

However, many artists and cultural institutions resisted censorship attempts and continued to create and display work related to the CAA and its implications. For example, the National Art Education Association (NAEA) in the United States issued a position statement on censorship and the arts, emphasizing the importance of freedom of expression and the role of art educators in confronting students with diverse art experiences. While not directly related to the CAA context in India, such statements reflect broader global concerns about artistic freedom in politically charged environments.

Role of Religious Literature in Shaping Public Opinion

Religious literature played a significant role in shaping public opinion about the CAA, with writers and scholars from various faith traditions contributing to the discourse through essays, opinion pieces, and longer works.

Many religious scholars and leaders penned articles and open letters critiquing the CAA from theological perspectives. These writings often emphasized religious teachings on hospitality, compassion, and the equal worth of all human beings, arguing that the CAA's exclusion of certain religious groups contradicted these fundamental principles. Such literature helped frame the debate in moral and ethical terms, appealing to readers' religious sensibilities.

Conversely, some religious writers produced literature supporting the CAA, arguing that it was necessary to protect persecuted religious minorities from neighbouring countries. These works often drew on historical narratives of religious conflict and displacement to justify the Act's provisions. The divergent interpretations of religious texts and traditions in relation to the CAA highlighted the complex interplay between religion, politics, and citizenship in contemporary India.

Poetry emerged as a powerful form of religious literature in response to the CAA. Poets drew on devotional traditions and mystical imagery to critique the Act and express hopes for unity and justice. For example, the widespread recitation of

Faiz Ahmed Faiz's "Hum Dekhenge" at protests demonstrated the enduring power of religiously inflected poetry to inspire social movements.

Religious literature also played a crucial role in educating the public about the implications of the CAA. Scholars and activists produced accessible guides and FAQs that explained the Act's provisions and potential consequences from various religious perspectives. These materials helped demystify the legal jargon and provided religious frameworks for understanding the citizenship debates.

The CAA controversy also spurred the creation of new interfaith literature that emphasized shared values and common struggles across religious lines. Writers collaborated on anthologies and online platforms that showcased diverse religious perspectives on citizenship, belonging, and national identity. These works sought to counter divisive narratives and foster greater understanding between different faith communities.

However, the role of religious literature in shaping public opinion was not without controversy. Some writers faced accusations of blasphemy or hurting religious sentiments for their critiques of the CAA, highlighting the sensitive intersection of religion and politics in India. These controversies sometimes led to calls for censorship or legal action against writers, raising concerns about freedom of expression in religious discourse.

In conclusion, the artistic and literary responses to the CAA demonstrated the profound impact of the legislation on India's religious and cultural landscape. Through diverse forms of expression, artists and writers grappled with complex questions of identity, belonging, and citizenship, often challenging dominant narratives and fostering interfaith dialogue. While these creative endeavors faced censorship and controversy, they also played a crucial role in shaping public opinion and providing alternative visions of religious coexistence in contemporary India.

The artistic and literary responses to the CAA reflect broader global trends in the intersection of religion, politics, and creative expression. As societies worldwide grapple with issues of citizenship, migration, and religious pluralism, the role of art and literature in fostering dialogue and challenging divisive narratives becomes increasingly significant. The Indian experience with the CAA offers valuable insights into the power of creative expression to articulate religious sentiments, foster interfaith collaboration, and shape public discourse on contentious political issues.

References:

1. Arikan, G., & Bloom, P. B. N. (2020). Religion and political attitudes: The impact of religiosity and religious context. In Oxford Research Encyclopedia of Politics. Oxford University Press.
2. Bhat, M. A. (2019). The constitutional case against the Citizenship Amendment Bill. Economic and Political Weekly, 54(3), 12-14.
3. Jayal, N. G. (2022). Citizenship imperilled: India's fragile democracy. Permanent Black.
4. Kalyvas, S. N., & Van Kersbergen, K. (2010). Christian democracy. Annual Review of Political Science, 13, 183-209.
5. Nagarwal, S. (2021). The Citizenship (Amendment) Act, 2019: A critique. Journal of the Indian Law Institute, 63(1), 114-131.
6. Ranjan, A., & Mittal, A. (2023). The Citizenship Amendment Act 2019: A critical analysis. Asian Journal of Law and Society, 10(1), 119-138.

CHAPTER 30: CAA AND RELIGIOUS PILGRIMAGES

The Citizenship Amendment Act (CAA) and its implications have had far-reaching effects on various aspects of Indian society, including religious pilgrimages. This chapter explores the multifaceted impact of the CAA on cross-border pilgrimages, changes in pilgrimage patterns within India, interfaith initiatives promoting harmony, and enhanced security measures for pilgrims in sensitive areas.

Impact on Cross-Border Pilgrimages

The implementation of the CAA has significantly affected cross-border pilgrimages, particularly those involving India and its neighbouring countries. The Act, which aims to provide citizenship to persecuted religious minorities from Pakistan, Bangladesh, and Afghanistan, has inadvertently created tensions that impact pilgrimage routes and accessibility.

One of the most notable impacts has been on the Kailash Mansarovar Yatra, a significant pilgrimage for Hindus, Jains, and Buddhists to Mount Kailash in Tibet. The yatra, which had been suspended due to various factors including the COVID-19 pandemic, has recently seen positive developments. India and China have agreed to resume the Kailash Mansarovar Yatra, signaling a thaw in bilateral relations. This agreement, reached during talks between National Security Advisor Ajit Doval and Chinese Foreign Minister Wang Yi, demonstrates the importance of pilgrimage in diplomatic relations and cross-border cooperation.

The resumption of the Kailash Mansarovar Yatra is expected to have several implications:

1. Improved Bilateral Relations: The agreement to resume the yatra indicates a willingness from both India and China to improve diplomatic ties, which could have positive ripple effects on other areas of cooperation.

2. Economic Impact: The resumption of the pilgrimage is likely to boost local economies along the pilgrimage route, benefiting communities in both countries.

3. Cultural Exchange: The yatra provides an opportunity for cultural exchange between Indian pilgrims and local Tibetan communities, fostering greater understanding and cooperation.

However, the CAA's implementation has also raised concerns about potential impacts on other cross-border pilgrimages, particularly those involving Muslim pilgrims traveling to and from Bangladesh and Pakistan. There are fears that the Act, combined with the proposed National Register of Citizens (NRC), could complicate travel for certain groups and potentially lead to a decrease in cross-border pilgrimages.

Changes in Pilgrimage Patterns within India: The CAA, along with other socio-political factors, has contributed to significant changes in pilgrimage patterns within India. These changes reflect both the evolving nature of religious tourism and the impact of government policies and initiatives.

Rise of Spiritual Tourism

India has witnessed a substantial increase in spiritual tourism, particularly in the post-COVID era. This trend is partly driven by a global shift towards mindfulness and conscious living, amplified by social media and a desire for self-improvement. Cities like Rishikesh have become synonymous with spiritual tourism, attracting an unprecedented influx of visitors due to their deep-rooted traditions in Ayurveda, yoga, and meditation.

The growth of spiritual tourism in India is characterized by:

1. Diversification of Pilgrimage Sites: While traditional pilgrimage sites continue to attract large numbers of devotees, new destinations are emerging, often associated with modern spiritual leaders or movements.

2. Integration of Technology: The use of digital tools and social media has revolutionized how pilgrims plan and experience their journeys, making spiritual practices more accessible and widespread.

3. Economic Impact: Pilgrimage and spiritual tourism now generate considerable revenue, supporting local economies and creating employment opportunities. It is estimated that spiritual tourism makes up nearly 60% of domestic tourism in India.

Government Initiatives: The Indian government has recognized the potential of pilgrimage tourism and has implemented several initiatives to promote and develop religious sites:

1. PRASHAD Scheme: The Pilgrimage Rejuvenation and Spiritual Augmentation Drive (PRASHAD) scheme, launched in 2014-2015, focuses on developing and identifying pilgrimage sites across India to enrich the religious tourism experience.

2. Infrastructure Development: There has been significant investment in improving infrastructure at pilgrimage sites, including road construction, accommodation facilities, and amenities for pilgrims.

3. Promotion of Religious Circuits: The government has been actively promoting various religious circuits, connecting multiple pilgrimage sites to create comprehensive spiritual

journeys.

These initiatives have led to a more organized and accessible pilgrimage experience for many devotees, potentially increasing the number of domestic pilgrims.

Interfaith Pilgrimage Initiatives Promoting Harmony

In the context of the CAA and broader concerns about religious tensions, several interfaith pilgrimage initiatives have emerged, aiming to promote harmony and understanding among different religious communities.

The Hajo Model: One notable example is the interfaith harmony demonstrated in Hajo, a community in Assam. Hajo has long been an ancient pilgrimage center for Hindus, Buddhists, and Muslims, considered a unique example of religious coexistence.

Key aspects of the Hajo model include:

1. Annual Interfaith Procession: Since 1993, Hajo has conducted an annual interfaith procession involving the Hayagriva Madhava Temple (Hindu, Buddhist) and the Powa Mecca (Muslim). This tradition began as a response to communal tensions elsewhere in India and has continued for over 25 years.

2. Inclusive Participation: The procession is open to people of various religious groups, fostering a sense of unity and shared spiritual experience.

3. Daily Coexistence: The harmony in Hajo extends beyond the annual procession, reflected in the daily activities and interactions of the community.

Other Interfaith Initiatives: Across India, various other interfaith pilgrimage initiatives have been implemented to promote harmony:

1. Joint Pilgrimages: Some organizations arrange joint pilgrimages where people of different faiths visit each other's sacred sites together, fostering understanding and respect.

2. Interfaith Dialogue Centers: Establishment of centers at major pilgrimage sites where visitors can learn about different religions and engage in interfaith dialogue.

3. Community Outreach Programs: Initiatives where pilgrimage organizers engage with local communities of different faiths, promoting cultural exchange and mutual understanding.

These interfaith initiatives serve as important counterpoints to religious tensions, demonstrating the potential for pilgrimage to be a unifying rather than divisive force in society.

Security Measures for Pilgrims in Sensitive Areas

The implementation of the CAA, along with other security concerns, has led to enhanced security measures for pilgrims, particularly in sensitive areas. The government and security agencies have implemented comprehensive strategies to ensure the safety of pilgrims.

Amarnath Yatra Security: The Amarnath Yatra, an annual pilgrimage to the Amarnath Cave shrine in Jammu and Kashmir, has seen significant security enhancements:

1. Three-Tier Security Arrangement: A robust security setup has been put in place by Jammu and Kashmir Police along with other security agencies to secure both the highway and the routes leading to the Amarnath Cave.

2. High-Tech Monitoring: Over 17 PTZ high-definition 360-degree view cameras have been placed along the routes from base camps to the cave, along with dozens of static cameras at key locations.

3. RFID Tagging: All registered pilgrims are equipped with Radio Frequency Identification (RFID) tags, allowing authorities to track their exact locations throughout the journey.

4. Quick Reaction Teams: Rapid response teams are stationed at sensitive locations to handle any unforeseen incidents.

Maha Kumbh 2025 Security Measures: For the upcoming Maha Kumbh in 2025, a comprehensive seven-tier security plan has been devised:

1. Multi-Level Screening: The security plan involves screening at various points, from the pilgrims' point of origin to the inner fair area.

2. Increased Manpower: A total of 37,611 police personnel will be deployed, a significant increase from previous events.

3. Gender-Specific Security: 1,378 women police officers will be specifically deployed for the safety of women devotees.

4. Technological Integration: The security plan incorporates modern technology for surveillance and rapid response.

General Security Enhancements: Across various pilgrimage sites, especially in sensitive areas, the following security measures have been implemented:

1. Intelligence Sharing: A robust mechanism for intelligence sharing among security agencies has been established.

2. Regular Safety Advisories: Authorities regularly issue safety advisories to inform and guide pilgrims.

3. Coordination Among Agencies: There is enhanced coordination of security efforts among various agencies to ensure comprehensive protection.

4. Infrastructure Improvements: Installation of CCTV cameras, deployment of drones, and establishment of check

posts at strategic locations have been undertaken to enhance security.

These security measures aim to provide a safe environment for pilgrims while maintaining the spiritual atmosphere of the pilgrimage sites. However, they also reflect the complex security challenges faced in certain regions and the need for a delicate balance between security and the pilgrimage experience.

In conclusion, the implementation of the CAA has had wide-ranging effects on religious pilgrimages in India. While it has created challenges, particularly for cross-border pilgrimages, it has also coincided with a period of growth in spiritual tourism and increased government focus on developing pilgrimage infrastructure. The rise of interfaith pilgrimage initiatives offers hope for promoting harmony in a diverse society, while enhanced security measures reflect the ongoing challenges in certain regions. As India continues to navigate these complex issues, the role of pilgrimage in fostering both spiritual growth and social cohesion remains significant.

References:

1. https://scroll.in/article/947458/the-caa-and-nrc-together-will-reopen-wounds-of-partition-and-turn-india-into-a-majoritarian-state
2. https://indianexpress.com/article/india/ajit-doval-wang-yi-india-china-special-representatives-talks-9732574/
3. https://www.diva-portal.org/smash/get/diva2:1602759/FULLTEXT01.pdf
4. https://kpmg.com/in/en/insights/2024/08/sacred-journeys-unfolding-the-evolution-and-growth-of-pilgrimage-and-spiritual-tourism-in-india.html
5. https://www.myscheme.gov.in/schemes/prashad
6. https://www.hyunjinmoon.com/hajo-a-local-model-

of-interfaith-in-india/

7.   https://www.dailyexcelsior.com/security-measures-to-protect-pilgrims-enhanced-mos-home/

8.   https://timesofindia.indiatimes.com/city/allahabad/enhanced-seven-tier-security-measures-for-pilgrim-safety-in-maha-kumbh-2025/articleshow/114515987.cms

9.   https://www.cnbctv18.com/views/caa-sparks-off-movement-on-indias-eastern-and-western-frontiers-5223961.htm

10.   https://zeenews.india.com/india/amarnath-yatra-2024-strong-security-measures-for-annual-pilgrimage-2760890.html

CHAPTER 31: RELIGIOUS COUNSELING IN THE WAKE OF CAA

The implementation of the Citizenship Amendment Act (CAA) in India has sparked widespread controversy and concern, particularly among religious minority communities. This chapter explores the critical role of religious counseling in addressing the psychological and emotional impacts of the CAA on affected communities, with a focus on interfaith initiatives, counselor training, and mental health support.

Addressing Community Fears and Anxieties

The CAA has generated significant fear and anxiety among religious minority groups in India, particularly Muslims. The Act, which provides a pathway to citizenship for non-Muslim migrants from Afghanistan, Bangladesh, and Pakistan, has been criticized for its perceived discrimination against Muslims. This has led to widespread protests and unrest, creating a climate of uncertainty and apprehension among affected communities.

Religious counselors play a crucial role in addressing these fears and anxieties. They must be equipped to provide accurate information about the CAA and its implications while offering emotional support to individuals and families grappling with concerns about their citizenship status and future in India. Counselors should focus on:

1. Providing factual information: Counselors must stay informed about the CAA and its implementation to provide accurate, up-to-date information to their clients. This includes

understanding the legal aspects of the Act and its potential impact on different communities.

2. Addressing misinformation: Given the complex nature of the CAA and the spread of misinformation, counselors should help clients distinguish between facts and rumors. This may involve guiding them to reliable sources of information and teaching critical thinking skills to evaluate news and social media content.

3. Validating emotions: It is essential for counselors to acknowledge and validate the fears and anxieties experienced by community members. Many individuals may feel marginalized or targeted by the CAA, and counselors should create a safe space for them to express these emotions without judgment.

4. Promoting resilience: Religious counselors can draw upon spiritual teachings and practices to help individuals and communities build resilience in the face of uncertainty. This may include emphasizing values such as faith, hope, and community solidarity.

5. Encouraging community engagement: Counselors can guide individuals towards constructive ways of engaging with the issue, such as participating in peaceful protests, engaging in interfaith dialogues, or advocating for their rights through legal channels.

Interfaith Counseling Initiatives

In the wake of the CAA, interfaith counseling initiatives have emerged as a powerful tool for promoting understanding, empathy, and solidarity across religious communities. These initiatives bring together counselors and religious leaders from various faiths to address the shared concerns and challenges faced by different communities affected by the CAA.

Key aspects of interfaith counseling initiatives include:

1. Collaborative approach: Interfaith counseling teams typically consist of representatives from multiple religious backgrounds, including Hinduism, Islam, Christianity, Sikhism, Buddhism, and Jainism. This diverse composition allows for a more comprehensive understanding of the issues faced by different communities.

2. Shared values: Interfaith counseling initiatives often emphasize common values and principles shared across religions, such as compassion, justice, and human dignity. This approach helps to build bridges between communities and foster a sense of unity in the face of divisive policies.

3. Cultural sensitivity: Counselors involved in interfaith initiatives must be trained in cultural competence to effectively address the unique needs and concerns of diverse religious communities. This includes understanding specific religious practices, cultural norms, and historical contexts that may influence individuals' responses to the CAA.

4. Conflict resolution: Interfaith counseling teams can play a crucial role in mediating conflicts and tensions that may arise between different religious groups in the wake of the CAA. By promoting dialogue and understanding, these initiatives can help prevent the escalation of communal tensions.

5. Public outreach: Many interfaith counseling initiatives organize public events, workshops, and seminars to educate the broader community about the CAA and promote interfaith harmony. These events can serve as platforms for open discussions and community building.

Training Religious Counselors on CAA-related Issues: To effectively address the challenges posed by the CAA, religious counselors require specialized training that equips them with the knowledge, skills, and sensitivity needed to support affected communities. Training programs should focus on:

1. Legal and policy understanding: Counselors must have a thorough understanding of the CAA, its provisions, and its potential implications for different religious communities. This includes knowledge of related policies such as the National Register of Citizens (NRC) and their intersections with the CAA.

2. Psychological impact: Training should cover the psychological effects of citizenship-related stress, including anxiety, depression, and trauma. Counselors should be equipped to recognize symptoms and provide appropriate interventions or referrals.

3. Interfaith competence: Given the diverse religious landscape of India, counselors should be trained in interfaith dialogue and understanding. This includes knowledge of different religious traditions, practices, and sensitivities.

4. Crisis intervention: The CAA has led to protests and social unrest in many parts of India. Counselors should be trained in crisis intervention techniques to support individuals and communities affected by violence, arrests, or other traumatic events related to CAA protests.

5. Ethical considerations: Training should emphasize the ethical responsibilities of religious counselors, including maintaining confidentiality, respecting client autonomy, and avoiding political bias in their counseling practice.

6. Resource navigation: Counselors should be familiar with legal, social, and community resources available to individuals affected by the CAA. This includes knowledge of pro bono legal services, advocacy groups, and support networks.

7. Self-care: Given the emotionally demanding nature of counseling in the context of the CAA, training programs should emphasize self-care strategies for counselors to

prevent burnout and maintain their own mental health.

Mental Health Support for Affected Religious Communities

The implementation of the CAA has had significant mental health implications for affected religious communities, particularly Muslims and other minority groups who feel marginalized or threatened by the Act. Religious counselors play a crucial role in providing mental health support tailored to the unique needs of these communities.

Key aspects of mental health support in the context of the CAA include:

1. Culturally sensitive approaches: Mental health support must be provided in a manner that respects and incorporates the cultural and religious beliefs of affected communities. This may involve integrating religious practices and teachings into counseling approaches.

2. Addressing collective trauma: The CAA has created a sense of collective trauma among some religious communities. Counselors should be prepared to address not only individual mental health concerns but also the broader psychological impact on entire communities.

3. Combating stigma: In many religious communities, there may be stigma associated with seeking mental health support. Religious counselors can play a crucial role in destigmatizing mental health issues and encouraging individuals to seek help when needed.

4. Group support: Organizing support groups for individuals affected by the CAA can provide a sense of community and shared experience. These groups can be facilitated by religious counselors and may incorporate religious teachings and practices as coping mechanisms.

5. Family-centered approaches: The CAA's impact often

extends to entire families. Mental health support should include family counseling to address intergenerational concerns and strengthen family resilience in the face of uncertainty.

6. Addressing youth concerns: Young people may be particularly affected by the CAA, facing concerns about their future and identity. Religious counselors should develop targeted mental health support programs for youth, addressing issues such as identity formation, educational aspirations, and social belonging.

7. Trauma-informed care: Given the potential for traumatic experiences related to the CAA (e.g., protests, detentions, family separations), counselors should be trained in trauma-informed care approaches to effectively support affected individuals.

8. Holistic well-being: Mental health support should address not only psychological symptoms but also the broader well-being of individuals and communities. This may include guidance on maintaining physical health, nurturing social connections, and engaging in meaningful activities.

In conclusion, religious counseling plays a vital role in addressing the complex challenges posed by the Citizenship Amendment Act in India. By addressing community fears and anxieties, promoting interfaith initiatives, providing specialized training for counselors, and offering culturally sensitive mental health support, religious counselors can contribute significantly to the resilience and well-being of affected communities. As India continues to grapple with the implications of the CAA, the role of religious counselors in fostering understanding, healing, and social cohesion will remain crucial.

References:

1. Bhat, M. A. (2019). The constitutional case against the Citizenship Amendment Bill. Economic and Political Weekly, 54(3), 12-14.

2. Guha, R. (2024). The Citizenship Amendment Act: A historical and legal analysis. Indian Journal of Constitutional Law, 15(2), 45-62.

3. Singh, R. (2024). Implementation challenges of the Citizenship Amendment Act. Public Policy Review, 18(3), 78-95.

CHAPTER 32: CAA'S IMPACT ON RELIGIOUS DEMOGRAPHICS

The Citizenship Amendment Act (CAA) of 2019 has sparked intense debate and controversy regarding its potential impact on India's religious demographics. This chapter examines the projected changes in religious population ratios, concerns about demographic shifts in border regions, the impact on religious minority populations, and the long-term implications for India's religious landscape.

Projected Changes in Religious Population Ratios

The implementation of the CAA is expected to have significant effects on India's religious composition, particularly in terms of the Hindu-Muslim population ratio. According to projections by the Pew Research Center, India's religious landscape is already undergoing gradual changes, with Muslims expected to grow as a share of the population in the coming decades.

As of 2020, Muslims were estimated to comprise about 15% of India's population, while Hindus represented 79%. The projections for 2050 suggest that Hindus may decrease to about 77% of the population, while Muslims could increase to 18%. These projections, however, do not account for the potential impact of the CAA, which could accelerate these demographic shifts.

The CAA provides a pathway to citizenship for non-Muslim refugees from Afghanistan, Pakistan, and Bangladesh who entered India before December 31, 2014. This selective inclusion of certain religious groups is likely to increase the proportion of Hindus, Sikhs, Buddhists, Jains, Parsis, and

Christians in India's population, while potentially decreasing the relative proportion of Muslims.

It is important to note that the actual impact of the CAA on religious demographics will depend on various factors, including:

1. The number of eligible non-Muslim refugees who apply for and receive citizenship

2. The rate of natural population growth among different religious groups

3. Migration patterns and their religious composition

4. The implementation and enforcement of the CAA

Concerns about Demographic Shifts in Border Regions

The CAA has raised significant concerns about potential demographic shifts, particularly in border regions and states with historically sensitive demographic balances. These concerns are especially pronounced in northeastern states like Assam, where fears of cultural and linguistic dilution have led to widespread protests.

Assam and the Northeast

The implementation of the CAA in Assam has been particularly contentious due to its potential to alter the delicate demographic balance in the state. The Assam Accord of 1985 had set March 24, 1971, as the cut-off date for terminating citizenship for illegal immigrants. However, the CAA extends this date to December 31, 2014, potentially allowing the legal settlement of thousands of Bangladeshi immigrants who entered the state between these dates.

This extension has sparked fears among the indigenous Assamese population about the erosion of their cultural and linguistic identity. The CAA's selective application to certain districts in Assam, particularly those with Hindu majorities, has further fueled suspicions of a targeted demographic engineering attempt.

Border Security and Infiltration Concerns

The CAA's implementation in border regions has also raised concerns about national security and illegal infiltration. Critics argue that the act might incentivize further illegal immigration from neighbouring countries, particularly Bangladesh, as non-Muslim migrants might view it as a potential pathway to Indian citizenship.

These demographic shifts in border areas could have significant implications for India's security apparatus, potentially altering the social and cultural fabric of these regions and complicating border management strategies.

Impact on Religious Minority Populations

The CAA's impact on religious minority populations in India is multifaceted and contentious. While the act purportedly aims to protect certain religious minorities from neighbouring countries, its implementation has raised concerns about the status and rights of existing minority communities within India.

Non-Muslim Refugees

For non-Muslim refugees from Afghanistan, Pakistan, and Bangladesh, the CAA offers a faster route to Indian citizenship. This provision is expected to benefit thousands of Hindu, Sikh, Buddhist, Jain, Parsi, and Christian individuals who have fled religious persecution in these countries. The act reduces the residency requirement for citizenship from 11 years to 5 years for these groups, potentially leading to a significant increase in their numbers within India's population.

Muslim Minorities

The exclusion of Muslim refugees from the CAA's provisions has raised concerns about discrimination and the potential marginalization of Muslim communities in India. While the government has stated that the CAA does not affect the citizenship status of Indian Muslims, critics argue that the act, combined with other measures like the proposed National Register of Citizens (NRC), could be used to target and disenfranchise Muslim populations, particularly in border regions.

The CAA's implementation has led to increased anxiety and insecurity among Muslim communities, with fears of being rendered stateless or facing increased scrutiny and discrimination. This perceived threat has resulted in widespread protests and social unrest, particularly in areas with significant Muslim populations.

Other Religious Minorities

The CAA's selective inclusion of certain religious groups has also raised questions about the status of other religious minorities not covered by the act. For instance, the exclusion of groups like Rohingya Muslims from Myanmar or Tamil Hindus from Sri Lanka has been criticized as inconsistent with the act's stated aim of protecting persecuted minorities.

Long-term Implications for India's Religious Landscape: The implementation of the CAA is likely to have far-reaching consequences for India's religious landscape, potentially altering the country's secular fabric and inter-religious dynamics.

Shift in Religious Demographics

Over the long term, the CAA could contribute to a gradual shift in India's religious demographics. While the extent of this shift is difficult to predict accurately, it is likely to reinforce the Hindu majority while potentially slowing the growth rate of the Muslim population relative to other groups. This demographic change could have significant political, social, and cultural implications for India's future.

Challenges to Secularism

The CAA has been criticized for potentially undermining India's constitutional commitment to secularism. By introducing religion as a criterion for citizenship, the act has been seen as a departure from the principle of treating all religions equally under the law. This shift could have long-lasting effects on India's identity as a secular democracy and its treatment of religious minorities.

Social Cohesion and Inter-religious Relations

The implementation of the CAA has the potential to strain inter-religious relations and social cohesion in India. The act's perceived bias against Muslims has already led to increased tensions and protests. In the long term, these tensions could lead to further polarization along religious lines, potentially affecting social harmony and national unity.

Political Implications

The demographic changes resulting from the CAA could have significant political implications. Shifts in religious population ratios may influence voting patterns and political representation, potentially altering the balance of power in certain regions and at the national level.

International Relations

The CAA's implementation and its impact on India's religious demographics could also affect India's international relations, particularly with neighbouring countries and those with significant Muslim populations. Concerns about the treatment of religious minorities in India may influence diplomatic ties and India's soft power on the global stage.

In conclusion, the Citizenship Amendment Act's impact on India's religious demographics is a complex and contentious issue with far-reaching implications. While the act aims to provide protection to certain persecuted religious minorities, its implementation raises significant questions about equity, secularism, and the future of India's diverse religious landscape. As India navigates these challenges, it will be crucial to balance national security concerns with the principles of inclusivity and religious freedom that have long been cornerstones of Indian democracy.

References:

1. Amnesty International. (2024). India: Citizenship Amendment Act is a blow to Indian constitutional values and international standards. Retrieved from https://www.amnesty.org/en/latest/news/2024/03/india-citizenship-amendment-act-is-a-blow-to-indian-constitutional-values-and-international-standards/

2. Economic Times. (2024). View: CAA is not a threat to Indian Muslims. Retrieved from https://economictimes.indiatimes.com/news/india/view-caa-is-not-a-threat-to-indian-muslims/articleshow/108526004.cms

3. Pew Research Center. (2021). Population growth and religious composition in India. Retrieved from https://www.pewresearch.org/religion/2021/09/21/population-growth-and-religious-composition/

4. Saikia, S. (2024). Border Communities and Citizenship: The NRC, CAA and the Erosion of Constitutional Values. Retrieved from https://blogs.law.ox.ac.uk/border-criminologies-blog/blog-post/2024/11/border-communities-and-citizenship-nrc-caa-and-erosion

5. The SVI. (2024). Impact of Citizenship Amendment Act (CAA) on Religious Minorities in India. Retrieved from https://thesvi.org/minority-rights-vs-majoritarian-rule-impact-of-citizenship-amendment-act-caa-on-religious-minorities-in-india/

CHAPTER 33: INTERFAITH FAMILIES AND CAA: NAVIGATING COMPLEXITIES

The intersection of interfaith families and the Citizenship Amendment Act (CAA) in India presents a complex landscape of legal, social, and personal challenges. This chapter explores the multifaceted issues faced by interfaith families in the context of the CAA, examining citizenship challenges, adoption and guardianship complexities, legal ambiguities for children, and available support systems.

Citizenship Challenges for Multi-Religious Families

The Citizenship Amendment Act of 2019 has introduced new complexities for interfaith families in India, particularly those involving Muslim and non-Muslim partners. The Act offers a pathway to citizenship for non-Muslim immigrants from Afghanistan, Bangladesh, and Pakistan who entered India before 2014, citing religious persecution as the reason. This selective approach to citizenship based on religion has raised concerns about its impact on interfaith families, especially those where one partner is Muslim.

Legal Ambiguities and Discrimination

Interfaith couples in India already face numerous legal and social challenges. The introduction of the CAA has added another layer of complexity to their situation. For instance, in cases where a Hindu individual is married to a Muslim partner who immigrated from one of the specified countries, the non-Muslim spouse might be eligible for expedited citizenship under the CAA, while the Muslim spouse would not. This disparity could potentially lead to situations where family members hold different citizenship statuses, creating legal and emotional strain within the family unit.

Impact on Family Unity

The CAA's religious-based criteria for citizenship could potentially threaten the unity of interfaith families. In extreme cases, it might lead to situations where one spouse faces deportation or denial of citizenship, while the other is granted legal status. This scenario not only impacts the couple but also has significant implications for their children, potentially leading to family separations or forcing difficult choices between family unity and legal status.

Societal Perceptions and Discrimination

The implementation of the CAA has occurred against a backdrop of increasing religious polarization in India. Interfaith couples, already facing societal stigma and family opposition, may find themselves under increased scrutiny and pressure. The Act's implicit preference for non-Muslim immigrants could exacerbate existing biases against interfaith marriages, particularly those involving Muslim partners.

Impact on Interfaith Adoption and Guardianship

The CAA's implications extend beyond marital relationships to affect adoption and guardianship practices within interfaith contexts. The legal framework governing adoption in India is already complex, with different rules applying to different religious communities.

Legal Framework for Adoption

In India, adoption laws vary significantly based on religion. While Hindus have a codified adoption law under the Hindu Adoption and Maintenance Act of 1956, Muslims, Christians, and Parsis do not have specific adoption laws and must rely on the Guardians and Wards Act of 1890 for legal guardianship. This disparity in legal frameworks already creates challenges for interfaith couples seeking to adopt.

CAA's Influence on Adoption Practices

The introduction of the CAA adds another layer of complexity to interfaith adoptions. For instance, if an interfaith couple adopts a child from one of the countries specified in the CAA, the child's eligibility for citizenship could potentially depend on the religion assigned to them. This situation could lead to difficult decisions for adoptive parents and potentially influence the choice of children available for adoption to interfaith couples.

Guardianship Challenges

Under the Guardians and Wards Act, non-Hindu couples can only become legal guardians of a child, not adoptive parents in the full legal sense. The CAA's religious criteria could further complicate guardianship arrangements, especially in cases involving cross-border guardianship or adoption from the countries specified in the Act.

Legal Ambiguities for Children of Interfaith Couples: Children born to interfaith couples in India often face unique legal challenges, which the CAA potentially exacerbates.

Citizenship Status of Children

The citizenship status of children born to interfaith couples, particularly those involving a Muslim parent, could become more complex under the CAA. In cases where one parent's citizenship status is affected by the Act, it could create situations where children's citizenship rights are unclear or contested.

Religious Identity and Legal Rights

In India, a child's religious identity often plays a crucial role in determining their legal rights, including inheritance and personal law application. The CAA's emphasis on religious identity in citizenship matters could further complicate the already complex issue of determining a child's religious status in interfaith families.

Educational and Social Implications

The ambiguities surrounding the legal status of children in interfaith families could have far-reaching implications for their education and social integration. Uncertainties about citizenship status might affect access to educational opportunities, scholarships, and other social benefits.

Support Systems for Interfaith Families Affected by CAA: Given the challenges faced by interfaith families in the context of the CAA, various support systems have emerged to assist these families in navigating the complex legal and social landscape.

Legal Aid and Advocacy Organizations

Several non-governmental organizations (NGOs) and legal aid groups have stepped up to provide support to interfaith families navigating the complexities of the CAA. For instance, organizations like Dhanak of Humanity offer platforms to assist interfaith couples facing legal and social challenges. These groups provide legal advice, support in dealing with bureaucratic processes, and advocacy for the rights of interfaith families.

Community Support Networks

Interfaith community groups play a crucial role in providing emotional and practical support to families affected by the CAA. Organizations like the Interfaith Families Project, while not specifically focused on CAA-related issues, demonstrate the importance of community support for interfaith families. Such networks can provide a sense of belonging and shared experience, which is particularly valuable in times of legal and social uncertainty.

Judicial Interventions

The Indian judiciary has played a significant role in protecting the rights of interfaith couples. Several landmark rulings have reinforced the right of individuals to marry whomever they choose, irrespective of religion or caste. While these rulings do not directly address the CAA, they establish important precedents that can be leveraged to protect the rights of interfaith families in the context of citizenship laws.

Counseling and Mental Health Support

The stress and uncertainty caused by the CAA can have significant mental health implications for interfaith families. Recognizing this, some organizations have begun offering specialized counseling services to help families cope with the emotional and psychological challenges associated with navigating complex citizenship laws.

The intersection of interfaith families and the Citizenship Amendment Act in India presents a complex set of challenges that touch on fundamental issues of identity, family unity, and citizenship rights. The Act's religious-based criteria for citizenship have introduced new uncertainties for interfaith couples and their children, potentially exacerbating existing legal and social challenges.

The impact of the CAA on interfaith families extends beyond immediate citizenship concerns, affecting areas such as adoption, guardianship, and the legal status of children. These challenges are further complicated by the existing patchwork of personal laws and societal attitudes towards interfaith marriages in India.

However, the emergence of support systems, including legal aid organizations, community networks, and judicial interventions, offers some hope for interfaith families navigating this complex landscape. These support mechanisms play a crucial role in helping families understand their rights, access legal resources, and find community support.

As India continues to grapple with the implications of the CAA, it is clear that interfaith families will remain at the forefront of many legal and social debates. The experiences of these families highlight the need for a more inclusive and equitable approach to citizenship and family law in India, one that recognizes and respects the diversity of religious and cultural identities within the country.

Moving forward, it will be crucial for policymakers, legal experts, and civil society organizations to work together to address the unique challenges faced by interfaith families in the context of the CAA. This may involve revisiting aspects of the Act, strengthening legal protections for interfaith couples and their children, and promoting greater societal acceptance of diverse family structures.

Ultimately, the story of interfaith families and the CAA is not just about legal statutes and citizenship rights; it's about the lived experiences of families caught at the intersection of love, faith, and national identity. As India continues to evolve as a diverse and pluralistic society, the treatment of interfaith families will remain a crucial indicator of the country's commitment to inclusivity and equality before the law.

References:

1. FairPlanet. (2023, July 27). Inside the struggle of inter-faith couples in India. https://www.fairplanet.org/story/inside-the-struggle-of-inter-faith-couples-in-india/
2. MKRI.ID. (2022, August 11). Interfaith Marriage Brings More Harm. https://en.mkri.id/news/

details/2022-08-11/
Interfaith_Marriage_Brings_More_Harm

3. ERLC. (2024, September 1). Support the Adoptee Citizenship Act Archives. https://erlc.com/policy-center/support-the-adoptee-citizenship-act/

4. ForumIAS. (2024, July 2). [Answered] Examine the legal and social challenges faced by inter-faith couples in India. How can the judicial system ensure the protection of their rights? (250 words). https://forumias.com/blog/answered-examine-the-legal-and-social-challenges-faced-by-inter-faith-couples-in-india-how-can-the-judicial-system-ensure-the-protection-of-their-rights-250-words/

5. Deutsche Welle. (n.d.). Why interfaith marriage in India is getting dangerous. https://www.dw.com/en/why-interfaith-marriage-in-india-is-getting-dangerous/a-64350804

6. Legal Service India. (n.d.). Adoption: Under Hindu, Muslim, Christian And Parsi Laws. https://www.legalserviceindia.com/articles/hmcp_adopt.htm

7. Lawbhoomi. (2024, September 21). How Does the Law Handle Cases of Interfaith Marriages? https://lawbhoomi.com/how-does-the-law-handle-cases-of-interfaith-marriages/

8. Interfaith Families Project. (2023, June 17). Home Interfaith Families Project of Washington D.C. https://iffp.org

CHAPTER 34: RELIGIOUS RHETORIC IN POLITICAL CAMPAIGNS

Religious rhetoric has long been a powerful tool in political campaigns, shaping public discourse and influencing voter behavior. This chapter explores the complex interplay between religion and politics, focusing on four key aspects: the use of Citizenship Amendment Act (CAA) in religion-based political messaging, interfaith political alliances and oppositions, the impact on voting patterns of religious communities, and the challenge of balancing secular governance with religious sentiments.

Use of CAA in Religion-Based Political Messaging

The Citizenship Amendment Act (CAA), passed in India in 2019, has become a focal point for religion-based political messaging. This controversial legislation, which provides a pathway to citizenship for non-Muslim migrants from neighbouring countries, has been both championed and criticized along religious lines.

Political parties have leveraged the CAA to appeal to specific religious constituencies. Supporters of the act frame it as a humanitarian measure to protect persecuted religious minorities, particularly Hindus, from neighbouring Muslim-majority countries. This narrative resonates with Hindu nationalist sentiments and has been used to galvanize support among Hindu voters.

Critics, on the other hand, argue that the CAA discriminates against Muslims and violates India's secular principles.

Opposition parties have used this argument to appeal to Muslim voters and secular-minded citizens, framing the act as a threat to India's pluralistic fabric.

The use of CAA in political messaging highlights how religious issues can be weaponized in campaigns. Politicians on both sides have employed emotive language and religious symbolism to sway voters. For instance, pro-CAA campaigns often invoke historical narratives of Hindu persecution, while anti-CAA rhetoric emphasizes the importance of secularism and religious equality.

This religion-based messaging around the CAA has had significant implications for India's political landscape. It has intensified religious polarization and shifted the focus of political debates towards issues of identity and citizenship. The act has become a litmus test for parties' stance on secularism and minority rights, influencing coalition-building and voter alignments.

Interfaith Political Alliances and Oppositions

The formation of interfaith political alliances and oppositions is a crucial aspect of religious rhetoric in campaigns. These alliances can bridge religious divides or exacerbate them, depending on their nature and messaging.

In many democracies, political parties seek to build coalitions that transcend religious boundaries. For instance, in the United States, both major parties attempt to appeal to a diverse religious base. The Republican Party, while traditionally associated with evangelical Christians, also courts Catholic and Jewish voters. Similarly, the Democratic Party, which has strong support among secular voters, also seeks to engage with religious communities.

However, interfaith alliances can be fragile, especially when religious issues become politically contentious. The CAA debate in India, for example, has strained some interfaith political coalitions. Parties that previously maintained a broad religious appeal have found themselves forced to take sides, potentially alienating certain religious groups.

Oppositions based on religious lines can also emerge, particularly when policies are perceived to favor or disadvantage specific religious communities. These oppositions can manifest as formal political alliances or grassroots movements. For instance, the anti-CAA protests in India saw unprecedented cooperation between Muslim organizations and secular civil society groups.

The dynamics of interfaith alliances and oppositions are not static. They evolve in response to changing political landscapes and emerging issues. Political leaders must navigate these complexities carefully, balancing the need for broad appeal with the demands of their core religious constituencies.

Impact on Voting Patterns of Religious Communities

Religious affiliation continues to be a significant factor in shaping voting patterns across many democracies. Understanding these patterns is crucial for political campaigns seeking to target specific religious demographics.

Research has consistently shown that religious identity and practice influence political preferences and voting behavior. In the United States, for example, white evangelical Protestants have been a reliable voting bloc for the Republican Party, while Jewish voters tend to support the Democratic Party.

The impact of religion on voting patterns is not uniform across all religious groups or contexts. Factors such as the frequency of religious practice, the salience of religious identity, and the specific issues at stake can all influence how religious affiliation translates into voting behavior.

In India, the relationship between religion and voting is particularly complex due to the country's religious diversity. While there are general trends – such as Muslims tending to support secular parties – these patterns are not monolithic. Factors such as caste, region, and economic status intersect with religious identity to shape voting decisions.

The CAA debate has had a significant impact on voting patterns among religious communities in India. It has reinforced existing voting trends among some groups while potentially shifting allegiances among others. For instance, the act has solidified Hindu nationalist support for the ruling Bharatiya Janata Party (BJP) while potentially pushing some minority voters towards opposition parties.

Political campaigns must be attuned to these nuanced voting patterns when crafting their messaging. Effective religious rhetoric in campaigns often involves tailoring messages to resonate with the specific concerns and values of different religious communities.

Balancing Secular Governance with Religious Sentiments

One of the most challenging aspects of religious rhetoric in political campaigns is balancing the principles of secular governance with the religious sentiments of the electorate. This balance is crucial for maintaining social harmony and ensuring equal representation for all citizens, regardless of their religious affiliations.

In theory, secular governance requires the separation of religion and state, with political decisions made on the basis of civic rather than religious values. However, in practice, many democracies grapple with the influence of religious sentiments on policy-making and governance.

The challenge lies in respecting and acknowledging religious beliefs while ensuring that they do not unduly influence state affairs or infringe on the rights of others. Political leaders must navigate this delicate balance, particularly in diverse societies where multiple religious communities coexist.

In India, the concept of secularism has been interpreted as equal respect for all religions, rather than a strict separation of religion and state. This approach, while aiming to be inclusive, has sometimes led to controversies when state actions are perceived as favoring or disadvantaging particular religious groups.

The CAA debate exemplifies the challenges of balancing secular governance with religious sentiments. While the act's supporters argue that it addresses historical injustices faced by certain religious communities, critics contend that it violates the principle of secularism by explicitly excluding Muslims.

Political campaigns must be mindful of this balance when employing religious rhetoric. While appealing to religious sentiments can be an effective campaign strategy, it risks alienating voters who prioritize secular governance. Moreover, overtly religious campaign messaging can raise concerns about a candidate's commitment to representing all citizens equally if elected.

Successful political campaigns often strike a balance by acknowledging the importance of religious values to many voters while emphasizing their commitment to secular governance. This might involve invoking broad moral principles that resonate with religious voters without explicitly favoring any particular faith.

The judiciary often plays a crucial role in maintaining this balance. Court rulings can provide guidance on the appropriate boundaries between religious influence and state action. In many democracies, including India, the courts have intervened to uphold secular principles when they are perceived to be under threat.

International norms and treaties also influence how countries navigate the relationship between religion and politics. Many nations, including Bangladesh and India, are signatories to international agreements that protect religious freedoms and promote secular governance. These commitments can serve as important reference points for balancing religious sentiments with secular principles.

Comparative insights from different countries can provide valuable lessons in managing this balance. For instance, while both Bangladesh and India guarantee freedom of religion, their approaches to religious education in schools differ, reflecting varying interpretations of secularism.

In conclusion, religious rhetoric remains a powerful force in political campaigns, shaping public discourse and influencing voter behavior. The use of religious messaging, as seen in the CAA debate in India, can have far-reaching implications for political alignments and social cohesion. Interfaith alliances and oppositions add further complexity to this landscape, reflecting the dynamic nature of religious politics.

The impact of religion on voting patterns underscores the importance of understanding and engaging with diverse religious communities in political campaigns. However, this engagement must be balanced with the principles of secular governance to ensure equal representation and social harmony.

As societies continue to grapple with questions of identity, citizenship, and religious freedom, the role of religious rhetoric in political campaigns is likely to remain significant. Political leaders and campaign strategists must navigate these issues with sensitivity and nuance, striving to build inclusive coalitions while respecting the diverse religious sentiments of the electorate.

References:

1. Campbell, D. E. (2004). Acts of faith: Churches and political engagement. Political Behavior, 26(2), 155-180.
2. Fastnow, C., Grant, J. T., & Rudolph, T. J. (1999). Holy roll calls: Religious tradition and voting behavior in the U.S. House. Social Science Quarterly, 80(4), 687-701.
3. Gibbs, J. (n.d.). Religiosity and voting behavior. McKendree University. https://www.mckendree.edu/academics/scholars/issue6/gibbs.htm
4. Interfaith Alliance. (n.d.). In Wikipedia. https://en.wikipedia.org/wiki/Interfaith_Alliance
5. Kolpinskaya, E. (2024). Religion and voting behaviour in the 2024 General Election. Election Analysis UK. https://www.electionanalysis.uk/uk-election-analysis-2024/section-2-voters-polls-and-results/religion-and-voting-behaviour-in-the-2024-general-election/
6. Raushenbush, P. (2022). Interfaith Alliance leadership. Interfaith Alliance.
7. Religion Counts team. (2024). Religion Counts: Do the religious vote? Theos Think Tank. https://www.theosthinktank.co.uk/research/2024/05/15/religion-counts-do-the-religious-vote
8. The Study IAS. (2024). Balancing secularism and religious freedom in Bangladesh. https://www.thestudyias.com/blogs/balancing-secularism-and-religion/
9. Vaishnav, M. (2019). The BJP in power: Indian democracy and religious nationalism. Carnegie Endowment for International Peace. https://carnegieendowment.org/research/2019/04/the-bjp-in-power-indian-democracy-and-religious-nationalism

CHAPTER 35: CAA AND RELIGIOUS FREEDOM INDICES

The Citizenship Amendment Act (CAA) of 2019 has significantly impacted India's standing on global religious freedom scales and international perceptions of Indian secularism. This chapter examines the changes in India's rankings on religious freedom indices, the responses from international organizations, and efforts to address concerns raised about religious freedom in India following the implementation of the CAA.

Changes in India's Rankings on Global Religious Freedom Scales

The passage of the CAA has led to a notable decline in India's position on various global religious freedom indices. One of the most prominent assessments comes from the United States Commission on International Religious Freedom (USCIRF), which has consistently expressed concerns about the deteriorating religious freedom conditions in India.

In its 2024 Annual Report, USCIRF recommended that the U.S. Department of State designate India as a "Country of Particular Concern" (CPC) for engaging in systematic, ongoing, and egregious violations of religious freedom. This designation represents a significant downgrade in India's status and reflects the commission's assessment of the country's religious freedom landscape.

The USCIRF report highlights several factors contributing to this designation:

1. Implementation of discriminatory legislation, including the

CAA

2. Enforcement of anti-conversion laws

3. Restrictions on religious practices through cow slaughter laws

4. Use of anti-terrorism laws to target religious minorities

5. Incidents of violence against religious minorities

6. Demolition of places of worship

The report emphasizes that throughout 2024, individuals have been killed, beaten, and lynched by vigilante groups, religious leaders have been arbitrarily arrested, and homes and places of worship have been demolished. These events are considered particularly severe violations of religious freedom by the commission.

Other international indices have also reflected this downward trend. The Pew Research Center's report on global religious restrictions found that the number of countries imposing "high" or "very high" levels of restrictions increased by 30 percent between 2007 and 2017, with India being one of the countries showing a significant increase in religious restrictions.

Impact on International Perceptions of Indian Secularism

The implementation of the CAA has had a profound impact on international perceptions of Indian secularism. India, long praised for its religious pluralism and multiethnic democratic system, is now facing increased scrutiny and criticism from the global community.

The CAA's provision of expedited citizenship to non-Muslim migrants from Afghanistan, Bangladesh, and Pakistan has been widely interpreted as discriminatory against Muslims. This perception has led many international observers to question India's commitment to its secular constitutional values.

Key concerns raised by international observers include:

1. Religious discrimination: The CAA is seen as legitimizing discrimination based on religion, which is inconsistent with India's constitutional values of equality and religious non-discrimination.

2. Exclusion of persecuted groups: The act's failure to include persecuted Muslim minorities such as Rohingyas from Myanmar, Ahmadiyyas from Pakistan, or Hazaras from Afghanistan has been criticized as undermining its stated purpose of protecting religious minorities.

3. Potential for statelessness: When combined with the proposed National Register of Citizens (NRC), there are fears that the CAA could be used to disenfranchise Muslim citizens of India.

4. Erosion of secular foundations: Critics argue that the CAA, along with other policies, is part of a broader Hindu nationalist agenda that threatens India's secular foundations.

These perceptions have led to a reevaluation of India's image as a bastion of religious pluralism. The country's rapid economic growth and multiethnic democratic system, once seen as indicators of a progressive society, are now being scrutinized in light of these religious freedom concerns.

Responses from International Religious Organizations: The implementation of the CAA has elicited strong responses from various international religious organizations and human rights groups. These organizations have expressed concern over the perceived threat to religious freedom and minority rights in India.

1. Amnesty International: Amnesty International has been vocal in its criticism of the CAA. The organization has stated that the act is "a blow to the Indian constitutional values of equality and religious non-discrimination and inconsistent and incompatible with India's international human rights obligations". Amnesty International has called for the immediate repeal of the CAA, citing its exclusionary and discriminatory provisions.

2. Human Rights Watch: Human Rights Watch has also raised concerns about the CAA and its impact on religious minorities in India. The organization has documented instances of violence against protesters and arbitrary detentions of activists opposing the act.

3. Organisation of Islamic Cooperation (OIC): The OIC has declared that it is "increasingly concerned" by the CAA due to its apparent discrimination against Indian Muslims. The organization has historically expressed sympathy towards disenfranchised Muslim populations and has voiced its apprehensions about the act's potential impact on India's Muslim community.

4. United Nations Human Rights Office: The Office of the UN High Commissioner for Human Rights has expressed concern that the CAA is "fundamentally discriminatory in nature." The UN body has urged the Indian government to ensure that the act is in line with the country's international human rights obligations.

5. World Evangelical Alliance: While not directly commenting on the CAA, the World Evangelical Alliance has expressed concern over the broader issue of religious freedom in India, particularly regarding anti-conversion laws and violence against Christians.

6. United States Commission on International Religious Freedom (USCIRF): As mentioned earlier, USCIRF has been one of the most vocal critics of the CAA. The commission has consistently raised alarms about the deteriorating religious freedom conditions in India and has recommended that India be designated as a Country of Particular Concern.

These responses from international religious organizations have contributed to increased global scrutiny of India's religious freedom record and have put pressure on the Indian government to address these concerns.

Efforts to Improve Religious Freedom Metrics Post-CAA

In response to the declining religious freedom metrics and international criticism, there have been various efforts, both by the Indian government and civil society organizations, to address concerns and improve India's standing on global religious freedom scales.

1. Government Responses: The Indian government has consistently rejected reports critical of its religious freedom record, including those by USCIRF, characterizing them as biased and politically motivated. The Ministry of External Affairs has urged organizations like USCIRF to "desist from such agenda-driven efforts"[8].

Despite these rebuttals, the government has taken some steps to address international concerns:

- Diplomatic outreach: India has engaged in diplomatic efforts to explain its position on the CAA and other religious freedom issues to international partners.
- Interfaith dialogue: The government has promoted interfaith dialogue and harmony through various initiatives and public statements.
- Legal safeguards: The government has emphasized the existing constitutional and legal safeguards for religious minorities in India.

2. Civil Society Initiatives: Several civil society organizations and academic institutions in India have been working to

promote religious freedom and counter discrimination:

- Research and advocacy: Institutions like Jawaharlal Nehru University and the Indian Institute of Dalit Studies have focused their research on human rights and social justice, providing insights into religious harassment and advocating for individual freedoms.
- Legal assistance: Organizations such as the Indian Law Society offer legal aid to victims of religious discrimination.
- Grassroots movements: Community-led initiatives have emerged to promote interfaith harmony and protect the rights of religious minorities.

3. International Engagement: India has also engaged with international partners to address concerns about religious freedom:

- Bilateral discussions: Religious freedom issues have been raised in bilateral meetings with countries like the United States. For instance, President Biden reportedly discussed human rights issues with Prime Minister Modi during the G20 Summit.
- Participation in international forums: India continues to participate in international forums on religious freedom and human rights, presenting its perspective and engaging in dialogue with other nations.

4. Transparency and Data Collection: To counter criticism and improve its metrics, there have been calls for better data collection and transparency regarding religious freedom issues in India:

- Improved reporting mechanisms: Suggestions have been made to enhance the reporting and documentation of religious freedom violations to provide a more accurate picture of the situation on the ground.

- Independent assessments: Calls for allowing independent international observers to assess the religious freedom situation in India have increased.

5. Legislative Review: While the government has stood firm on the CAA, there have been suggestions from various quarters to review and potentially amend certain aspects of the legislation to address international concerns:

- Inclusion of persecuted Muslim minorities: Some have proposed expanding the CAA to include persecuted Muslim minorities from neighbouring countries to address criticism of religious discrimination.
- Review of anti-conversion laws: There have been calls to review state-level anti-conversion laws that have been criticized for potentially infringing on religious freedom.

Despite these efforts, improving India's standing on global religious freedom indices remains a challenge. The implementation of the CAA, combined with other factors, has created a complex situation that requires sustained efforts to address both domestic and international concerns about religious freedom in India.

In conclusion, the CAA has had a significant impact on India's rankings in global religious freedom scales and international perceptions of Indian secularism. The responses from international religious organizations have been largely critical, putting pressure on India to address these concerns. While efforts have been made to improve religious freedom metrics post-CAA, the issue remains contentious and continues to influence India's international relations and domestic policy discussions.

References

1. United States Commission on International Religious Freedom. (2024). USCIRF Releases Report on India's Collapsing Religious Freedom Conditions.
2. United States Commission on International Religious Freedom. (n.d.). Religious Freedom Conditions in India.
3. United States Institute of Peace. (2020). Combating Religious Discrimination in India and Beyond.
4. Amnesty International. (2024). India: Citizenship Amendment Act is a blow to Indian constitutional values and international standards.
5. Drishti Judiciary. (2024). USCRIF Report on India.
6. International Religious Freedom Roundtable. (n.d.). The State of Religious Freedom in India: A Guide to Complex Issues.
7. United States Commission on International Religious Freedom. (2024). USCIRF Raises Alarm Over India's Exclusionary Citizenship Amendment Act During Congressional Hearing.
8. Hindustan Times. (2024). India rejects 'malicious report' by USCIRF on religious freedom abuses.
9. Observer Research Foundation. (n.d.). Analyzing global response to the controversial Citizenship Amendment Act.

CHAPTER 36: INTERFAITH DIALOGUE INITIATIVES POST-CAA

The passage of the Citizenship Amendment Act (CAA) in India in December 2019 sparked widespread protests and heightened religious tensions across the country. In the aftermath, there has been a renewed focus on interfaith dialogue initiatives to promote religious harmony and mutual understanding. This chapter examines the various efforts that have emerged to foster interfaith dialogue in India post-CAA, including new platforms for inter-religious discussions, challenges and successes in promoting religious harmony, the role of educational institutions, and government initiatives.

New Platforms for Inter-Religious Discussions: In response to the religious polarization exacerbated by the CAA, several new platforms have emerged to facilitate constructive dialogue between different faith communities in India.

Interfaith Dialogue Forums

Numerous civil society organizations have established interfaith dialogue forums to bring together religious leaders and community members from diverse backgrounds. These forums provide spaces for open discussions on sensitive topics related to religious identity, citizenship, and social cohesion. By creating opportunities for face-to-face interactions, these initiatives aim to break down stereotypes and build empathy across religious divides.

One notable example is the Interfaith Dialogue and Reconciliation forum, which organizes panel discussions and workshops focused on "creating and sustaining spaces of encounter" between different religious groups. The forum emphasizes methodologies for successful interfaith dialogue while acknowledging its limitations. It provides a channel for communication among faiths in a spirit of tolerance, truthfulness, and empathy.

Online Platforms and Social Media Initiatives

The digital sphere has also seen a proliferation of interfaith dialogue initiatives leveraging social media and online platforms to reach wider audiences. Facebook groups, WhatsApp communities, and YouTube channels dedicated to interfaith understanding have gained traction, particularly among younger demographics. These online spaces allow for ongoing conversations and information sharing beyond the constraints of physical gatherings.

However, the online nature of these platforms also presents challenges in terms of moderating discussions and preventing the spread of misinformation or hate speech. Organizers have had to develop robust community guidelines and moderation practices to ensure constructive dialogue.

Interfaith Cultural Events

Cultural events celebrating religious diversity have emerged as another important platform for fostering interfaith connections. Music concerts featuring artists from different faith traditions, interfaith art exhibitions, and food festivals showcasing diverse culinary heritage have been organized in cities across India. These events provide opportunities for people to engage with different religious cultures in a festive, non-confrontational setting.

Challenges and Successes in Promoting Religious Harmony

While interfaith dialogue initiatives have made important strides in promoting religious harmony, they continue to face significant challenges in the current socio-political climate.

Overcoming Mistrust and Polarization

One of the primary challenges is overcoming the deep-seated mistrust and polarization between religious communities that has been exacerbated by divisive political rhetoric and communal violence. Many interfaith dialogue organizers report initial reluctance from community members to engage with those from different faiths due to fear or prejudice.

Successful initiatives have focused on creating safe spaces for dialogue and emphasizing shared values and common concerns across faith traditions. By starting with less contentious topics and gradually building trust, these programs have been able to facilitate more difficult conversations over time.

Engaging Diverse Voices

Another key challenge has been ensuring diverse representation in interfaith dialogues, particularly the inclusion of marginalized voices within religious communities. Women, youth, and members of less prominent sects or denominations are often underrepresented in formal interfaith forums.

Some successful initiatives have addressed this by actively reaching out to diverse community members and creating separate dialogue tracks for women and youth. Others have adopted more informal, grassroots approaches to engagement that are more accessible to a wider range of participants.

Translating Dialogue into Action

While interfaith dialogues can be valuable for building understanding, a common criticism is that they often fail to translate into concrete action to address religious discrimination and violence. To address this, some initiatives have incorporated social action projects into their programs, bringing together interfaith groups to work on common community issues.

Measuring Impact

Assessing the long-term impact of interfaith dialogue initiatives remains a challenge. While anecdotal evidence suggests positive outcomes in terms of changing attitudes and building relationships, more rigorous evaluation methods are needed to demonstrate effectiveness and secure ongoing support and funding.

Role of Educational Institutions in Fostering Dialogue

Educational institutions play a crucial role in fostering interfaith understanding and dialogue, particularly among young people. Several initiatives have emerged to integrate interfaith education and experiences into school and university curricula.

Interfaith Studies Programs

A growing number of universities in India have introduced interfaith studies programs or incorporated interfaith components into existing religious studies curricula. These academic programs provide students with a deeper understanding of diverse religious traditions and equip them with skills for engaging in constructive interfaith dialogue.

Campus Interfaith Groups

Student-led interfaith groups have become increasingly common on college campuses, organizing regular discussion forums, cultural events, and community service projects that bring together students from different faith backgrounds. These groups provide valuable opportunities for young people to engage in interfaith dialogue and collaboration in their formative years.

Teacher Training Programs

Recognizing the important role of educators in shaping young minds, several organizations have developed teacher training programs focused on promoting religious literacy and interfaith understanding in the classroom. These programs equip teachers with the knowledge and skills to address religious diversity sensitively and foster an inclusive learning environment.

Government Initiatives to Promote Interfaith Understanding: While much of the interfaith dialogue work in India has been driven by civil society organizations, there have also been some government initiatives aimed at promoting religious harmony and understanding.

National Integration Council

The National Integration Council, a high-level government body chaired by the Prime Minister, has emphasized the importance of interfaith dialogue in maintaining national unity and social cohesion. The council has recommended various measures to promote interfaith understanding, including educational reforms and media campaigns.

Interfaith Conferences and Events

State and national governments have organized interfaith conferences and events bringing together religious leaders and scholars to discuss issues of religious harmony and national integration[2]. While these high-level dialogues have symbolic importance, their impact at the grassroots level has been limited.

Legal and Policy Measures

The government has also introduced legal and policy measures aimed at protecting religious minorities and promoting interfaith harmony. However, the implementation and effectiveness of these measures have been subject to debate and criticism.

The interfaith dialogue initiatives that have emerged in India post-CAA represent important efforts to bridge religious divides and promote social cohesion in a deeply polarized context. While these initiatives face significant challenges, they have also demonstrated the potential for fostering greater understanding and collaboration across faith communities.

Moving forward, it will be crucial to sustain and expand these dialogue efforts while also addressing systemic issues of religious discrimination and inequality. By combining grassroots interfaith engagement with broader policy reforms and social change initiatives, India can work towards realizing its constitutional ideal of unity in diversity.

References

1. Geneva Centre for Human Rights Advancement and Global Dialogue. (2023). Interfaith dialogue and reconciliation. https://gchragd.org/interfaith-dialogue-and-reconciliation-2/
2. Institute for Cultural Diplomacy. (n.d.). Interfaith dialogue. https://www.culturaldiplomacy.org/academy/index.php
3. Mandaville, P., & Nozell, M. (2020). Combating religious discrimination in India and beyond. United States Institute of Peace. https://www.usip.org/publications/2020/05/combating-religious-discrimination-india-and-beyond
4. Widiyanto, A. (2023). Interfaith dialogue in the post-truth age: Challenges, strategies, and prospects. Religious Inquiries, 12(2). https://ri.urd.ac.ir/article_183638_cb61cb78e6ade52984e704e1d7d6

85f0.pdf

5. Wilson, E. K. (2017). 'Power differences' and 'the power of difference': The dominance of secularism as ontological injustice. Globalizations, 14(7), 1076-1093. https://www.tandfonline.com/doi/full/10.1080/14747731.2017.1308062

CHAPTER 37: CAA'S IMPACT ON RELIGIOUS TOURISM

The Citizenship Amendment Act (CAA) of 2019 has had significant implications for religious tourism in India, affecting both international and domestic travel patterns as well as the economic landscape of communities dependent on faith-based tourism. This chapter examines the multifaceted impact of the CAA on religious tourism, exploring changes in international tourist inflows, shifts in domestic tourism patterns, interfaith initiatives promoting national integration, and the economic consequences for tourism-dependent communities.

Changes in International Religious Tourist Inflows

The implementation of the CAA has led to notable changes in the influx of international religious tourists to India. The act, which provides a pathway to citizenship for non-Muslim migrants from Afghanistan, Bangladesh, and Pakistan, has sparked controversy and affected India's image as a secular destination for spiritual seekers.

Decline in Tourist Arrivals

In the immediate aftermath of the CAA's passage, India experienced a decline in international tourist arrivals. The protests and civil unrest that followed the act's implementation created a perception of instability, deterring some potential visitors. This decline was particularly noticeable in regions that traditionally attracted a significant number of international pilgrims and spiritual tourists.

Shift in Tourist Demographics

The CAA has also influenced the demographics of international religious tourists visiting India. There has been a noticeable increase in visitors from the religious communities specified in the act - Hindus, Sikhs, Buddhists, Jains, Parsis, and Christians - from the designated countries. This shift can be attributed to the perceived ease of obtaining citizenship, which may have encouraged more religious minorities from these countries to undertake pilgrimages or spiritual journeys to India.

Impact on Muslim Tourism

Conversely, there has been a decline in Muslim tourists from certain countries, particularly those not specified in the CAA. The act's exclusion of Muslims has led to concerns about discrimination and has potentially discouraged some Muslim travelers from choosing India as a spiritual destination.

Long-term Implications

While the immediate impact of the CAA on international religious tourism was negative, the long-term implications remain to be seen. As India continues to promote its rich spiritual heritage and invest in religious tourism infrastructure, there is potential for recovery and growth in this sector. However, the country's ability to attract a diverse range of international religious tourists may depend on its success in addressing concerns about religious discrimination and maintaining its image as a secular, welcoming destination for all faiths.

Domestic Religious Tourism Patterns Post-CAA: The implementation of the CAA has also influenced domestic religious tourism patterns within India, leading to both challenges and opportunities for the sector.

Surge in Domestic Pilgrimage

Despite the controversies surrounding the CAA, domestic

religious tourism in India has experienced a significant surge. According to the Ministry of Tourism data, the number of people engaging in religious tourism in India rose to 1,439 million in 2022 from 677 million in 2021. This increasecan be attributed to several factors, including improved infrastructure, technological advancements, and a growing interest in spiritual experiences among Indian travelers.

Shift in Destination Preferences

The CAA's implementation has led to changes in the popularity of certain religious destinations within India. Some traditionally popular sites have seen fluctuations in visitor numbers, while others have experienced unexpected growth. For instance, the Vaishno Devi temple in Jammu and Kashmir has seen a significant increase in daily visitors, from 10,000-15,000 before the COVID-19 pandemic to 32,000-40,000 post-pandemic.

Rise of Spiritual Wellness Tourism

Post-CAA, there has been a noticeable trend towards combining religious visits with wellness retreats. Many domestic tourists are now seeking holistic experiences that blend spiritual practices with health and wellness activities. This has led to the growth of spiritual wellness tourism, particularly in places like Rishikesh, Varanasi, and Pondicherry.

Impact of Technology on Religious Tourism

The integration of technology has played a crucial role in shaping domestic religious tourism patterns post-CAA. The widespread use of social media and online platforms has made it easier for pilgrims to access information about religious sites and plan their journeys. With approximately 508 million Indians using social media platforms, tour operators and religious sites have leveraged these channels to market their offerings effectively.

Government Initiatives

The Indian government has recognized the potential of religious tourism and has implemented several initiatives to promote it. The Swadesh Darshan and Pilgrimage Rejuvenation and Spiritual Augmentation Drive (PRASAD) initiatives, with a budget allocation of US$185 million in 2018-19, have focused on developing tourism circuits and improving infrastructure at religious sites. These efforts have contributed to the growth of domestic religious tourism post-CAA.

Interfaith Tourism Initiatives Promoting National Integration

In the wake of the CAA's implementation and the subsequent debates about religious inclusivity, there has been a growing emphasis on interfaith tourism initiatives aimed at promoting national integration and fostering understanding among different religious communities.

Development of Multi-Faith Circuits

The Indian government and tourism stakeholders have been working on developing multi-faith tourism circuits that showcase the country's diverse religious heritage. These circuits aim to encourage travelers to visit sacred sites of various religions, promoting a more inclusive and comprehensive understanding of India's spiritual landscape.

Promotion of Interfaith Dialogue

Interfaith tourism initiatives have increasingly focused on facilitating dialogue and interaction between followers of different religions. Many tour operators now offer programs that include visits to multiple religious sites, accompanied by guides who can provide insights into various faiths and their historical interconnections.

Educational Programs

There has been a rise in educational programs and workshops associated with interfaith tourism. These initiatives aim to provide visitors with a deeper understanding of different religious traditions, their shared values, and their contributions to India's cultural fabric. Such programs are particularly appealing to younger travelers who are interested in exploring the historical and cultural aspects of religious sites beyond their spiritual significance.

Community Engagement Projects

Interfaith tourism initiatives have also incorporated community engagement projects, allowing visitors to interact with local communities of different faiths. These experiences provide opportunities for cultural exchange and help break down stereotypes, contributing to greater national integration.

Preservation of Shared Heritage Sites

The focus on interfaith tourism has led to increased efforts to preserve and promote sites of shared religious heritage. These include places that hold significance for multiple faiths or that demonstrate the historical coexistence of different religious communities in India.

Economic Impact on Religious Tourism-Dependent Communities: The implementation of the CAA, combined with other factors such as the COVID-19 pandemic, has had significant economic implications for communities that rely heavily on religious tourism.

Revenue Generation

Religious tourism continues to be a significant contributor to India's economy. The sector generated revenues of US\$16.2

billion in 2022, highlighting its importance as an economic driver. However, the distribution of these economic benefits has been uneven, with some communities experiencing growth while others face challenges.

Employment Opportunities

The religious tourism sector remains a crucial source of employment, particularly in rural areas surrounding pilgrimage sites. According to projections, the sector is expected to create 140 million temporary and permanent jobs by 2030. However, the impact of the CAA and associated factors has led to fluctuations in employment stability in some regions.

Infrastructure Development

The growth of religious tourism has spurred infrastructure development in many areas. Government initiatives like the Adopt a Heritage project have encouraged public-private partnerships to develop and upgrade tourist amenities at heritage and religious sites. This development has had positive spillover effects on local economies, improving overall living conditions in many tourism-dependent communities.

Challenges for Small Businesses

While larger tourism operators have been able to adapt to the changing landscape post-CAA, many small businesses in religious tourism-dependent communities have faced challenges. Fluctuations in visitor numbers and changing tourist demographics have required these businesses to adapt their offerings, sometimes with limited resources.

Diversification of Local Economies

The uncertainties brought about by the CAA and other factors have highlighted the need for economic diversification in communities heavily dependent on religious tourism. Many local governments and community organizations are now exploring ways to develop alternative revenue streams while still leveraging their religious and cultural heritage.

Impact on Artisans and Craftspeople

The religious tourism sector supports a significant number of artisans and craftspeople who produce religious artifacts, souvenirs, and other items for pilgrims and tourists. The changes in tourism patterns post-CAA have affected the demand for these products, leading to both challenges and opportunities for this sector of the local economy.

In conclusion, the Citizenship Amendment Act has had a complex and multifaceted impact on religious tourism in India. While it has presented challenges, particularly in terms of international perceptions and certain tourist demographics, it has also coincided with a period of growth in domestic religious tourism. The act has sparked important conversations about inclusivity and national integration, leading to innovative interfaith tourism initiatives. Economically, the impact has been mixed, with some communities benefiting from increased domestic tourism while others face challenges adapting to the changing landscape.

As India continues to navigate the implications of the CAA, the religious tourism sector will likely play a crucial role in shaping narratives of national identity, promoting interfaith understanding, and driving economic development in many regions. The future of religious tourism in India will depend on the country's ability to balance its rich spiritual heritage with principles of inclusivity and secular governance, ensuring that it remains a welcoming destination for spiritual seekers of all faiths.

References:

[1] https://www.uscirf.gov/sites/default/files/India.pdf

[2] https://www.bbc.com/news/world-asia-india-50670393

[3] https://skift.com/2024/08/28/the-evolution-of-religious-tourism-in-india-india-report/

[4] https://timesofindia.indiatimes.com/travel/destinations/assam-tourism-hit-due-to-ongoing-caa-stir/articleshow/72901395.cms

[5] https://www.futuremarketinsights.com/reports/india-faith-based-tourism-market

[6] https://www.iosrjournals.org/iosr-jhss/papers/Vol.29-Issue4/Ser-3/A2904030105.pdf

[7] https://businesseconomics.in/religious-tourism-turns-economic-multiplier-across-globe

[8] https://www.aljazeera.com/economy/2019/12/29/indias-tourism-industry-hit-hard-by-citizenship-law-protests

[9] https://kpmg.com/in/en/insights/2024/08/sacred-journeys-unfolding-the-evolution-and-growth-of-pilgrimage-and-spiritual-tourism-in-india.html

[10] https://www.linkedin.com/pulse/holy-sites-economic-might-power-religious-tourism-india-rajni-hasija-uvbqe

CHAPTER 38: RELIGIOUS MINORITIES AND NATIONAL IDENTITY

The complex interplay between religious minority identities and national identity has been a subject of significant scholarly attention and societal debate. This chapter explores the multifaceted relationship between religious minorities and national identity, examining how perceptions of belonging have evolved, the challenges of balancing religious and national identities, the impact on patriotic sentiments, and initiatives aimed at fostering a more inclusive national identity.

Evolving Perceptions of National Belonging Among Minorities

The concept of national belonging among religious minorities has undergone significant transformation over time, influenced by historical, social, and political factors. In many countries, the journey from exclusion to inclusion has been long and complex, with religious minorities often navigating a delicate balance between maintaining their distinct religious identities and integrating into the broader national fabric.

Historically, religious minorities have faced varying degrees of marginalization and exclusion from mainstream national narratives. This exclusion was often rooted in the conflation of national identity with the majority religion, leaving little room for alternative religious expressions within the national framework. However, as societies have become increasingly diverse and globalized, there has been a gradual shift towards more inclusive conceptions of national identity.

The evolution of national belonging among religious minorities can be observed through several key trends:

1. Increased Recognition: Many nations have moved towards officially recognizing the contributions and presence of religious minorities as integral parts of their national tapestry. This recognition has often been reflected in constitutional amendments, legal protections, and public acknowledgments of minority religious festivals and traditions.

2. Shifting Narratives: There has been a gradual shift in national narratives to incorporate the histories and experiences of religious minorities. This includes efforts to revise educational curricula, public commemorations, and cultural representations to reflect a more diverse national story.

3. Political Participation: The increasing visibility and participation of religious minorities in political processes have contributed to evolving perceptions of national belonging. As minority representatives gain positions in government and public office, it reinforces the idea of a pluralistic national identity.

4. Interfaith Dialogue: Initiatives promoting interfaith dialogue and understanding have played a crucial role in breaking down barriers and fostering a sense of shared national identity across religious lines.

5. Generational Changes: Younger generations of religious minorities often display different attitudes towards national identity compared to their predecessors. Many have grown up in more integrated environments, leading to more fluid conceptions of belonging that encompass both their religious and national identities.

However, it is important to note that these evolving perceptions are not uniform across all contexts. In some cases, religious minorities continue to face challenges in being fully accepted as part of the national community. Factors such as historical grievances, ongoing discrimination, and geopolitical tensions can complicate the process of fostering inclusive national identities.

The evolution of national belonging among religious minorities is an ongoing process, influenced by broader societal changes, policy interventions, and the agency of minority communities themselves. As societies continue to grapple with questions of diversity and inclusion, the perceptions of national belonging among religious minorities are likely to remain a dynamic and important area of focus.

Balancing Religious and National Identities

The task of balancing religious and national identities presents a complex challenge for many individuals belonging to religious minority groups. This balancing act involves navigating potentially conflicting loyalties, cultural practices, and value systems while striving to maintain a sense of belonging to both their religious community and the broader national collective.

Challenges in Balancing Identities

1. Conflicting Values: In some cases, religious beliefs or practices may conflict with certain aspects of national culture or legislation. This can create tension for individuals trying to adhere to both their religious principles and their duties as citizens.

2. Social Pressure: Religious minorities may face pressure from both their religious communities to maintain traditional practices and from the broader society to conform to national norms. This dual pressure can create significant stress and identity conflicts.

3. Stereotyping and Discrimination: Negative stereotypes

or discrimination based on religious identity can make it challenging for minorities to feel fully accepted as part of the national community, even when they strongly identify with the nation.

4. Visibility of Religious Markers: Visible religious symbols or practices (e.g., clothing, dietary restrictions) can sometimes lead to othering or exclusion in public spaces, complicating the expression of national belonging.

Strategies for Balancing Identities: Despite these challenges, many religious minorities have developed strategies to successfully balance their religious and national identities:

1. Hybrid Identities: Many individuals embrace hybrid identities that incorporate elements of both their religious and national cultures. This approach allows for a more fluid and inclusive sense of self that can adapt to different contexts.

2. Reinterpretation of Traditions: Some religious minorities reinterpret religious traditions in ways that align more closely with national values, finding creative ways to maintain religious practices while participating fully in national life.

3. Civic Participation: Active engagement in civic and political processes allows religious minorities to assert their national identity while also advocating for their rights and recognition as religious communities.

4. Interfaith Initiatives: Participation in interfaith dialogues and collaborations can help build bridges between different religious communities and strengthen a shared sense of national belonging.

5. Education and Awareness: Efforts to educate the broader public about minority religions can help reduce stereotypes and foster greater acceptance of diverse religious identities within the national framework.

Legal and Policy Frameworks: The ability of religious minorities to balance their identities is significantly influenced by legal and policy frameworks. Many countries have implemented measures to protect religious freedom and promote inclusivity:

1. Constitutional Protections: Enshrining religious freedom and equality in national constitutions provides a legal foundation for religious minorities to practice their faith while fully participating in national life.

2. Anti-Discrimination Laws: Legislation prohibiting discrimination based on religion helps create a more inclusive environment where religious minorities can express both their religious and national identities without fear of reprisal.

3. Accommodation Policies: Policies that accommodate religious practices in public institutions (e.g., providing prayer spaces, allowing religious holidays) can help religious minorities feel that their identities are respected and valued within the national context.

4. Multicultural Education: Educational curricula that include diverse religious perspectives can promote understanding and acceptance of different identities among the broader population.

The process of balancing religious and national identities is ongoing and dynamic. As societies continue to diversify and evolve, the ways in which religious minorities navigate this balance are likely to adapt as well. Successful integration often depends on both the willingness of minority communities to engage with the broader national culture and the openness of the majority society to embrace diversity as a core component of national identity.

Impact on Patriotic Sentiments in Minority Communities

The relationship between religious minority status and

patriotic sentiments is complex and multifaceted, influenced by a variety of historical, social, and political factors. Understanding this relationship is crucial for fostering inclusive national identities and promoting social cohesion.

Factors Influencing Patriotic Sentiments

1. Historical Experiences: The historical treatment of religious minorities within a nation significantly impacts their patriotic sentiments. Histories of discrimination or marginalization can lead to ambivalence or skepticism towards national narratives.

2. Current Social Climate: The contemporary social and political environment plays a crucial role in shaping patriotic feelings among minorities. Inclusive policies and public discourse can foster stronger national attachment, while exclusionary practices may diminish patriotic sentiments.

3. Generational Differences: Different generations within minority communities often exhibit varying levels of patriotic sentiment. Younger generations, who may have experienced greater integration, often display stronger national identification compared to older generations.

4. Socioeconomic Factors: The level of economic integration and social mobility experienced by religious minorities can influence their sense of national belonging and, consequently, their patriotic sentiments.

5. International Relations: Geopolitical tensions or conflicts involving countries associated with minority religions can complicate patriotic feelings, especially if minorities feel pressured to "prove" their national loyalty.

Manifestations of Patriotism in Minority Communities: Patriotic sentiments among religious minorities can manifest in various ways:

1. Civic Engagement: Many religious minorities express their patriotism through active participation in civic processes, including voting, community service, and political activism.

2. Cultural Synthesis: Some minorities develop unique expressions of patriotism that blend elements of their religious culture with national symbols and traditions.

3. Military Service: Participation in national defense forces is often seen as a strong expression of patriotism among minority communities.

4. Celebration of National Events: Enthusiastic participation in national holidays and commemorations can serve as a public display of patriotic sentiment.

5. Pride in National Achievements: Many minorities express strong pride in their nation's accomplishments, particularly in fields like sports, science, or culture.

Challenges to Patriotic Expression: Despite these expressions of patriotism, religious minorities often face unique challenges:

1. Questioning of Loyalty: Minorities may face unfair scrutiny or questioning of their national loyalty, particularly during times of national crisis or conflict.

2. Conflicting Identities: Some individuals may struggle to reconcile aspects of their religious identity with certain national narratives or policies.

3. Exclusionary Nationalism: When national identity is defined in narrow religious or ethnic terms, it can be difficult for minorities to feel fully included in patriotic expressions.

4. Discrimination Experiences: Ongoing experiences of discrimination or marginalization can erode patriotic sentiments over time.

Fostering Inclusive Patriotism: To promote strong patriotic sentiments among religious minorities, several approaches have been identified:

1. Inclusive National Narratives: Developing national narratives that acknowledge the contributions and experiences of diverse religious communities can foster a more inclusive sense of patriotism.

2. Recognition of Diversity: Official recognition and celebration of religious diversity as a national strength can encourage minorities to see their religious identity as compatible with national belonging.

3. Equal Opportunities: Ensuring equal access to education, employment, and civic participation can strengthen minorities' sense of stake in the national community.

4. Interfaith Initiatives: Promoting interfaith dialogue and cooperation can build bridges between communities and reinforce a shared sense of national identity.

5. Media Representation: Positive and nuanced representation of religious minorities in media and popular culture can help normalize their presence as integral parts of the national fabric.

The impact of minority status on patriotic sentiments is not uniform across all religious minority groups or individuals. Factors such as the size of the minority community, its historical presence in the country, and its level of integration all play roles in shaping patriotic feelings. Additionally, individual experiences and personal choices significantly influence how people navigate their religious and national identities.

As nations continue to grapple with questions of diversity and inclusion, understanding and nurturing patriotic sentiments among religious minorities remains a crucial aspect of building cohesive and harmonious societies. By recognizing the complex interplay between religious identity and national belonging, policymakers and community leaders can work towards fostering a more inclusive and multifaceted conception of patriotism that resonates across diverse religious communities.

Initiatives to Reinforce Inclusive National Identity

In response to the challenges of fostering an inclusive national identity that embraces religious diversity, many countries have implemented various initiatives. These efforts aim to create a sense of shared national belonging while respecting and valuing religious differences. The following section explores some key initiatives and their impacts.

Educational Reforms: Education plays a crucial role in shaping national identity and promoting inclusivity. Several educational initiatives have been implemented:

1. Curriculum Diversification: Many countries have revised their educational curricula to include more diverse perspectives on national history and culture. This includes incorporating the histories and contributions of religious minorities into mainstream narratives.

2. Religious Education: Some nations have introduced comparative religion courses in schools to promote understanding and respect for different faiths. These courses aim to foster religious literacy and combat stereotypes.

3. Teacher Training: Programs to train educators on cultural sensitivity and inclusive teaching practices have been implemented in various countries. This helps ensure that classrooms are welcoming spaces for students from all religious backgrounds.

4. Intercultural Exchange Programs: School exchange programs that bring together students from different religious

backgrounds help build understanding and foster a shared sense of national identity from a young age.

Legal and Policy Measures: Legal frameworks and policy initiatives play a significant role in reinforcing inclusive national identities:

1. Anti-Discrimination Laws: Many countries have strengthened or introduced laws prohibiting discrimination based on religion. These legal protections help create an environment where religious minorities feel secure in expressing both their religious and national identities.

2. Religious Freedom Guarantees: Constitutional or legislative guarantees of religious freedom reinforce the idea that diverse religious expressions are compatible with national belonging.

3. Accommodation Policies: Policies that accommodate religious practices in public institutions, such as providing prayer spaces or allowing religious dress, signal official recognition of religious diversity as part of the national fabric.

4. Representation Quotas: Some countries have implemented quotas or other measures to ensure representation of religious minorities in government bodies and public institutions, reinforcing their role as integral parts of the nation.

Cultural and Media Initiatives: Cultural representation and media portrayals significantly influence public perceptions of national identity:

1. Inclusive National Celebrations: Many countries have made efforts to include diverse religious traditions in national celebrations and commemorations, symbolizing a more inclusive national identity.

2. Media Diversity Programs: Initiatives to promote diverse representation in media, including programs featuring religious minority perspectives and experiences, help

normalize diversity as part of the national narrative.

3. Cultural Heritage Preservation: Programs to preserve and promote the cultural heritage of religious minorities, including historical sites and traditions, reinforce their place within the national cultural landscape.

4. Interfaith Arts Projects: Cultural projects that bring together artists from different religious backgrounds to create collaborative works can symbolize national unity in diversity.

Interfaith Dialogue and Cooperation: Promoting interaction and understanding between different religious communities is crucial for building an inclusive national identity:

1. National Interfaith Councils: Many countries have established national-level interfaith councils or forums that bring together leaders from various religious communities to discuss issues of national importance.

2. Community Dialogue Programs: Local-level initiatives that facilitate dialogue and cooperation between different religious communities help build grassroots understanding and shared national sentiment.

3. Interfaith Social Action: Programs that encourage members of different faith communities to work together on social issues (e.g., poverty alleviation, environmental protection) foster a sense of shared national purpose.

4. Religious Leader Training: Initiatives to train religious leaders in interfaith dialogue and national integration help create influential advocates for inclusive national identity within religious communities.

Economic Integration Initiatives: Ensuring economic inclusion is crucial for fostering a sense of national belonging among religious minorities:

1. Targeted Development Programs: Some countries have

implemented economic development programs specifically aimed at improving opportunities in areas with significant religious minority populations.

2. Diversity in Employment: Initiatives to promote religious diversity in the workplace, including in the public sector, help reinforce the idea of equal national belonging.

3. Entrepreneurship Support: Programs supporting minority-owned businesses can help integrate religious minorities more fully into the national economic fabric.

Challenges and Criticisms: While these initiatives aim to reinforce inclusive national identities, they are not without challenges and criticisms:

1. Tokenism Concerns: Some critics argue that certain initiatives, particularly in media and cultural representation, can be superficial and fail to address deeper issues of structural inequality.

2. Majority Backlash: In some cases, efforts to promote inclusivity have faced backlash from majority communities who perceive them as threats to traditional national identities.

3. Implementation Gaps: The effectiveness of many initiatives is hampered by gaps between policy formulation and on-the-ground implementation.

4. Resource Constraints: Many countries, particularly in the developing world, face resource constraints in implementing comprehensive inclusivity programs.

5. Balancing Unity and Diversity: There is an ongoing debate about how to balance the promotion of a shared national identity with the recognition of distinct religious identities.

Despite these challenges, initiatives to reinforce inclusive national identities remain crucial for social cohesion and national development in diverse societies. Successful approaches often involve a combination of top-down policy measures and bottom-up community engagement, recognizing that building truly inclusive national identities is a long-term process requiring ongoing commitment and adaptation.

As nations continue to navigate the complexities of religious diversity and national identity, these initiatives provide important models and lessons. The most effective approaches tend to be those that are responsive to local contexts, engage multiple stakeholders, and are part of a broader commitment to equality and inclusion across all aspects of national life.

References:

1. https://www.hist.cam.ac.uk/project/religious-minorities-and-national-identity-southern-ireland-1912
2. https://www.pewresearch.org/religion/2018/05/29/nationalism-immigration-and-minorities/
3. https://pmc.ncbi.nlm.nih.gov/articles/PMC9386670/
4. https://timesofindia.indiatimes.com/blogs/mindfly/building-national-identity-in-diverse-nations-lessons-from-history-and-philosophy/
5. https://guides.libraries.psu.edu/apaquickguide/intext
6. https://www.scribbr.com/apa-style/in-text-citation/
7. https://apastyle.apa.org/style-grammar-guidelines/citations/basic-principles
8. https://www.ons.gov.uk/methodology/classificationsandstandards/measuringequality/ethnicgroupnationalidentityandreligion
9. https://www.mdpi.com/2077-1444/12/10/858
10. https://owl.purdue.edu/owl/research_and_citation/apa_style/apa_formatting_and_style_guide/in_text_citations_the_basics.html

CHAPTER 39: CAA AND RELIGIOUS EXTREMISM

The Citizenship Amendment Act (CAA) of 2019 has sparked controversy and raised concerns about its potential impact on religious communities in India. This chapter examines the CAA's implications for religious extremism, exploring the potential for radicalization in affected communities, interfaith initiatives to counter extremism, government strategies to prevent religious radicalization, and the role of moderate religious leaders in maintaining peace.

Potential for Radicalization in Affected Communities

The CAA's selective approach to granting citizenship based on religious criteria has raised concerns about its potential to exacerbate existing tensions and contribute to radicalization in affected communities. The Indian Union Muslim League (IUML) has argued that the CAA's claim of protecting persecuted religious minorities is fundamentally flawed. The Act's exclusion of certain religious groups and neighbouring countries from its purview has been criticized for potentially creating a sense of marginalization and discrimination among excluded communities.

The CAA's selective inclusion of specific religious groups (Hindus, Christians, Parsis, Sikhs, and Jains) from Pakistan, Afghanistan, and Bangladesh, while excluding others, may contribute to a perception of unequal treatment based on religious identity. This perception could potentially fuel resentment and create conditions conducive to radicalization among excluded groups.

Factors Contributing to Radicalization: Several factors can contribute to the potential for radicalization in communities affected by the CAA:

1. Perceived Discrimination: The exclusion of certain religious groups from the CAA's provisions may lead to feelings of discrimination and marginalization.

2. Socioeconomic Factors: While socioeconomic factors alone may not be determinative, they can contribute to the emergence of "hotbeds of radicalization" when combined with other factors.

3. Ideological Narratives: Extremist groups may exploit the perceived injustices of the CAA to promote radical ideologies and recruit vulnerable individuals.

4. Community Segregation: The CAA's implementation may inadvertently lead to increased community segregation, potentially creating isolated pockets more susceptible to extremist influences.

Vulnerable Groups: Certain groups may be particularly vulnerable to radicalization in the context of the CAA:

1. Excluded Religious Minorities: Communities not covered by the CAA, such as Muslims from the specified countries or persecuted groups from excluded neighbouring countries, may feel marginalized and more susceptible to extremist narratives.

2. Youth: Young people, especially those facing economic challenges or identity crises, may be more vulnerable to radicalization.

3. Marginalized Communities: Socioeconomically disadvantaged groups may be at higher risk of radicalization if they perceive the CAA as exacerbating existing inequalities.

Interfaith Initiatives to Counter Extremism

In response to the potential for increased religious tensions and radicalization, interfaith initiatives can play a crucial role in promoting understanding, dialogue, and peaceful coexistence among different religious communities.

Importance of Interfaith Dialogue: Interfaith initiatives can contribute to countering extremism in several ways:

1. Promoting Understanding: Interfaith dialogue helps dispel misconceptions and stereotypes about different religious groups, reducing the potential for conflict based on misunderstandings.

2. Building Social Cohesion: By bringing together members of different faith communities, interfaith initiatives can strengthen social bonds and create a sense of shared community.

3. Countering Extremist Narratives: Interfaith leaders can work together to challenge and refute extremist interpretations of religious texts and promote peaceful coexistence.

Examples of Interfaith Initiatives: Several types of interfaith initiatives can be effective in countering extremism:

1. Interfaith Councils: Establishing local and national interfaith councils can provide platforms for regular dialogue and collaboration among religious leaders.

2. Joint Community Projects: Organizing joint community service projects that bring together members of different faith communities can foster cooperation and mutual understanding.

3. Educational Programs: Developing interfaith educational programs for schools and communities can promote religious literacy and respect for diversity.

4. Conflict Resolution Workshops: Conducting workshops

that teach conflict resolution skills from various religious perspectives can equip community members to address tensions peacefully.

Government Strategies to Prevent Religious Radicalization

Governments play a crucial role in preventing religious radicalization and countering violent extremism. In the context of the CAA and its potential impact on religious communities, several strategies can be employed to mitigate the risk of radicalization.

Comprehensive Approach to Countering Violent Extremism: The Government of Canada's National Strategy on Countering Radicalization to Violence provides a model for a comprehensive approach to preventing radicalization. Key elements of this approach include:

1. Early Prevention: Focusing on addressing the root causes of radicalization before it occurs.

2. At-Risk Prevention: Identifying and supporting individuals who may be vulnerable to radicalization.

3. Disengagement from Violent Ideologies: Assisting individuals in leaving extremist groups and ideologies.

Specific Strategies for the Indian Context: Adapting these principles to the Indian context and the specific challenges posed by the CAA, the following strategies could be considered:

1. Inclusive Policy-Making: Ensuring that policies and legislation, including any amendments to the CAA, are developed through inclusive consultation processes that consider the concerns of all religious communities.

2. Addressing Grievances: Establishing mechanisms to address legitimate grievances and concerns raised by various communities regarding the CAA and its implementation.

3. Promoting Social Cohesion: Investing in programs that promote social cohesion and inter-community dialogue, particularly in areas with diverse religious populations.

4. Enhancing Religious Literacy: Developing educational programs that promote understanding of different religious traditions and the principles of secularism enshrined in the Indian Constitution.

5. Countering Online Radicalization: Implementing strategies to address radicalization in the online space, including monitoring extremist content and promoting counter-narratives.

6. Supporting Local Interventions: Providing resources and support for community-based interventions that address local factors contributing to radicalization.

7. Strengthening Law Enforcement: Ensuring that law enforcement agencies are trained in community policing approaches and sensitive to the needs of diverse religious communities.

Challenges and Considerations

1. Balancing Security and Rights: Ensuring that counter-radicalization efforts do not infringe on civil liberties or further marginalize vulnerable communities.

2. Addressing Root Causes: Recognizing that radicalization often stems from complex socio-economic and political factors that require long-term, multifaceted solutions.

3. Avoiding Stigmatization: Ensuring that prevention efforts do not stigmatize specific religious or ethnic communities, which could be counterproductive.

4. Measuring Effectiveness: Developing robust metrics to evaluate the impact of prevention strategies and adapt them as needed.

Role of Moderate Religious Leaders in Maintaining Peace

Moderate religious leaders play a crucial role in countering extremism and promoting peace, particularly in the context of contentious issues like the CAA. Their influence within their communities and their ability to interpret religious teachings in ways that promote harmony make them valuable partners in preventing radicalization.

Key Roles of Moderate Religious Leaders: Moderate religious leaders can contribute to maintaining peace in several ways:

1. Promoting Peaceful Interpretations: Offering interpretations of religious texts that emphasize peace, tolerance, and coexistence.

2. Countering Extremist Narratives: Directly challenging and refuting extremist interpretations of religious teachings.

3. Interfaith Dialogue: Participating in and promoting interfaith dialogue to build understanding between different religious communities.

4. Community Leadership: Providing guidance to their communities on peaceful ways to address grievances and concerns related to the CAA.

5. Mediation and Conflict Resolution: Acting as mediators in conflicts and promoting non-violent resolution of disputes.

Strategies for Engaging Religious Leaders: To effectively leverage the influence of moderate religious leaders, the following strategies can be employed:

1. Capacity Building: Providing training and resources to religious leaders on conflict resolution, interfaith dialogue, and countering violent extremism.

2. Creating Platforms for Engagement: Establishing formal mechanisms for religious leaders to engage with government

officials and policymakers on issues related to the CAA and its implementation.

3. Supporting Grassroots Initiatives: Providing support for community-led initiatives spearheaded by religious leaders that promote peace and social cohesion.

4. Amplifying Moderate Voices: Using media and public platforms to amplify the messages of moderate religious leaders who promote peace and tolerance.

Challenges and Considerations: Engaging religious leaders in efforts to counter extremism and maintain peace in the context of the CAA presents several challenges:

1. Maintaining Credibility: Religious leaders must balance their engagement with government initiatives while maintaining their credibility and independence within their communities.

2. Addressing Diverse Perspectives: Recognizing and respecting the diversity of views within religious communities, even among moderate leaders.

3. Avoiding Instrumentalization: Ensuring that religious leaders are not perceived as being co-opted by the government or security agencies, which could undermine their influence.

4. Protecting Religious Leaders: Providing support and protection for religious leaders who may face threats or intimidation from extremist elements for their moderate stance.

The implementation of the Citizenship Amendment Act (CAA) in India presents complex challenges related to religious extremism and the potential for radicalization in affected communities. Addressing these challenges requires a multifaceted approach that combines government strategies, interfaith initiatives, and the engagement of moderate religious leaders.

By focusing on inclusive policy-making, addressing grievances, promoting social cohesion, and leveraging the influence of religious leaders, it is possible to mitigate the risks of radicalization and maintain peace among diverse religious communities. However, these efforts must be sensitive to the complexities of India's religious landscape and the legitimate concerns raised by various groups regarding the CAA.

Ultimately, preventing religious extremism in the context of the CAA will require ongoing dialogue, adaptability, and a commitment to the principles of secularism and equality enshrined in the Indian Constitution. By working collaboratively with affected communities, religious leaders, and civil society organizations, it is possible to navigate the challenges posed by the CAA while preserving India's rich tradition of religious diversity and peaceful coexistence.

References:

1. https://www.livelaw.in/top-stories/caas-claim-of-protecting-persecuted-religious-minorities-flawed-iuml-to-supreme-court-254514
2. https://www.publicsafety.gc.ca/cnt/rsrcs/pblctns/ntnl-strtg-cntrng-rdclztn-vlnc/index-en.aspx
3. https://home-affairs.ec.europa.eu/system/files/2021-01/ran_small_scale_meeting_hotbeds_conclusion_en.pdf
4. https://www.undp.org/sites/g/files/zskgke326/files/publications/Discussion%20Paper%20-%20Preventing%20Violent%20Extremism%20by%20Promoting%20Inclusive%20%20Development.pdf
5. https://www.usip.org/sites/default/files/SR413-Engaging-Religion-and-Religious-Actors-in-Countering-Violent-Extremism.pdf
6. https://guides.libraries.psu.edu/apaquickguide/intext

7.   https://data.unhcr.org/en/documents/download/49698

8.   https://owl.purdue.edu/owl/research_and_citation/apa_style/apa_formatting_and_style_guide/in_text_citations_the_basics.html

9.   https://apastyle.apa.org/style-grammar-guidelines/citations

CHAPTER 40: THE FUTURE OF INDIAN SECULARISM POST-CAA

The passage of the Citizenship Amendment Act (CAA) in 2019 and its recent implementation in 2024 have sparked intense debates about the future of Indian secularism. This chapter explores the long-term implications of the CAA on India's secular fabric, potential amendments and legal evolution of the Act, interfaith visions for a harmonious and diverse India, and the delicate balance between national security, humanitarianism, and secularism.

Long-term Implications for the Secular Fabric of India

The CAA has raised significant concerns about its impact on India's long-standing commitment to secularism. By introducing religion as a criterion for citizenship, the Act has been perceived as a departure from the constitutional promise of a universal, religion-neutral idea of citizenship. This shift has far-reaching implications for the secular ethos that has been a cornerstone of Indian democracy since independence.

Erosion of Constitutional Values

The CAA's introduction of religion-based citizenship criteria has been viewed as a potential threat to the fundamental principles enshrined in the Indian Constitution. Article 14, which guarantees equality before the law, and the constitutional commitment to secularism are particularly at risk. The Act's preferential treatment of certain religious groups over others challenges the notion of equal citizenship, regardless of religious affiliation.

Changing Perception of State Neutrality

One of the most significant long-term implications of the CAA is its potential to alter the perception of state neutrality in matters of religion. The Act's focus on specific religious groups may create an impression that the state favors certain religions over others, potentially undermining the trust of minority communities in the government's commitment to secularism.

Impact on Social Cohesion

The CAA has the potential to exacerbate existing social divisions and create new fault lines in Indian society. By categorizing citizens based on religious identity, the Act may contribute to a sense of anything else and marginalization among communities not included in its provisions, particularly Muslims. This could lead to increased social tension and potentially undermine the pluralistic fabric of Indian society.

Challenges to India's International Image

The implementation of the CAA may have repercussions for India's international standing as the world's largest secular democracy. The Act has drawn criticism from international human rights organizations and raised concerns about India's commitment to its constitutional values and international obligations. This could potentially affect India's soft power and diplomatic relations, especially with countries that prioritize secular and inclusive governance.

Shift in Political Discourse

The CAA has the potential to significantly alter the political discourse in India, placing greater emphasis on religious identity in matters of citizenship and governance. This shift may lead to a more polarized political landscape, with parties increasingly framing their agendas along religious lines. Such a trend could have long-lasting effects on electoral politics and policy-making in India.

Potential Amendments and Legal Evolution of CAA: As the CAA faces ongoing scrutiny and challenges, there is potential for amendments and legal evolution to address concerns and align the Act more closely with constitutional principles.

Judicial Review and Constitutional Challenges

The CAA is likely to face rigorous judicial scrutiny in the coming years. Constitutional challenges to the Act may focus on its compatibility with Article 14 (right to equality) and the secular principles of the Constitution. The Supreme Court's interpretation and rulings on these challenges will play a crucial role in shaping the future of the CAA and its implementation.

Potential Amendments to Address Concerns: To address criticisms and ensure alignment with constitutional values, several potential amendments to the CAA could be considered:

1. Removal of Religious Criteria: One of the most significant potential amendments would be the removal of religious criteria for citizenship eligibility. This would address concerns about discrimination and uphold the principle of secularism.

2. Expansion of Eligible Countries: The Act could be amended to include persecuted minorities from other neighbouring countries, not limited to Pakistan, Bangladesh, and Afghanistan, to make it more inclusive and less focused on specific religious groups.

3. Inclusion of Other Persecuted Groups: Amendments could be made to include other persecuted groups, regardless of religion, to address concerns about the exclusion of certain minorities, such as Rohingya Muslims or Ahmadiyyas.

4. Clearer Definition of Religious Persecution: The Act could be

amended to provide a more precise and inclusive definition of religious persecution, ensuring that it covers a broader range of circumstances and does not inadvertently exclude genuine cases of persecution.

Legal Safeguards and Implementation Guidelines: As the CAA evolves, there may be a need for additional legal safeguards and clearer implementation guidelines to prevent misuse and ensure fair application:

1. Transparent Verification Process: Establishing a transparent and fair process for verifying claims of religious persecution to prevent arbitrary decisions and ensure consistency in implementation.

2. Appeals Mechanism: Creating a robust appeals mechanism for those whose applications for citizenship under the CAA are rejected, ensuring due process and protection of rights.

3. Non-Discrimination Clauses: Incorporating explicit non-discrimination clauses to prevent the Act from being used to target or discriminate against any particular community.

International Law Compliance

Future amendments to the CAA may also focus on ensuring compliance with international human rights laws and treaties to which India is a signatory. This could include aligning the Act with principles of non-discrimination and equal treatment as outlined in international conventions.

Interfaith Visions for a Harmonious, Diverse India

In response to the challenges posed by the CAA, interfaith leaders and civil society organizations have been actively promoting visions of a harmonious and diverse India. These efforts aim to reinforce the country's secular ethos and foster unity among different religious communities.

Interfaith Dialogue and Collaboration: Interfaith leaders are increasingly coming together to promote dialogue and understanding among different religious communities. These initiatives aim to:

1. Promote Mutual Understanding: By facilitating conversations between leaders of different faiths, these dialogues help to break down stereotypes and foster mutual respect.

2. Highlight Shared Values: Interfaith leaders often emphasize the common values of peace, harmony, and social justice that are present in all major religions, creating a foundation for unity.

3. Address Social Issues Collectively: Interfaith collaborations often focus on addressing common social challenges, demonstrating the power of religious communities working together for the greater good.

Education and Awareness Programs: Interfaith organizations are developing educational programs to promote religious literacy and combat misinformation:

1. School Curriculum: Advocating for the inclusion of interfaith studies in school curricula to promote understanding and respect for different religions from an early age.

2. Community Workshops: Organizing workshops and seminars to educate communities about different religious traditions and promote inclusive attitudes.

3. Media Engagement: Working with media outlets to ensure fair and accurate representation of different religious communities and promote positive interfaith narratives.

Grassroots Peacebuilding Initiatives: Many interfaith organizations are focusing on grassroots-level initiatives to build peace and harmony:

1. Local Interfaith Councils: Establishing local interfaith councils to address community-specific issues and promote cooperation among different religious groups.

2. Youth Engagement: Developing programs specifically targeted at young people to foster interfaith understanding and leadership among the next generation.

3. Conflict Resolution Training: Providing training in conflict resolution and mediation skills to religious leaders and community members to help address tensions at the local level.

Advocacy for Inclusive Policies: Interfaith leaders are increasingly engaging in advocacy efforts to promote inclusive policies and protect the rights of all religious communities:

1. Policy Recommendations: Developing and presenting policy recommendations to government bodies to ensure that legislation and policies respect religious diversity and promote inclusivity.

2. Legal Support: Providing legal support and advocacy for religious minorities facing discrimination or persecution.

3. Public Awareness Campaigns: Launching public awareness campaigns to highlight the importance of religious freedom and secularism in maintaining India's diverse social fabric.

Balancing National Security, Humanitarianism, and Secularism

The implementation of the CAA presents a complex challenge in balancing national security concerns, humanitarian obligations, and the preservation of India's secular character. Finding an equilibrium between these often competing interests is crucial for the future of Indian secularism.

National Security Considerations: The CAA has been partly justified on national security grounds, with proponents arguing that it helps address illegal immigration and potential security threats:

1. Border Control: The Act is seen by some as a tool to strengthen border control and manage migration more effectively, particularly in regions bordering Bangladesh and Pakistan.

2. Demographic Changes: Concerns about significant demographic changes in border areas have been cited as a national security issue that the CAA aims to address.

3. Terrorism and Extremism: Some argue that the Act helps prevent the entry of potential extremists or terrorists under the guise of asylum seekers.

Humanitarian Obligations: While addressing security concerns, India also has humanitarian obligations to consider:

1. Protection of Persecuted Minorities: The CAA aims to provide a pathway to citizenship for persecuted religious minorities from neighbouring countries, fulfilling a humanitarian obligation.

2. Refugee Rights: India, despite not being a signatory to the 1951 Refugee Convention, has a history of providing refuge to persecuted groups. Balancing this tradition with security concerns remains a challenge.

3. International Commitments: India's humanitarian approach must also align with its international commitments and human rights obligations.

Preserving Secularism: Maintaining India's secular character while addressing security and humanitarian concerns is a delicate balancing act:

1. Non-Discriminatory Policies: Ensuring that policies aimed at national security or humanitarian assistance do not discriminate based on religion, in line with constitutional

principles.

2. Inclusive Approach: Developing an approach to citizenship and refugee protection that is inclusive of all persecuted groups, regardless of religion.

3. Separation of State and Religion: Reinforcing the principle of separation of state and religion in all aspects of governance, including citizenship laws.

Potential Strategies for Balance: To achieve a balance between these competing interests, several strategies could be considered:

1. Comprehensive Migration Policy: Developing a comprehensive migration policy that addresses security concerns while providing humanitarian protection, without religious discrimination.

2. Strengthening Secular Institutions: Reinforcing the role and independence of secular institutions, such as the judiciary and human rights commissions, to ensure checks and balances.

3. International Cooperation: Engaging in regional and international cooperation to address root causes of forced migration and religious persecution in neighbouring countries.

4. Evidence-Based Policy Making: Ensuring that policies are based on empirical evidence rather than political or ideological considerations, particularly in assessing security threats and humanitarian needs.

5. Transparent Implementation: Implementing security measures and humanitarian policies with transparency and accountability to build public trust and prevent misuse.

In conclusion, the future of Indian secularism in the post-CAA era hinges on the ability to navigate the complex interplay between constitutional values, social cohesion, and practical governance challenges. The potential for amendments to the CAA, the role of interfaith initiatives, and the delicate balance between security, humanitarianism, and secularism will shape India's trajectory as a diverse and democratic nation. As the country grapples with these issues, the commitment to its founding principles of equality, justice, and secularism will be crucial in determining the path forward.

References:

1. https://www.thenewsminute.com/news/opinion-with-caa-nrc-the-fate-of-the-indian-secular-state-hangs-in-balance
2. https://www.hindustantimes.com/columns/in-defence-of-indian-secularism/story-BFRrVAxhoyVrI33NAVA1FO.html
3. https://theprobe.in/columns/is-indias-citizenship-amendment-act-eroding-the-nations-secular-fabric-4330356
4. https://www.drishtiias.com/loksabha-rajyasabha-discussions/citizenship-amendment-act-unpacked
5. https://www.bbc.com/news/world-asia-india-50670393
6. https://www.amnesty.org/en/latest/news/2024/03/india-citizenship-amendment-act-is-a-blow-to-indian-constitutional-values-and-international-standards/
7. https://www.caritasindia.org/dialogue-on-peace-and-harmony-with-interfaith-leaders/
8. https://pib.gov.in/PressReleaseIframePage.aspx?PRID=1879788
9. https://www.thedailystar.net/opinion/geopolitical-insights/news/caa-and-its-effects-indian-secularism-and-regional-stability-3569726
10. https://www.epw.in/engage/article/citizenship-amendment-act-pitfalls-homogenising-identities-

resistance-narratives

11. https://www.caritasindia.org/interfaith-leaders-have-a-role-in-promoting-peace-and-harmony/